BAPTISTS AND
THE CATHOLIC
TRADITION

BAPTISTS AND THE CATHOLIC TRADITION

Reimagining the Church's Witness
in the Modern World

SECOND EDITION

BARRY HARVEY

Baker Academic
a division of Baker Publishing Group
Grand Rapids, Michigan

Published by Baker Academic
a division of Baker Publishing Group
PO Box 6287, Grand Rapids, MI 49516-6287
www.bakeracademic.com

First edition published in 2008 under the title *Can These Bones Live? A Catholic Baptist Engagement with Ecclesiology, Hermeneutics, and Social Theory* by Brazos Press

Printed in the United States of America

Library of Congress Cataloging-in-Publication Data
Names: Harvey, Barry, 1954– author.
Title: Baptists and the Catholic tradition : reimagining the church's witness in the modern world / Barry Harvey.
Other titles: Can these bones live
Description: Second edition. | Grand Rapids, MI : Baker Academic, a division of Baker Publishing Group, [2020] | Revision edition of: Can these bones live? : a Catholic Baptist engagement with ecclesiology, hermeneutics, and social theory / Barry Harvey. c2008. | Includes bibliographical references and index.
Identifiers: LCCN 2019027441 | ISBN 9781540960795 (paperback)
Subjects: LCSH: Church. | Church renewal. | Christian sociology.
Classification: LCC BV600.3 .H445 2020 | DDC 280/.042—dc23
LC record available at https://lccn.loc.gov/2019027441

ISBN 978-1-5409-6267-6 (casebound)

Chapter 6 contains a quotation from Micheal O'Siadhail's poem "Freedom," in *Poems, 1975–1995* (Newcastle upon Tyne: Bloodaxe Books, 1999), 117. Used with permission.

20   21   22   23   24   25   26   7   6   5   4   3   2   1

To John

CONTENTS

Preface to the Revised Edition   ix

Acknowledgments   xi

Introduction   1

1. Where, Then, Do We Stand? The Church
   as the Presupposition of Theology   11

2. Can These Bones Live? The Dismembering
   of Christ's Body   23

3. Caught Up in the Apocalypse: God's Incursion
   into the World in Israel and Christ   51

4. Let Us Be like the Nations: Becoming
   Entangled in the Ways of the World   91

5. Sacramental Sinews: The Re-membering
   of Christ's Body   123

6. Holy Vulnerable: Spiritual Formation
   for a Pilgrim People   161

7. Dwelling Again in Tents: Living in Tension
   with the Earthly City   195

Bibliography   213

Scripture Index   231

Subject Index   235

PREFACE TO THE REVISED EDITION

When Baker Academic approached me about doing a revision of my 2008 book *Can These Bones Live?*, I readily agreed. Though the first edition was read and reviewed thoughtfully by many when it was published, both Protestants and Catholics, several people at Baker were of the opinion that external factors had hindered a wider reception and response. I am grateful for the opportunity to revisit, restate, and revise what I wrote previously, the basic contours of which I still affirm (with some changes and additions).

This revision gives me the chance to clarify what I sought to do in the previous work, which I wrote with my fellow Baptists (and free church sisters and brothers more generally) principally in mind as the first tentative moves in a study of how Baptists might best move toward full communion with the other traditions of the church. I did not, however, make my purpose as explicit as I should have, and so I remedy that oversight here. I am indebted to those of my fellow Baptists who have undertaken the work of ecumenical dialogue, and they are to be commended, but I worry about what I take to be an inordinate concern among many of them to preserve cherished denominational distinctives in their proposals. As a consequence, they seem to enter into these deliberations with a determination to protect what they regard as true and genuine Baptist identity, which they then argue is commensurate with the small-*c* church catholic. I pursue a different tack, which is to acknowledge our part in the evil of schism, examine self-critically our many positions (there is no one Baptist position, regardless of how hard one tries to imagine that there is), and be ready to be forgiven by and learn from the other strands in the Christian tradition.

As I reviewed the first edition in preparation for this revision, I also realized that I needed to sharpen the connections between ecclesial concerns and what is happening in the wider social world to which God has sent us as the place where we live, move, have our being, and seek its welfare. As I say in more detail in the introduction, as a missional movement the church is sent by God into the world, there to "play away from home," engaging with other forms of life and language, other political and cultural standpoints. The church is the creation of God's activity in Christ and the Holy Spirit and also an empirical, historical social entity that shares in the achievements and corruptions of a fallen world. As such, the church needs an adequate ecclesiology in order to hold on to the one without letting go of the other. My treatment of race, for example, was woefully inadequate.

In addition to a variety of modifications and amendments to the text, I have removed two chapters from the first edition. The first of these chapters, "Lovers, Madmen, and Pilgrim Poets," dealt with the role that imagination and memory play in the type of scriptural reasoning that informs and directs the thinking, feeling, and acting of the church as the body of Christ in a post-Christendom world. The second chapter, "Doctrinally Speaking," emphasized the central role that sound doctrine, including metaphysical surmises, exercises in the life, witness, and words of the Christian community. My editor, Dave Nelson, persuaded me that we could safely remove these two chapters and retain the integrity of the argument, and at the same time make it more accessible. That said, I stand by what I wrote in those chapters and would commend them to the reader.

Again, I am grateful to Baker for the opportunity to return to the topics in this book and offer this revision to all to read and weigh as we seek to "travel the street of love together as we make our way toward him of whom it is said, 'Seek his face always.'"[1]

---

1. Augustine, *De Trinitate* 1.3.5, quoted in Wilken, *Spirit of Early Christian Thought*, 107.

ACKNOWLEDGMENTS

Countless people—family, mentors, colleagues, and students—make vital contributions to the writing of a book. In the case of this book, I particularly want to thank my Baylor University colleague Jenny Howell, who took the time to read and comment on a preliminary draft. Her suggestions greatly improved what the reader finds here. In addition, my thanks to Laura Lysen for her assistance with the page proofs.

I also wish to express my gratitude to all those at Baker Academic, especially to Dave Nelson, who believed in what I had written previously and encouraged me to revise the first edition, and to Brian Bolger for his keen editorial eye.

My wife, Sarah, daughter, Rachel, and grandchildren, Audi, Ella, Lexus, and Porsche, continue to be my delight and comfort. I shudder to think of what life would be without their love, friendship, and support.

I dedicate this book to John. I doubt there is a father who takes more joy in his son than I do. To him and to all my family, friends, and colleagues, and above all to the God of mercy and grace, I give thanks.

INTRODUCTION

In an interview prior to his election as Pope Benedict XVI, Joseph Ratzinger stated that in the future the church can no longer expect to be the form of life for a whole society (an aspiration that, as I argue below, Baptists have also nurtured). It must now assume different configurations that identify it less with great civilizations and more with minorities. In these new formats the members of Christ's body will work whenever possible with the status quo, but they should also be spiritually prepared when necessary to stand over against it in solidarity with the poor and the persecuted. "But precisely in this way," he said, believers "will, biblically speaking, become the salt of the earth again. In this upheaval, constancy—keeping what is essential to man from being destroyed—is once again more important, and the powers of preservation that can sustain him in his humanity are even more necessary."[1]

These comments are astounding, coming as they do from one who was to become the temporal head of the world's only true transnational community, a social body that had for centuries claimed that it constituted the organizing center of "a single civilization homogeneously and integrally Christian."[2] It is nothing short of revolutionary for the pope to state that the church should see itself not as the spiritual fulcrum around which the entire human world revolves, nor as one of the well-connected institutions collaborating principally with the rich and powerful, but as "small, seemingly insignificant groups that nonetheless live in an intensive struggle against evil and bring the good into the world—that let God in."[3]

1. Ratzinger, *Salt of the Earth*, 164, 222.
2. Taylor, *Secular Age*, 744.
3. Ratzinger, *Salt of the Earth*, 16.

The work of reimagining the church for this task is more urgent than it was even a few years ago, as churches in Europe, Australia, and North America are struggling to come to terms with the demise of that complex and variegated social arrangement known as Christendom, a social reality to which those who came before us had become accustomed for over a millennium. Though the details of this cooperative pact with the earthly *res publica* were constantly being reworked down through the centuries, the church as an integral element in an overarching system of social relations was a constant. But changes unlike anything that has occurred since the earliest centuries of Christianity are well underway, and there is no going back. Things that our grandparents took for granted—the need to belong to a church to succeed in a profession or occupation, theological sanctions for what counted as civic morality, the privileged social standing that came with being a Christian—either have already vanished or will soon do so.

The task is complicated by the fact that the last few centuries have been riddled by divisions between the Catholic church and an ever-expanding list of groups descended from the Protestant Reformation. I need to add a second word of caution here, as a veritable cottage industry has arisen seeking to lay the blame for our present circumstances solely or principally at the feet of the Protestant Reformation. Such assertions are no more justified than are claims that the church lost its soul with the conversion of the emperor Constantine in the fourth century. First, it was never the aim of the Protestant Reformers to break up Christendom. The sixteenth-century Reformation, contends Jaroslav Pelikan, was a tragic necessity of history. Its necessity resided in the Reformers' desire to affirm what they regarded as the highest and the best in the Catholic tradition and in "their obligation to summon Rome back to it." Pelikan goes so far as to say that "the Reformation began because the reformers were too catholic in the midst of a church that had forgotten its catholicity." It was tragic because each side lost something of what they were trying to defend, leading to an outcome that neither wanted.[4]

Catholic historian Joseph Lortz agrees with Pelikan, stating that the events of the sixteenth century were a social and historical necessity. He offers a laundry list of offenses and misdeeds in the Catholicism of the day that gave rise to the "protest," including a series of bad popes, the divided papacy, structural flaws including the intrusion of political and economic interests in the life of the church (indulgences being at the top of the list), simony, and the arbitrariness and hedonism of the clergy, particularly at the highest levels. According to Lortz,

4. Pelikan, *Riddle of Roman Catholicism*, 46.

Whether we recall that Erasmus was able to hear in the Pope's own chapel on Good Friday an ostentatious piece of humanistic oratory in which Our Lord and His Passion were not even mentioned, while the speaker displayed his learning and the glories of pagan antiquity; or whether we note that papal ambassadors were merely diplomats who operated solely in diplomatic, not a religious context even when purely religious matters were involved (as Alexander at the Diet of Worms in 1521), no one was in the least surprised at this way of acting; the picture of profound secularization in the holy places remains the same.[5]

It is also the case that Protestantism as we know it today was not the inevitable result of the Reformation. Other outcomes are both conceivable and plausible, for example, had Martin Luther and Ulrich Zwingli been able to reach a consensus at Marburg, or had the Catholic church responded more prudently, patiently, and charitably to the concerns of these Reformers. Moreover, the conflicts unfolding within the church during the sixteenth century did not occur in isolation from other momentous shifts in the social landscape of Europe. In its efforts to retain temporal authority in response to the rise of embryonic nation-states, the church responded by redefining its own power in legal and corporate rather than in sacramental terms.[6] Canon lawyers, at the behest of the pontiff, appropriated the Roman legal concept of the right of property in connection with the late medieval doctrine of the church as Christ's mystical body to posit the theory of "the absolute and universal jurisdiction of the supreme authority, and . . . the doctrine of the *plenitudo potestatis* [the fullness of jurisdictional power] of the Pope."[7] This claim became the basis for the attempt on the part of the popes to reassert their authority in a world where "secular control was rapidly on the rise and the political unity of Christendom was being fragmented into sovereign nation-states."[8] Protestant groups only accelerated a movement that was well underway by the time they appeared on the stage of history.

The question before us, therefore, is not where to place the blame or how to specify when the critical misstep took place, but how do we, Protestants and Catholics together, go forward toward the unity that is Christ's mandate? Some have devised detailed plans for moving forward toward full reunion. Peter Leithart, for example, has written what he calls an ecclesiological program to move primarily conservative evangelical Protestant churches down this path in obedience to Christ. My fear is that, regardless of how well thought

5. Lortz, *Reformation*, 75–76, 78.
6. Kantorowicz, *King's Two Bodies*, 200–206.
7. Figgis, *Studies of Political Thought*, 4.
8. Cavanaugh, *Torture and Eucharist*, 218.

out and carefully written such proposals are, they will quickly be shelved under the category of interesting thought experiments.

Others have suggested a path that is similar but would allow them to protect certain denominational "distinctives." For example, a small but grow-ing number of Baptist and other free church clergy, scholars, and laypeople note with considerable concern the divisions in our ranks, the changed social standing of Christianity in the wider society, and the impoverished theological understanding and insight that prevail within our denominations. They have wisely begun to look beyond our provincial borders to reconnect with historic patterns of faith, practice, and order shared by believers down through history and across the globe. Those who have taken up these efforts contend that we Baptists and our free church cousins not only have deep roots in the historic Christian tradition that need to be uncovered and nourished but also have an abiding stake in reconnecting with that heritage, not only for our own sake but also for the worldwide community of Christians.[9] To this extent I can only applaud these efforts.

The proposals offered by these Baptists differ at various points, but they frequently share a common feature, which is a concern to chart a course to full communion that does not conflict with what they regard as true and genuine Baptist identity, which they take to be commensurate with the small-*c* church catholic. Several problems emerge in this approach that render it suspect, beginning with the fact that there is disagreement as to what qualifies as true and genuine Baptist (or in James McClendon's version, "baptist") identity, which then shapes how one construes what can be assigned to the essence of the church catholic. A concern to preserve cherished denominational distinc-tives should not drive our participation in ecumenical deliberations. This is not to say that the institutions, practices, and convictions that developed since Luther first posted his theses should be discarded wholesale (though I can think of a few that would be better left on the scrap heap of history).

Also standing in the way of expanded ecumenical efforts on the part of Baptists are the ahistorical sensibilities that many of us share with more than a few of our Protestant kin. In his influential work on the development of doctrine, John Henry Newman writes, "To be deep in history is to cease to be a Protestant." He challenges us to show him where our system of doctrine might be found in the early centuries of the church, and he states that if it ever existed, all evidence of it "has been clean swept away as if by a deluge,

9. See, for example, Bullard, *Re-membering the Body*; Freeman, *Contesting Catholicity*; Harmon, *Baptist Identity and the Ecumenical Future*; D. Hatch, *Thinking with the Church*; McClendon, *Doctrine*; McClendon, *Ethics*; McClendon, *Witness*; E. Newman, *Attending the Wounds on Christ's Body*.

suddenly, silently, and without memorial."[10] Even if I were to concede that Newman is indulging here in hyperbole, Protestants in general, and Baptists more specifically, often do not see their faith as organically related to and dependent on that of past generations. This dislocation from any connection to the past is a pattern that is not limited to the history of Christianity, but extends to the chosen people of God, both biblical Israel and the ongoing existence of Israel, the Jewish people. We too often have regarded our relationship to the lives, struggles, doubts, failures, and sufferings of past generations as illustrative rather than constitutive of our place within the body of Christ. This is especially true of Baptists who affirm soul competency, congregational autonomy, and the sole sufficiency of Scripture as the foundation of their beliefs, for whom there is no actual social body to which they are necessarily related.

I recognize that what I am proposing may be worrisome to some, leaving them wondering whether the path to full communion requires at the outset a wholesale repudiation of all that they have held dear. My response is no, for it has taken us five hundred years to get to this point, and any suggestion that we simply ignore or jettison what has transpired during that time will never get out of the starting gate. Baptists and other free church traditions need not leave behind our love for Scripture, the fellowship of the local congregation, or our zeal for evangelization. As Ratzinger puts it, Protestants and Catholics must seek "the truth together with the firm intention of imposing nothing which does not come from the Lord on the other party, and of losing nothing entrusted to us by him. In this way our lives advance toward each other because they are directed toward Christ."[11] The person and lordship of Jesus Christ, crucified and risen, is the cantus firmus around which Protestant and Catholic alike add their voices in the polyphony of faith, hope, and love that is moving, slowly and tentatively, toward the advent of *olam haba*, the age to come.

The thorniest problem, however, is that the notion of a small-*c* catholicism is an abstraction without social embodiment or substantial historical precedents. On the one hand, it closely resembles the idea of Judeo-Christianity that some were promoting in the middle of the twentieth century as a more inclusive form of civil religion in the United States.[12] On the other hand, it resembles C. S. Lewis's "mere Christianity," a phrase that sounds inviting and generous but for which there is no real agreement. This concept of small-*c* catholicism was a by-product of American-style Protestantism that sought to legitimate the separated status of the various denominations as in some sense

10. J. Newman, *Essay on the Development of Christian Doctrine*, 8.
11. Ratzinger, *Church, Ecumenism, and Politics*, 87.
12. See, for example, Herberg, *Protestant, Catholic, Jew*.

permanent—not just their separation from Rome and the East but also from other Protestant bodies—while allowing us the comfort of believing that we still participated in a wider, though more vague, entity.[13] As a vestige of denominationalism, apart from which it loses much of its rationale, the concept of "church catholic" is ultimately unsustainable. In the end, therefore, I agree with Leithart's conclusion that denominationalism "is the institutionalization of division. It enables us to be complacent about defining ourselves not by union with our brothers [and sisters] but by our divisions."[14]

The reader will not find in what follows a detailed proposal of ecumenical convergence or a blueprint for a future restoration of catholicity between the divided church bodies. Rather, I commend what might be called an ecumenical posture, in hopes of taking a tentative step or two toward a family reconciliation. This posture, as Herbert McCabe says, begins with the recognition that the divisions within the body of Christ, though disastrous in themselves, "have their place in the mysterious plan of God, that perhaps certain Christian insights could never have been achieved without the painful cycle of a separation followed on both sides by a groping towards reconciliation." The way forward, he adds, is for all concerned to repent of their role in the evil of schism, examine self-critically their respective positions, and be ready to be forgiven by and learn from the others.[15] And as Walter Kasper rightly observes, the proper orientation in both ecumenical dialogues and intradenominational conversations needs to be "the conversion of all to Jesus Christ. As we move nearer to Jesus Christ, in him we move nearer to one another."[16]

If as free church people we are to reflect on what might be involved in moving nearer to Christ, we need some sense of how we all got from where our pilgrimage began with Jesus and the Twelve to where we are, having been diverted over the years, like the prodigal, to a "far country." In the words of Charles Taylor, "Our past is sedimented in our present, and we are doomed to misidentify ourselves, as long as we can't do justice to where we come from."[17] Determining where we currently stand thus depends on the story that narrates this journey and how it might be possible for us to make our way back to the crucified and risen Lord.

In chapter 1, we discover from retrospective history, first, that Christendom is a hard habit to break, not just for so-called magisterial Protestant churches but for Baptists and for other free churches as well. In the nascent American republic

13. Taylor, *Secular Age*, 449–50.
14. Leithart, *End of Protestantism*, 4.
15. McCabe, "Comment," 229.
16. Kasper, "Current Problems in Ecumenical Theology."
17. Taylor, *Secular Age*, 29.

in particular, our forebears thought they had solved the problem of establishment, persuaded as they were that the principle of the separation of church and state would liberate faith from all political entanglements. They failed to recognize that the formal separation of these institutions took place under the auspices of a social construct that stipulated a de facto moral and cultural identity between a certain type of Protestant Christianity and the new nation. The church is institutionally separated from the bureaucratic and coercive powers we typically associate with the state, but for most Baptists their congregations remain firmly bound together with nation. We bought into the notion that the relationship between the church and earthly commonwealths in the past was clearly deficient (seldom pausing to take into consideration the changing social and material conditions that fueled the development of that relationship over the centuries), but that now, with the definitive solution to the problem of past regimes well in hand, "we finally got it right!" Like so many before us, we succumbed to the seductive possibility of a more perfect Christendom through the endorsement of and cooperation with the American experiment.

As Baptists and other like-minded free church folks were busy reinventing the Christendom model, we also mishandled another aspect of faith, which is that matter matters. The crucified and risen Christ comes to us through the work of the Holy Spirit, in and through the material world, beginning with the most basic of elements: water, bread, and wine. Through these sacramental signs we are put in a position to learn something of what is at stake in our relationships with one another and with the earth. To recall McCabe's assertion about what needs to happen for all of us to move forward, the aspect of our Baptist heritage most in need of self-critical examination is our neglect of the material world, of which human life is inextricably a part. To be sure, there have been exceptions along the way, but for the most part we have not adequately recognized the importance that these signs play in our pilgrimage toward the city of God.

In chapter 2, I contrast the general understanding of nature and history proposed by the patristic and medieval church, according to which all created things are also signs that refer to their beginning and end in God, with new social configurations that arose with the modern world and that stipulate that the intelligibility of nature, the meaningfulness of history, and the purposefulness of human existence no longer require these sorts of references. I then provide an initial sketch of the interpretive art that allows us to follow God's critical, decisive, and final action and purpose for the world in the apocalypse of the long-awaited reign of God in Jesus Christ.

Chapter 3 develops the apocalyptic motif that initially formed the heart of the church's interpretive activity. The first group of disciples who followed the way of Jesus found themselves caught up in a set of allegiances, convictions, dispositions, and loves that put them in the middle of the divine struggle with and triumph over temporal powers and principalities that sought to usurp divine sovereignty over creation. God's intrusion, in the incarnation, into a world enslaved to sin and death marks the continuation of the story of Abraham and Sarah's offspring, but under radically new and distinct circumstances. The body politic of Christ initially took form as an apocalyptic fellowship constituted through the power of the Holy Spirit, its membership taken from every tribe and language, people and nation on earth, to serve as sign, instrument, and foretaste of creation's destiny, forged on a Roman cross, in the age to come. The messianic incursion of God into the world did not, however, appear out of a social or historical vacuum, as the early followers of Jesus understood themselves to be the continuation of God's election of Israel and, in particular, the continuation of the promise to Abraham that in the chosen people God would bless all the families of the earth (Gen. 12:3).

Many in our age have an aversion to apocalyptic imagery, in part for its supposedly "otherworldly" character and for advocating withdrawal from the everyday world where people deal with the necessities of eating, drinking, marrying and giving in marriage, having children, burying parents, acquiring and disposing of property, and exchanging goods. Associations of apocalyptic thought with otherworldliness can be traced to an erroneous assumption, which is that apocalyptically minded Jews in the years leading up to the first century CE expected the imminent collapse of the domain of time and space, and with it all sense of history. This misperception is due, to some degree, to an inherent ambiguity in the English word *end*, which can signify either a termination of some kind or the goal of an act, and often it can refer to both. In apocalyptic thought there is an intrinsic relationship between purpose and finality, between speaking of the aim of life and its limits, between the course that creation is taking in history and the consummation that awaits it. The "eschaton" marks that toward which everything tends, giving shape and direction to history—indeed, marking the passage of time *as* history.

In chapter 4 I discuss in more detail how the church was dismembered as the body politic of Christ. It began when the Christian community exchanged its distinctive way of life as a company of nomads assembled from every tribe and language, every people and nation, to serve the nations as a sign and instrument of God's eternal commonwealth, for a power-sharing arrangement with the rulers and authorities of the earthly city. Folding up its tents, the church got caught up in an unfolding series of disciplinary regimes that effectively domesticated, marginalized, and exploited its life, language, and witness.

In chapters 5 and 6 I turn to the question of how the church might by God's grace be gathered together once again and re-membered by the power of the Spirit as the body of Christ. I say "might," for we can never ensure the presence of Christ by means of a formal institution that connects the present with the past, as though it were the working-out of an immanent historical process. We cannot compel the grace of God through some sort of procedural or ritualistic alchemy. God's messianic reign comes to gather the church *epicletically*, through our invocation of the Holy Spirit to re-remember the presence of the messianic age in our midst, and through us to the rest of the world. Historical continuity as such is no guarantee that Christ is present. We believe that the end of the age rules over creation from beginning to end, but it is our hope that in the lives of the penitent faithful, God promises to enact that end as sign and foretaste in the midst of time.[18]

A people cannot set out on a pilgrimage and reasonably expect to survive, much less make progress, without being properly trained and provisioned. We must constantly be kept together so that we will not scatter along the way; we must learn how to take our bearings so that we know where we are, where we are headed, and how to get from the one to the other; we must be disciplined so that we keep our eyes trained on what lies before us and not be tempted to return to the fleshpots of Egypt; and we must learn how to distinguish among the variety of social regimes we shall encounter in the earthly city along the way. For Christians, then, this is a question that brings us to the work of the Third Person of the Trinity, the Holy Spirit, who binds us to Christ and to one another, sanctifying and sustaining his earthly-historical body in its work and witness, principally through baptism and Eucharist. As I suggest in chapter 5, these sacramental signs constitute the material point of entry of God's apocalyptic regime into the day-to-day life of this world, creating in the body of Christ an alternative social grammar for creaturely existence. Baptism and Eucharist, by incorporating us into the mystery of God's redemptive presence and activity in the world, propel us beyond the boundaries within which state and market seek to confine us, gathering us together in a new political body through which the age to come confronts the powers of this age.

With its intrusion into the disordered loves of a fallen world, the apocalypse of God in the midst of history radically restructures our life together. In order for the members of Christ's body to make this alternative social grammar our own, however, we must undergo a lifelong process of spiritual discipline, in which we give ourselves daily to God as we live "fully in the midst of life's tasks, questions, successes and failures, experiences, and perplexities."[19] In chapter 6, then, I examine some of the ways that practices generally associated

---

18. Cavanaugh, *Torture and Eucharist*, 270; Zizioulas, *Being as Communion*, 204–8.
19. Bonhoeffer, *Letters and Papers from Prison*, 486.

with spiritual formation—prayer, confession, fasting, hospitality, the giving and receiving of counsel, rites of forgiveness and reconciliation, and the works of mercy—incorporate the habits and skills of the church's interpretive art into our bodies. The telos of these practices is unselfing, being unmade so that we can be remade. Unselfing interrupts the solidifying of our identities as disembodied consumers and faceless producers promoted by the state and the global market, in order to cultivate a new human within the politics of the Spirit, one that is not confined by humankind's "Adamic" past but liberated for its future in the messianic kingdom.

As a missional movement, the church must also consider how its own life must "play away from home" and engage with other forms of life and language, other political and cultural standpoints, in "a search for what recognizably—however imperfectly—shares in the same project that the Gospel defines." In the process perhaps we can rediscover the import of our own story in the deeds and aspirations of others.[20] In the concluding chapter, therefore, I examine some of the recurring tendencies in the social grammar of the present age that set the context in which the members of Christ's body must practice the art of pilgrimage. In one way or another these tendencies are linked to what Augustine calls the *libido dominandi*, the lust for mastery that is predicated on the possession, threat, and use of coercive force, and thus on death and the fear of death. The desire to control our world manifests itself most destructively in war, but coercion and violence also find their way into activities overseen by the state and the market that are connected to the needed goods of daily life, and this same tendency appears in the intimate circles of families and churches.

To learn something of what it means to play away from home as witnesses to the gospel's proclamation that life and not death, love and not hate, peace and not strife, will have the final word, those who would practice the art of pilgrimage well must cultivate good habits of reasoning so that we might discern which aspects of the earthly commonwealth are open to God's irruption into the disordered cosmos in Christ and can therefore be thought of as natural, and which are closed to Christ and must be regarded as unnatural. As artisans of the age to come, Christians must be discriminating connoisseurs of reason, mindful that the intrinsic powers of rationality given to us by God are now typically caught up within the structures of nation-state and neoliberal market and embedded in a cultural ethos that no longer seeks to habituate its citizens in a shared set of customs and habits, trusting instead in the alchemical fantasy that process can transform itself into substance.[21]

20. Williams, *On Christian Theology*, 38–39.
21. Beiner, *What's the Matter with Liberalism?*, 22; Mensch and Freeman, *Politics of Virtue*, 5.

1

WHERE, THEN, DO WE STAND?

The Church as the Presupposition of Theology

Theology is a laborious attempt to explain the joke about this ordinary physical, political world.

Herbert McCabe, *God Matters*

The desire to ask about the beginning, writes Dietrich Bonhoeffer, is the innermost passion of our thinking as creaturely beings, imparting reality to every genuine question we ask. And yet no sooner is the question of the beginning put before us than our thinking is thrown back on itself, spending its strength like huge breakers crashing upon a rocky shore. In its desire to reach back to the beginning, human reasoning cannot help but pound itself to pieces. We are intractably located in the middle, knowing neither the end nor the beginning.[1]

In contrast to the delusion that there is a Gnostic "spark of breath" in each of us going back "to before the Creation,"[2] we always find ourselves somewhere, heirs to patterns of speaking and acting set within a context formed by the time, place, and people of which we are a part. Indeed, if others are to

1. Bonhoeffer, *Creation and Fall*, 25–28.
2. Bloom, *American Religion*, 22.

take what we say or do seriously, we must take up and consistently maintain some standpoint, and they must do likewise,[3] for it is only in and through some particular stance that "the world and ourselves are opened to us."[4] The theological task facing the church, then, is not to try to find a universal starting point or method that can lift us out of our time and place so that we might see all the kingdoms of the world as though we were gods. It is instead to help a fallen world take its bearings here in the middle, to understand something of what went before, to learn about the way things developed in the past that led to the way they are now. Instead of asking where sound theology begins, those who would practice the art of pilgrimage would do well to ask, "Where, then, do we stand?"[5]

This question can, of course, be parsed in several different ways. It can be taken in an epistemic sense: What are the warrants for our claims to know something significant about ourselves? It also suggests a historical referent: it has been a commonplace for a time now to say that we live in a "postmodern" era, though increasingly it is far from certain what is meant by that notion. This question can also be addressed by noting that much of the inhabited world, both human and nonhuman, now works, consumes, lives, and dies within a neoliberal[6] matrix of nation-state, market, and cultural ethos in which every person, thing, product, and activity that we might have once said was good, true, and beautiful is now evaluated as a formal value predicated on its usefulness and exchange potential, thus "flattening all hierarchies to formal equivalences."[7]

Though these are important considerations that I take up in what follows, for Christians the question of where we now stand is principally set within an eschatological trajectory narrated by the apocalyptic images and motifs of the New Testament. As citizens of another city that is to come (Heb. 13:14), we have no permanent standpoint or proper place in the present time. We are on pilgrimage through history, looking with anticipation for the coming of the commonwealth whose architect and builder is the triune God (Heb. 11:10; cf. Phil. 3:20). When we ask where we now stand, we do so as a people

---

3. McClendon, *Doctrine*, 172.

4. Grant, *Time as History*, 6–7.

5. Lash, *Believing Three Ways in One God*, 2.

6. In what follows, *neoliberalism* refers to the complex nexus of institutions and practices, rules, habits, and procedures, both formal and informal, that shape and discipline individual bodies so that they will engage in conduct that will effectively support and reproduce the current regime of production, accumulation, and consumption. This regimen seeks to keep women, men, and children in their place as producers and consumers, stripped of the resources of memory and imagination that might allow them to question the legitimacy of this regime.

7. Long, *Divine Economy*, 262.

seeking to go on and go further toward that future that summons all of God's creatures, and especially humankind. In this regard Bonhoeffer rightly states that the visible church is the presupposition for theology.[8]

I need to add a word of caution at this point, one that I presuppose about the church throughout this work. Though I believe that this motley mob of misfits and malcontents is a reality of revelation established and animated by the missions of the triune God, it is never so in a straightforward and unambiguous sense. It is, has always been, and will remain until the final consummation a "sesquiguous" reality,[9] both (1) a social order set apart by the Spirit to embody concretely the presence and activity of the crucified and risen Christ before a hurting and waiting world and (2) an impure and sinful community constantly in need of the grace and forgiveness it proclaims. In no wise am I arguing that the empirical church possesses the reality of the new humanity in Christ or has decisively left behind humankind's "Adamic" past, but in faith it sesquiguously embodies habits and relations of the new human in tension with that past.[10]

I thus contend that the church, by being what in the power of the Holy Spirit it is—the earthly-historical body of Christ—constitutes an interpretive surmise about creaturely life as lived before God and the world, and is that not just for itself but for the whole cosmos. The existence of this people is grounded in a distinctive performance of life and language that is a socially embodied, historically extended interpretation of the world in general and of human life in particular. The answer to the question of what is signified by the word *God* cannot be adequately ascertained by the kind of conceptual clarification practiced by analytic philosophers (though that might be helpful at certain points), but only by observing how this community orders its life together through its worship, teaching, witness, and work.[11] This hermeneutical dimension is implicit in the understanding of the church as a sacrament—that is, as "a sign and instrument . . . of communion with God and of unity among men."[12]

Another way to put this is to say with John Milbank that theology can be practiced only by way of explicating Christian practice: "The Christian God can no longer be thought of as a God first seen, but rather as a God first

---

8. Bonhoeffer, "Nature of the Church," 290.

9. A "sesquiguous" sign or utterance, writes Herbert McCabe, is one that "lies between the *ambiguous* and the *plonking* or flat statement." More specifically, it is "one in which the speaker both commits himself to a position and is simultaneously aware of the inadequacy of what he is saying, and of his own position in saying it." McCabe, *God Matters*, 176 (emphasis original).

10. See Mawson, *Christ Existing as Community*, 126–32.

11. Williams, *On Christian Theology*, xii, 135.

12. *Lumen Gentium*, 68–69.

prayed to, first imagined, first inspiring certain actions, first put into words, and always already thought about, objectified, even if this objectification is recognised as inevitably inadequate."[13] This interdependence of theory with practice is not unique to theology, for any attempt at interpretation or explanation is an unpacking of already existing activities.

This book is therefore an exercise in theological hermeneutics, though not in the narrow sense of formulating a general theory of meaning that establishes normative rules, procedures, and standards for the interpretation of written texts. It has to do instead with the possibilities of human action, fulfillment, and happiness made possible by what God accomplishes in our midst, encompassing ethics, politics, poetics, rhetoric, cosmology, and metaphysics. Theology has a vested interest in all these areas of investigation, but it attends to them in the course of asking how to carry on with a specified message at that point in life "where past hearing turns to new speaking."[14]

Theological hermeneutics asks, What do the life, death, and resurrection of the man Jesus of Nazareth and the sending of the Holy Spirit have to do with this life that we now live? If we are to grasp the significance of Christ and his earthly-historical body for our lives, living as we do in a different time and place, in circumstances that are marked by their own particularity and contingency, it is necessary that we learn how to narrate our lives both as distinct from his story and, at the same time, as a continuation of it. To this end theologians engage in three interpretive tasks, involving, first, the Scriptures as the book of the church; second, the practices of the church; and third, the political and economic regime, cultural ethos, and forms of knowledge that distinguish our particular time and place in history.

Theology's "venture of an overall view"[15] subsists in the doctrinal, liturgical, and spiritual convictions and in moral dispositions and activities that have been handed on to us within the Christian community by our mothers and fathers in the faith. We take up and develop this heritage so that we might learn how to speak truthfully and live faithfully in our own circumstances and then hand it on in good working order to our spiritual offspring. This book is therefore also a work in ecclesiology, with emphases, first, on the originating mission and character of the church and its subsequent history, and second, on three of the constitutive practices of the church: baptism and Eucharist and spiritual formation. These practices cultivate the mission and sustain the distinctive form of life that characterizes the body of Christ in the world, which is the topic of the last chapter.

13. Milbank, "'Postmodern Critical Augustinianism,'" 226–27.
14. Jenson, *Triune God*, 14.
15. Ritschl, *Logic of Theology*, 202.

Any attempt at theological hermeneutics grounded in the life and language of the church immediately encounters a serious problem in the fact of the dismembered body of Christ. Given that the visible church is the presupposition of this hermeneutics, these divisions may make theology as a public endeavor virtually impossible, since the proper agent of such hermeneutics does not exist, unless one simply declares that one particular branch totally comprehends that reality. The assumption that theology can flourish apart from some degree of unity in the church in actuality threatens to reduce theology's teachings on matters of faith and practice to "the nonbinding character of a general moral exhortation." When theology is deprived of its unified public character, we are left with little more than the private concerns of individual professors.[16]

If we are to go on and go further as the nomadic people of God in the context of a divided church (assuming it can happen at all), writes Robert Jenson, then we must confess that "we live in radical self-contradiction and that by every churchly act we contradict that contradiction. Also theology must make this double contradiction at and by every step of its way."[17] This need not be a pessimistic assessment, since the members of Christ's body live by hope in the coming kingdom of God. And so we wait in the knowledge that it is a blessing to theology that we need not wait for the church to be completely re-membered to do our work.

Some may object that proceeding from the standpoint of the church community and its intellectual tradition entails suppressing the critical and speculative side of our rational nature, but these fears are unfounded. When inquiring after knowledge generally, writes John Henry Newman, "we must assume something to prove anything, and can gain nothing without a venture."[18] Human beings must make an interpretive surmise of one sort or another to know or do anything at all, from the most mundane tasks to the most elaborate research programs in science, and such ventures are always subject to subtle reworking, substantive revision, or outright rejection. The church is not exempt from this principle, and it is the work of theology to test the convictions of its interpretive venture, to criticize and transform them when warranted, and to take account of the differences and disputes that exist between the church and other human associations.[19]

Theologians must therefore refuse as illusory the notion that there is an unsullied beginning point, a "mid-air" position that we can occupy through

---

16. Peterson, *Theological Tractates*, 17, 25.
17. Jenson, *Triune God*, vii.
18. J. Newman, "Nature of Faith in Relation to Reason," 215.
19. McClendon and Smith, *Convictions*, 9.

the application of some sort of critical method, allowing us—without our feet touching the ground, so to speak—to judge which claims are true and which are not. We should not confuse what William of St. Thierry refers to as the hesitations of thought (*haesitationes cogitationum*) that invariably accompany the thoughts of faith (*fidei cogitationes*) with the sort of dishonest rationality (*rationalitas improba*) that adopts an antagonistic attitude to faith.[20] The skepticism that arises from this kind of antagonism necessarily leads to either despair or cynicism, or to both in alternation.[21]

Dismembering the Body of Christ

So then, where *do* we in the body of Christ currently stand? Obviously, not where our mothers and fathers in the faith once stood. They saw the world in which they lived as followable, as a "book" authored by God, with the events of history unfolding in the manner of a dramatic narrative. The complex plot and many subplots of this story were detailed for the faithful in God's other work, the Bible, according to which all things ultimately find their significance in their being either receptive to or closed off from the work of God in Christ's life, passion, and resurrection.

The church's venture of an overall view of things was not confined to the privatized realm of "religion," sequestered from the everyday world of politics, economics, and the like. It was interwoven with a complex (and admittedly messy) social space that was composed of intersecting associations—church institutions, civil authorities of all sorts, clans, monasteries and other religious groups, guilds, and towns. The obligations, immunities, and entitlements that men and women owed to one another within these *societates* were not conferred by an omnicompetent, centralized nation-state, but subsisted within these overlapping associations of which they were members. Each person and association was regarded as an integral whole that also constituted a part of a larger whole, generating a complex conception of space that was conceived on the Pauline theology of the body of Christ.

Over the last several centuries, however, reconfigurations of world and self trained women and men to think, feel, and act quite differently in every sphere of life. A vast technological apparatus—the emergence of the state as the normative form of political community; the commodification of property, goods, and labor; the development of complex monetary systems; the rise to social

20. William of St. Thierry, *Mirror of Faith*, 38, 65; cf. de Lubac, *Mystery of the Supernatural*, 170.
21. Tillich, *Dynamics of Faith*, 19.

prominence of managerial expertise; and radical changes in political and moral discourse—uprooted the social relationships and personal identities previously embedded in local associations. In place of these encumbrances, modern institutions sought to establish a direct and unmediated relationship between the sovereign power of the state and the unencumbered individual whose only necessary identity was as a unit of production and consumption, and for whom other individuals were only variables in the calculation of self-interest.

The peoples of Christendom were thus gradually divested of the practices, dispositions, and institutions that had bound them to one another and enabled them to follow the world as an ensemble of signs uttered and intended by God. The accumulated social capital—the moral habits, customs, and beliefs about what made for human flourishing—was reinvested in a series of political, economic, and cultural projects that stipulated that the social mediation of transcendence was no longer needed to ascend to truth, goodness, and beauty. Set free from the constraints of a shared past and the claim of others on their lives to fashion their own stories (except not, of course, free from the authority of the state, which promised to ensure that freedom in exchange for unquestioned sovereignty over every aspect of their lives), progress would be measured solely by the degree to which individuals realized independence from any relationship or authority outside themselves.

Of all the relationships that needed to be dismantled for the modern project to go forward, none was more crucial than those once located within the church. The political and economic regime that separated the day-to-day lives of women and men from the social ligatures of family, clan, guild, estate, and village also severed the ecclesial sinews that bound them to the risen Christ and to each other. Working gradually and methodically, the new order of things dismembered the body of Christ by abating its common life and vitiating its witness to the triune God. The substance of Christian faith was separated from the constitutive practices that made it possible for women and men, in the power of the Spirit, to participate in the economy of God's redemptive work in the world, with the capacity to imagine, reason, desire, feel, and act as members of Christ's true body.

Apart from these practices and the habits they cultivated, Christians were increasingly subject to the political whims and machinations of the state, with little sense of the difference between the obligations they owed to God and those owed to the state. We also became caught up in habits of consumption that no longer served any higher purpose but became ends in themselves, to be desired for their own sake. Ensnared by stunted imaginations and unfettered appetites, we still routinely confuse having a plethora of choices with being free. These desires and habits not only are out of proportion to what men and women need to flourish as creatures made in the image of God but substantially transform the character of their relations with others, not only within the body of Christ but also with those outside the fellowship of the church.

The dismembering of the body of Christ had a significant impact on the earthly commonwealth as well, for the institutions that for centuries constituted the social fabric of Western Europe, Australia, and North America were fostered by the church. Though we might finally judge this arrangement to be theologically deficient, it provided a measure of moral coherence and direction to a succession of temporal regimes that helped, to one degree or another, preserve a fallen world for the gathering-together of all things in Christ at the end of the age. People can only go about their business on the tacit assumption that error, deception, self-deception, irony, and ambiguity, though everywhere present in these interactions, will not finally render reliable reasoning and coherent action impossible.[22] These assumptions are formed and sustained by the stock of activities, stories, habits, and institutions that foster a common life and language within a society. These practices and habits enable the members of a community to engage one another in meaningful transactions by allowing them to make inferences about future behavior and present intentions from premises about past behavior.

When these shared customs and habits no longer bind men and women together into a community of shared interest, and mutually incompatible accounts of what is going on around them multiply exponentially, but with none achieving a critical mass, the result is the kind of social fragmentation that we see with the demise of Christendom in Europe, Australia, and North America. An ever-widening gap or wound has opened up in the secular body politic, "which neither conventional right nor conventional left are currently doing much to recognise or repair." In lieu of shared patterns of life that allow people to determine what they can reasonably do and say together to foster a just and equitable common life and language, the dominant regime of nation-states and global markets offers political discourse dominated by the marketing of slogans and sound bites and by the calculation of short-term advantages.[23] These tendencies are not only incapable of sustained deliberations about the basic conditions of our humanity; they also create the breeding ground for the nationalist and authoritarian movements that have emerged at many places across the globe in recent history.

22. MacIntyre, "Epistemological Crises, Dramatic Narrative, and the Philosophy of Science," 139.
23. Williams, *Lost Icons*, 2–3, 9.

Christians cannot assign the blame for this state of affairs solely to the advent of modernity. The *corpus Christianum* had been sagging under its own accumulated weight for several centuries, and the final supports are now giving way to the stress of a rapidly secularizing world. With its collapse, its patterns of relating to the world are rapidly deteriorating as well. Nations in Europe, Australia, and North America delayed for a time the dehumanizing effects of this process by selectively drawing on a residual stock of practices, convictions, and dispositions held over from the traditions of medieval Christendom. But as the contents of this reserve were disconnected from the practices and institutions that had nurtured them over the centuries, their intelligibility and credibility began to unravel, somewhat slowly at first, and then more rapidly as the era of "enlightenment" and "progress" unfolded.

The compliment typically paid to this situation, cobbled together from the debris left by the *ancien régime*, is that it is pluralistic and multicultural, but this is hollow praise indeed, for these are but names for the reduction of all values to those that can be marketed as commodities in the global market. In place of a stock of images and ideas, inscribed in a shared body of texts, that foster a rich common life, the ruling consortium seeks merely to secure a pragmatic minimum of coexistence between unencumbered individuals and their mutually tangential projects by means of a combination of managerial skills and economic policies.[24] The euphemisms of *pluralism* and *multiculturalism* serve as a façade to hide the incoherence and antagonism that afflict all. Many now wonder whether there is anything at all genuinely and intrinsically human beyond their momentary appetites and desires, and any identity they might share in common resides not in a positive good that commands their assent but in suspicion of and hatred for their enemies, both real and imagined.

The dismembering of Christ's body must therefore be conceived diachronically as well as synchronically. The logic of separation that emerged in the sixteenth and seventeenth centuries and gained momentum in the modern era has its origins much earlier, when the church joined forces with the rulers and authorities of the present age to govern the *saeculum*, the temporal period between fall and *eschaton*, and after the coming of Christ the overlap of the two ages in the here and now. The division of the church must be examined in conjunction with the emergence, development, and demise of the social project of Christendom. In addition to being a work in hermeneutics and ecclesiology, then, this book also engages the much-contested domain of social theory.

24. Williams, "Between Politics and Metaphysics," 4; Williams, *On Christian Theology*, 34.

Re-embarking on Pilgrimage

As we prepare to take our bearings for the future from what went before us, what lessons should we learn from our present circumstances? First, we need to be careful, lest we romanticize the past and find ourselves caught up in nostalgic longing for what has been. Though nostalgia can be a potent form of social criticism, the church cannot simply rebel against the modern in an effort to return to the simplicity and pristine faithfulness supposedly proffered by the premodern era. We cannot return, moreover, because modernity was shaped by the deliberate rejection of the past, and modernity is part of our past.[25] Rebellion against rebellion imprisons us within an insidious antithetical bondage. Indeed, part of the modern world's genius was its ability to conscript its adversaries into its modes of regulating behavior, which rely not so much on explicit coercion as on widely diffused modes of regulation that train us how to think, feel, and act in ways appropriate to its basic modes of governance and accumulation.

Nostalgia also clouds the fact that the social arrangements of Christendom failed to a significant degree because the church for most of its history "endeavored to be not what it is but what it is not." These arrangements failed not only the church, in that it set aside the art of pilgrimage and thus lost sight of itself as "the sacrament of the Kingdom, a holy community, God's eschatological vehicle of passage for this world through time into the world to come," but also the world to which the church was sent as sign and instrument. The failure was twofold. First, in its efforts to redeem and sanctify the existing social order, the church forgot its earlier understanding of the world as both (1) created and therefore good and (2) fallen and therefore a mortally sick order. Second, when the church accepted its status as a juridical and hierarchical institution within the established order, it forfeited its calling as a free community of faith whose presence in the world is both a judgment on and a boundary to the claims of every worldly authority and power.[26]

The passing of Christendom presents a timely opportunity for the church to recover its missional status as another city making its way toward the age to come. The laments and prophetic rebukes in Scripture remind us that among the remnants of the failed kingdoms of Israel and Judah, there was a struggle to understand what had happened, and out of their humiliation they revised their own history, seeing it as "a story of unceasing resistance to and rebellion against God." They nonetheless concluded that God had not utterly abandoned them, but in his faithfulness had instead folded the destruction

25. Bottum, "Christians and Postmoderns," 28–29.
26. Guroian, *Incarnate Love*, 146–47; cf. Harvey, *Another City*, 64–69.

of the Northern Kingdom, the fall of Jerusalem, the exile to Babylon, and the dispersion of the chosen people among the nations back into the saving history of Israel. In their affliction they learned to "recognize their guilt and turn back to God, thus correcting the direction they [were] going. The very crisis of the people of God would then be one of the reasons why God's cause does not fail, but instead goes forward as a history of salvation." The end of the monarchy in Israel did not spell Israel's end but led instead "to a rebirth of the people of God," thus making the event of the exile part of "a *saving* history and a step into the future."[27]

Unfortunately, the church, particularly in North America, seems more oblivious to its precarious situation than were the exiles in Babylon. One must look long and hard for similar retrospectives on the part of the church with respect to its own history. On the contrary, writes Gerhard Lohfink, "the faith for which Israel still struggled and over which it wrangled is dissolving in the current decades . . . almost without resistance, and unnoticed by a great many, into religion: a religion that permits everything, that surrenders to everything, that has countless gods but no longer a history with the biblical God."[28] In our feeble efforts to hold on to the remnants of the *ancien régime*, too many accommodate the substance of the faith to the demands of a world that no longer is interested in what the church has to say.

Nevertheless, we have the opportunity to rediscover our history with the God of Israel, to acknowledge our failures and guilt, and to return to our first love, so that we too might learn to see what has happened over the past few centuries as part of God's redemptive history and thus as a way forward. The turn of fortune that has thrust the church back outside the city gate (Heb. 13:12), so that it no longer has a portfolio in the ruling regime, is an occasion once again to take our cues from the story of God's revelation in Jesus Christ and to reclaim our identity as an eschatological commonwealth whose allegiance is vested not in institutions that are condemned to pass away but in the world to come.

Before we can reflect on what might be involved in moving nearer to Christ, we need a better sense of how we got from where our pilgrimage began with the people of Israel and with Jesus and the Twelve to where we find ourselves, having journeyed, like the prodigal, to a "far country." Determining where we stand depends on the story that narrates this journey and how it might be possible for us to make our way back to the crucified and risen Lord. Only by tracing how we made our way to where we are, the many contingent steps

27. Lohfink, *Does God Need the Church?*, 96, 105 (emphasis original).
28. Lohfink, *Does God Need the Church?*, 96–97.

involved in bringing us to this place, do we realize that there is no inexorable historical process that led us to our present situation. In virtually every facet of life—ecclesial, political, economic, cultural—matters could have turned out much differently.

In what follows in the next chapter, then, I say something about why this calling of the church to be a sign, instrument, and witness of God's invasion of the world, which is challenging under the best of conditions, is now much more difficult because we have been separated from each other and from the interpretive art that allows us to be attentive to the ways of Christ in a world that is fallen but nonetheless still cherished by its Creator.

2

CAN THESE BONES LIVE?

The Dismembering of Christ's Body

But the incarnate Son of God needs not only ears or even hearts; he needs actual, living human beings who follow him. That is why he called his disciples into following him bodily. His community with them was something everyone could see.

Dietrich Bonhoeffer, *Discipleship*

I t was a gruesome scene envisioned by the prophet Ezekiel: a valley littered with human skeletons bleached dry by the sun. "Mortal," said God, "these bones are the whole house of Israel. They say, 'Our bones are dried up, and our hope is lost; we are cut off completely.'" Very little remained of the tribes of the Lord after their defeat at the hands of Assyria and Babylon. A remnant had survived the carnage, but of these many had been scattered to the four winds. Those left behind in the small towns and villages that dotted the countryside, the so-called people of the land, struggled as always to eke out a meager subsistence, but now they did so under foreign domination. As Ezekiel surveyed the disturbing panorama, God asked him, "Can these bones live?" Seemingly at a loss for an answer, the prophet could only respond, "O Lord God, you know" (Ezek. 37:1–3, 11).

A people that once had come on the scene with such promise had apparently met a tragic end. Many years before, their ancestors left home, family, and friends to go to a land far away. For centuries they struggled with their neighbors and among themselves to survive and flourish in what could be a harsh and unforgiving land and—perhaps unknowingly—to realize a fragment of that promise. During that time Israel weathered famines and withstood marauders, witnessed the rise of powerful kings and faced threats from foreign invaders, enduring much suffering and no little bloodshed in the process. Now some found themselves refugees and exiles, carted off to a strange land where they were compelled to "serve other gods made by human hands, objects of wood and stone that neither see, nor hear, nor eat, nor smell" (Deut. 4:28). Those who remained in the land bore the brunt of occupation. The possibility that these two groups would ever be brought back together again to live as one people in their own land must have seemed remote.

And yet the Jewish people did not disappear from the pages of history. They persevered against incredible odds, sustained in exile, occupation, and dispersion by their memory of the land their ancestors once possessed and a hope that God would at some point in the future gather them together and return the scattered tribes to their true homeland. As they struggled to understand not only what had happened to them but what their ongoing existence meant for themselves and the world, they developed a distinctive way of communal life that often made them suspect in the eyes of their gentile neighbors. It was this life together that constituted a socially embodied, historically extended interpretation of the world as lived in relation to God, such that the answer to the question What is the meaning of this word *God*? could be ascertained only by observing the way they worshiped and ordered their life together.[1]

The church presently finds itself in circumstances similar to those suffered by the Jews in Ezekiel's day. It was not war, however, that was responsible for the fragmentation of the church's life and witness. Instead, powerful political structures, economic forces, and social movements have severed the sinews that bound the members of the risen Christ's earthly-historical body to one another and to the crucified and risen Lord. For most people faith has been reconfigured from its biblical specifications encompassing the whole of bodily life and concerns into a purely private, inward, and "spiritual" matter, and the community of word, sacrament, and discipleship has been reconfigured into a vendor of spiritual goods and services. The dry bones of the church are now beholden to "spirits" to which, ironically, Christians helped give birth and which now exercise a usurped authority over them that God had reserved

---

1. Williams, *On Christian Theology*, xii, 135.

for the work of the Holy Spirit. The question that left the prophet perplexed, "Can these bones live?" is thus one that is posed to us as well.

Christians can find a measure of hope in the response of God to the question posed by the prophet. In spite of Israel's disobedience and punishment, God said that he would remain faithful to this people and to the mission for which they had been called. God then commanded Ezekiel to prophesy to the bones and say to them: "O dry bones, hear the word of the LORD. Thus says the Lord GOD to these bones: I will cause breath to enter you, and you shall live. I will lay sinews on you, and will cause flesh to come upon you, and cover you with skin, and put breath in you, and you shall live; and you shall know that I am the LORD" (Ezek. 37:4–6). Ezekiel obeyed the injunction to prophesy, and in his vision he saw these bones—this people—joined together by sinew, covered with flesh, reanimated by the breath of God, and thus made to live again.

Dry bones being brought back to life by the breath of God afford an apt figure around which to develop a theological account of some of the constitutive practices that are necessary to *re-member* the scattered followers of Jesus as the earthly-historical form of the crucified and risen Christ. If by means of these activities the church reclaims convictions and dispositions that allow it to strip off the practices of the old human and clothe itself with the new human, "which is being renewed in knowledge according to the image of its creator" (Col. 3:10), the world may yet see communities of faith, hope, and charity reanimated by the Spirit and made to live again. The church may once again become a people able to interpret the persons, structures, and institutions that constitute the present world by comparing them to its own social practice, which manifests (imperfectly, to be sure) the form of community that alone truly deserves the title of peace: the city of God.[2]

If this is to happen, however, we will need to reckon with political, economic, and cultural developments that have relegated matters of the "spirit" to what has to do with the soul as opposed to the body, divorcing them from issues related to the production and reproduction of life in all its dimensions.[3] By contrast, the doctrine of the incarnation, God made flesh, authorizes the followers of Christ to live unreservedly in the material world without losing ourselves in it.[4] The significance of this one man's existence for everyday life, in all of its diversity, is reconstituted time and again within the earthly-historical body of Christ. This community, gathered together by the Spirit from every tribe and nation, offers to all peoples a social grammar in terms of which the beauty, goodness, and truth of the world can be followed.

2. Augustine, *City of God* 19.17.
3. McGinn, "Letter and the Spirit," 3.
4. Bonhoeffer, *Discipleship*, 55–56.

A Glimpse of the Beauty of Truth

As I mentioned in chapter 1, our mothers and fathers in the faith regarded the world as a book authored by God, with the events of nature and history unfolding in the manner of a dramatic story. People, objects, and events had their own integrity and relative independence, but they were also seen as signs of God and his intentions for creation. The transactions and relationships that composed nature and history were linked together within this narrative frame of reference, constituting either anticipations or rejections of the gathering-up of all things, both in heaven and on earth, in Christ. And as in all good stories, the role played by the exchanges and associations in this drama would not be fully revealed until the ending. Historical judgments were provisional in nature, typically cast in terms of a figural contrast between the present age and the age to come, the flesh and the Spirit, the earthly city and the city of God. All this was predicated on the conviction that the form of this world was passing away and that they, the pilgrim people of God, were to make wise use of its goods and to endure patiently its hardships as they made their way to the world to come.

The complex plot and many subplots of this story were detailed for the faithful in God's other text, the Bible, according to which all things ultimately find their significance in their convergence upon or divergence from the person and work of Christ. Were it not for sin, "the symbol of the world, in its unspoiled transparency, would have sufficed." But after the fall, humans need the help of Scripture to decipher it.[5] "The whole created world is now covered in a veil," writes Dietrich Bonhoeffer; "it is silent and lacking explanation, opaque and enigmatic."[6] In the words of John Scotus Erigena, "the surface of the Scriptures" and "the sensible forms of the world" are now the two garments of Christ. They are like two veils that filter the overwhelmingly brilliant light of his divinity. But they are also signs that, through their "reason" or "spirit," allow women and men to catch a glimpse of the beauty of truth itself.[7]

The church taught that the persons, places, events, and objects of the world were traces of the beginning and end of all things, and of rational beings in particular. On their own, however, human beings were too weak to find the truth by natural reason alone and "needed the authority of the sacred scriptures."[8] With the help of the Bible, all creatures could truthfully be seen as "signs of the possibility of communion, covenanted trust and the

5. De Lubac, *Medieval Exegesis*, 77.
6. Bonhoeffer, *Creation and Fall*, 126.
7. Erigena, *De divisione naturae*, bk. 3, cited in de Lubac, *Medieval Exegesis*, 77.
8. Augustine, *Confessions* 6.5.8.

recognition of shared need and shared hope."[9] Catherine of Siena states, for example, that God desires that we love him in the same way God loves us, but then she concedes that this is not possible, for God loves us gratuitously, but we love him out of duty. This is why God put us among our neighbors, so that we can do for them what we cannot do for God: "Love them without any concern for thanks and without looking for any profit for [ourselves]."[10]

Augustine sets forth the details of this interpretive surmise in *De doctrina Christiana*, where he states that all reality should be provisionally classified as either *res* (thing) or *signum* (sign) and that each *res* that human beings encounter acts upon their willing in one of two ways. A thing may be regarded as complete in itself and thus could be enjoyed (*frui*) for its own sake, or it may be used (*uti*) as a means to a greater and more proper satisfaction and thus as intending more than itself. The people, places, and things that human beings enjoy and use in their daily comings and goings are also signs that direct their attention to God, who alone is to be enjoyed for his own sake.[11]

God alone is truly *res*, and yet not actually some thing or some body, but that which is beyond all specification. As Anselm would finally conclude, "That than which nothing greater can be thought" is in actuality "greater than can be thought."[12] (This is what makes it so difficult to use the word *God* intelligibly, for it is not the name of some person or object that makes itself available for our inspection.) Nevertheless, by God's own initiative there is a *signum* of the divine reality in the Word made flesh that not only refers to God but is God's own self-communication. Because of the embodiment of the divine utterance, God could be truly and truthfully named and enjoyed by women and men as the one true end of desire. The incarnation thus decisively discloses the nature of the world as "sign" or trace of its Creator.

The Word made flesh "instructs us once and for all that we have our identity within the shifting, mobile realm of representation, non-finality, growing and learning, because it reveals what the spiritual eye ought to perceive generally— that the whole creation is uttered and 'meant' by God, and therefore has no meaning in itself." But apart from this imaginative venture, humans invariably seek or fashion finalities within the created order that would block off the processes of learning about and desiring God. It is only when we know that we live in a world of signs that we are "set free for the restlessness that is our destiny as rational creatures."[13] The distinctive use of things by Christians

9. Williams, *On Christian Theology*, 218.
10. Catherine of Siena, *Dialogue*, 121.
11. Augustine, *Teaching Christianity* 1.1–40.
12. Anselm, *Proslogion* 2.15.
13. Williams, "Language, Reality and Desire in Augustine's *De Doctrina*," 141.

was thus a part of and contributed to the church's ongoing interpretation of human existence lived in relation to the triune God.

The literary work that in the Middle Ages exemplified this figure for the world as a book authored by God was Dante Alighieri's *Divine Comedy*. All things that took place on earth, under the earth, and in heaven, past, present, and future, were mysteriously ordered toward the beatific vision; and the story of the poet's journey through the punishments of the Inferno, up the penitential path of Mount Purgatory, and into the celestial rose of Paradise recapitulated in poetic form the pilgrimage of the soul to its beginning and end in God. Along the way the political intrigues and personal animosities, the friendships and the rivalries that characterized Dante's rough-and-tumble world, were vividly displayed in their orientation either away from or toward "the Love that moves the sun and the other stars."[14]

The church thus engaged the world of time and space in the context of divine mystery and providence and, more precisely, as the issue of God's "speech." Were it not for the fall, creation's testimony to God's "eternal power and divine nature" (Rom. 1:20) would be followable to all. As it now stood, however, the "text" of God's speech had been effaced by our usurpations of power, making it unintelligible to humankind's natural abilities. In a postlapsarian world, men and women needed the Bible to make sense of it and of themselves. The church's contemplation of the triune mystery of God was sustained by the practice of scriptural reasoning—the imaginative process of figuring and refiguring the world depicted in the Bible—carried out in the context of eucharistic worship. Figural interpretation enabled exegetes to locate the whole sweep of history within the providential scope of divine rule.[15]

The beauty of truth (and of goodness) manifested in a world uttered and meant by God was eternal, but the church did not think the ability to trace it to its source and consummation in God was commonly available to all. The eucharistic communion, which constituted the body of Christ in its earthly-historical or ecclesial form, comprised the "site on which universal truth was produced, and it was clear to them that truth was not produced universally."[16] The practices and institutions of the body of Christ were therefore needed if men and women were to participate as fully as the mind of a rational animal was able in the triune life of the One who had created the world. Only those who had achieved a sufficient level of competence in the skills and virtues of the ecclesial household would be capable of truthfully following the movements and motifs of history as elements of a dramatic story. "Whoever enters

14. Dante, *Paradise* 33.145.
15. De Lubac, *Scripture in the Tradition*, 6.
16. Asad, *Genealogies of Religion*, 45n29; cf. 35.

Jesus's house is his true disciple," writes Origen. "He comes in by thinking with the Church, by living according to the Church."[17]

Christians thus did not regard the patterns and rhythms of history as givens, a sort of universally accessible text that anyone with a modicum of intelligence could use to decode the meaning of human existence. The practices, virtues, and skills of the ecclesial body of Christ, through which beauty, truth, and goodness were mediated to a fallen yet cherished world, were required if human beings were to respond truthfully to the Love who is the author of all things, who moves both the sun and the other stars, and who cherishes the creature specially made in Love's image. This ascent of the mind to the divine Love ultimately depended on God's prior act of gathering together the commonwealth of Israel, from which came the Messiah and into which his gentile followers have been grafted to form the church (Eph. 2:12–13; Rom. 11:17). Apart from this community and tradition the nations would continue in the futility of their minds and remain alienated from the life of God (Eph. 4:17–18).

A New Configuration

The assertion that human beings must be apprenticed within a particular community and tradition to follow the truth, goodness, and beauty of this world was deeply offensive to modern sensibilities. Increasingly it was thought that humans unencumbered by such impediments could in actuality get to the bottom of things, that the only limits that mattered were the limits of being itself, which were identical to the limits of human reason.[18] They thus sought a vantage point that would transport men and women beyond the limits of mere creatureliness to see all the kingdoms of the world in an instant. These epistemic moves were accompanied by a pronounced shift in how determination and contingency were depicted, with human choices, natural causes, and random chance replacing cosmologies such as one finds in the *Divine Comedy*.

The chief architects of modernity continued to assume that the intelligibility of nature, the meaningfulness of history, and the purposefulness of human existence would not be seriously disturbed by the changes being made. They did think, however, that the world was the real text on which God's writing was inscribed, regarding the Bible as simply the republication of natural religion. The book of nature had its own independent intelligibility, invested with indisputable authority for interpreting the meaning and truthfulness

17. Origen, "Dialogue of Origen with Heraclides and His Fellow Bishops," 69.
18. De Lubac, *Mystery of the Supernatural*, 171.

of the sacred texts, written as they were in merely human language.[19] The church and its practices were no longer essential to see what was true, good, or beautiful.

There was a great deal of disagreement among these pioneers, to be sure, over the precise nature of the plot and the identity of the author of the book of nature, but until recently relatively few seriously doubted whether it finally made sense. In a provocative essay that appeared in the fall of 1989, for example, Francis Fukuyama argues that the collapse of the Soviet Union and its sphere of influence, symbolized by the dismantling of the Berlin Wall, represented the "unabashed victory of economic and political liberalism" in its ideological struggle with Marxism, signaling "the end of history as such . . . the end point of mankind's ideological evolution and the universalization of Western liberal democracy as the final form of human government."[20] Although things would obviously continue to happen, the world would now witness the culmination of ideological conflict and development, and in this sense it now stands at the end of history.[21]

The formal features of Fukuyama's faith in a book of nature that is followable were bequeathed to him by modernity's Jewish and Christian forebears, who cultivated their stories about creation with care over the centuries. In addition to these precedents, however, there are yet other traditions of thought that are at least as significant. In North America, for example, a powerful proposal for a meaningful history was put forward when elements of the Christian hope for the future were detached from their ecclesial context and their material specifications in the Scriptures and grafted onto another narrative to form what is often referred to as the American dream. Progress became a kind of cosmic imperative, the necessity of which could be asserted with certainty even if we do not presently see evidence of it.[22]

The theme of progress merges seamlessly with the apparent success of the continental takeover by Western European immigrants, "the first and most successful specimen of the worldwide colonial expansion of European travel and technology." The seemingly inexhaustible supply of natural resources (once "liberated" from the purview of the previous inhabitants of this continent, who did not "choose to develop" them as they "should" have) and the ability and the willingness of the immigrants to exploit them as they sought to fashion a new and powerful civilization from a "wilderness" (again, those who once lived here did not count) "reinforced still further the ethnocentric

19. Asad, *Genealogies of Religion*, 41.
20. Fukuyama, "End of History?," 3–4.
21. Boyle, *Who Are We Now?*, 76.
22. Yoder, *For the Nations*, 128–29.

self-confidence which European culture had enough of to begin with and gave to the notion of a religiously founded civilizing mission the powerful amplification of several generations of impressive success."[23]

The development of the idea of nature as followable *etsi deus non daretur*, as if God does not exist, did not occur all at once and certainly did not happen according to some grand conspiracy. Galileo Galilei, René Descartes, and Isaac Newton did not want to dispense with what they regarded as the unquestioned "given" of morality that seemed to be jeopardized by their new scientific accounts of nature. Their intellectual heirs—Jean-Jacques Rousseau, Immanuel Kant, and G. W. F. Hegel—attempted to do this by seeking a way of discriminating between the human world of freedom and purpose and the "natural" world of seemingly blind cause and effect, and they settled on the notion of history. George Grant writes in this regard:

> It was indeed in this intellectual crisis (the attempt to understand the modern, scientific conception of nature that excluded any idea of final purpose, and to relate that conception to human purposiveness) that the modern conception of history first made its appearance. . . . "History" was used to describe the particular human situation in which we are not only made but make. In this way of speaking, history was not a term to be applied to the development of the earth and animals, but a term to distinguish the collective life of man (that unique being who is subject to cause and effect as defined in modern science, but also a member of the world of freedom).[24]

"History" as the sphere of activity over which humanity would gain strategic sovereignty as their permanent dwelling came about as a result of a series of interrelated developments, many of which predate the Enlightenment by several centuries. A partial list would include medieval nominalism's depiction of an undifferentiated deity; the demise of traditional forms of biblical exegesis, particularly figural interpretation; the bisection of the concept of the literal, giving birth both to the heretofore unheard-of notion that the literal sense stands over against metaphor, analogy, and the like, and eventually to the idea that the mind is an incorporeal mirror that merely represents reality; the world as a stock of resources that exist solely for our enjoyment; the introduction in predominantly Catholic circles of the concept of "pure nature," which regards the world as "a closed and self-sufficient whole," created with an end that is proportionate to humankind's natural powers; the invention of "religion" as a discrete and essentially private aspect of

23. Yoder, *For the Nations*, 128–29.
24. Grant, *Time as History*, 11–12.

human life; and the emergence of the state as the sole legitimate bearer of political authority.

A crucial aspect in the turn to "History" as the matrix of what is genuinely human was a confidence in the ability of the modern subject to make reliable value judgments about the exigencies of history. Ernst Troeltsch, in *The Social Teaching of the Christian Churches*,[25] asserted that modern historians could extrapolate from these exigencies ideal types that identified what is and is not of enduring value and significance. These ideal types in history were based on historians' experiences, allowing them to discern "what is normative and of enduring significance in history through a sensitivity to the needs of the present. In other words, the past is rendered intelligible and meaningful precisely by its implicit relationship to the present."[26]

These historians and theorists developed different narratives to track the plot of history refigured around the institutions of the nation-state and a capitalist market—social contract, manifest destiny, the inevitable triumph of science, liberal democracy, world socialism or global capitalism, and so on—all of which sought to reinforce the conviction that we inhabited a world possessing the properties of a unitary story that had no need of any transcendent frame. But with the passing of time this belief became increasingly difficult to sustain, as each attempt to identify a convincing replacement for God in the narrative progress of history only served to contribute another chapter to the chronicle of modernity's increasingly frantic effort to hold on to its inherited faith in a followable world. The forms of reasoning that distinguished the modern era from all that had gone before it proved to be a powerful corrosive, eating away at the assumption that human beings could, at least in principle, become like gods and distinguish between universal rationality and local acculturation, between the permanent truths of reason and temporary truths of facts, and between religion, myth, and tradition, on the one hand, and something ahistorical, common to all human beings qua human, on the other. Humans, as it turns out, are "historical contingency all the way through."[27] What remains of the New Testament proclamation of judgment and redemption, the passing of the old and the advent of the new in Christ, are merely "modulations within an order of things finally left undisturbed, a collection of dramatic tropes for 'naming and symbolizing what we take to be of significance in existence' in an 'outsideless' world, that, for all its flux, is ever essentially just one damn thing after another."[28]

25. Troeltsch, *Social Teaching of the Christian Churches*, 1:21.
26. Mawson, *Christ Existing as Community*, 18–20.
27. Rorty, "Priority of Democracy to Philosophy," 267.
28. Ziegler, *Militant Grace*, 5–6.

The historicist referral to "History" with its ideal types and value judgments is further complicated by the fact that the various plotlines invoked to sustain a sense of a coherent story were all grounded, in various and sundry ways, in the colonialist conquests and racial reasoning of European and North American powers, nowhere more apparent than in "the deep contradiction in the heart" of the United States, its founding documents committing it "to the idea that all people are created equal and to a system of race-based chattel slavery."[29] Sadly, the church, by aligning itself with these sorts of immanent frames, implicates itself in the "egregious moral failure" of Christendom's latest venture. Americans have taken pride in doing right, says Walker Percy, but "in the one place, the place which hurts the most and where charity was most needed, they have not done right. White Americans have sinned against the Negro from the beginning and continue to do so, initially with cruelty and presently with an indifference which may be even more destructive."[30] The dual legacy of colonialism and racial reasoning, aptly summed up by the trope of "whiteness," is part and parcel of our "outsideless" world.

The Church and the Modern World

These new configurations of human life, which were conceived in Europe but first executed in North America, sought to maintain an abiding faith in an underlying order to the book of nature, and especially a faith in the purposefulness of human history, while gradually disassociating themselves from the God who had been its beginning and end and from the practices and traditions of the church that bore witness to God.[31] According to Richard Rorty, notables such as Walt Whitman and John Dewey (designated by Richard Neuhaus as the chief apostles of American civil religion[32]) "hoped to separate the fraternity and loving kindness urged by the Christian scriptures from the ideas of supernatural parentage, immortality, and providence, and—most important—sin. They wanted Americans to take pride in what America might, all by itself and by its own lights, make of itself, rather than in America's obedience to any authority—even the authority of God."[33]

Though they obviously did not wish to separate fraternity and loving-kindness from the Christian tradition, many Protestant groups in the United States increasingly relied on the coherence and intelligibility of these new

29. T. Smith, *Weird John Brown*, 39.
30. Percy, *Message in the Bottle*, 117.
31. Jenson, "How the World Lost Its Story," 21.
32. Neuhaus, "Three Constellations of American Religion," 72.
33. Rorty, *Achieving Our Country*, 15–16.

social configurations as they made themselves at home in this new social order. They embraced the promise and possibility of a new and more perfect Christendom, a conviction that was exemplified in the title of a book by Walter Rauschenbusch, *Christianizing the Social Order*. The preeminent voice in the social gospel movement in the first half of the twentieth century, Rauschenbusch declares that social progress—by which he meant the spread of democracy—"is more than natural. It is divine." He commends Baptists, Congregationalists, Disciples, Unitarians, and Universalists in particular, stating that they "represent the principles of pure democracy in church life. That is their spiritual charisma and their qualification for leadership in the democratization of the social order."[34]

A contemporary of Rauschenbusch makes the connection between Christian faith and democratic habits and institutions more explicit. E. Y. Mullins likens the "fundamental principles of true religion" to a stalactite descending from heaven to earth. The most important of these principles is "soul competency," which asserts that individuals unencumbered by any social practice or convention possess a timeless inner source of spiritual insight that makes them competent to judge for themselves the state of their relationship to God. American political society, in turn, is the stalagmite, with its base on the earth rising to meet the stalactite. Both the stalactite and the stalagmite are formed from the same life-giving stream of water that flows from the throne of God down to humankind. "When the two shall meet," he writes, "then heaven and earth will be joined together and the kingdom of God will have come among men. *This is the process that runs through the ages*."[35] History is approaching its true telos in the convergence of these principles of religion and the institutions of procedural democracy. When this process is concluded it will mark nothing less than the presence of God's reign on earth.

Rauschenbusch and Mullins, together with countless others, perpetuate the ancient Stoic assumption that the "natural" and the "social" orders form a single entity,[36] and thus there exists at present one all-encompassing cosmopolis, one universal community made up of all human beings, within which the church properly functions as one of a number of secondary subsystems. When the church feels relatively at home in the world as it is, it becomes easier to assume that everyone is Christian, or at least shares essentially the same set of moral ends and virtues. When one asks what Christians should do, one also asks what society as a whole should do. The moral expectations of the church for its own members must then be consistent with what is required

34. Rauschenbusch, *Christianizing the Social Order*, 23, 30.
35. Mullins, *Axioms of Religion*, 274 (emphasis added).
36. See Toulmin, *Cosmopolis*, 67–69; Nussbaum, *Cultivating Humanity*, 58–59.

of those who maintain society's principles and directives: the diplomat, the investment banker, the soldier, the chairman of the board, the social worker, the factory manager. Ethical obligations are aligned with what is needed to maintain the given order of things, not with what might be entailed in the apocalyptic intrusion of God into that order. Not surprisingly, over the centuries the outlines of the body of Christ become less distinct, and the day-to-day existence of Christians becomes coextensive with, and thus indistinguishable from, that of any other citizen.

Though the kinds of assumptions we can credibly make about history are very different from those that Rauschenbusch and Mullins thought they could make in the first half of the twentieth century when they spoke confidently about a fundamental harmony between Christian identity and American society, there are still some who continue to make similar claims about the convergence of Christianity and the secular regime. Max Stackhouse, a theologian influenced by Rauschenbusch, argues that the Old Testament's prophetic vision of a single created realm where all peoples live under a divine law and toward a divine end is being realized in the economic process of globalization. He declares unequivocally that "God is in globalization."[37] For the most part, however, we live in a world that no longer feigns allegiance to the God whom Rauschenbusch and Mullins worshiped in all sincerity; neither does it believe that the bits and pieces that remain from Christendom's breakup are still needed to keep the wheels of unconstrained commerce and conspicuous consumption turning. The so-called mainline churches that once dominated the American social landscape have been pushed to the periphery of a culture of aimless production and narcissistic consumption, where they continue to make periodic pronouncements, as if they still enjoyed a monopoly in American religious life, while at the same time constantly adapting themselves to a world they still hope they control.[38]

The gradual separation of the book of nature from the plot, setting, and characters of the Bible—dramatically reenacted time and again by the people of God—thus may have for a time retained a residual sense of the coming to be and passing away of history that seemed coherent and convincing, but this sense has become progressively thinner and less persuasive as the years have gone by.[39] As a result, the assertion that we are at the end of history may not signify that there is a meaningful plot to human existence, provided we are clever enough to know where to look for it. On the contrary, it could mean that the world is unfollowable and that our hopes for an enduring meaning

37. Stackhouse, "Public Theology and Political Theology in a Globalizing Era," 179.
38. Copenhaver, Robinson, and Willimon, *Good News in Exile*, 31–32.
39. See Loughlin, *Telling God's Story*, 127–38.

and purpose may in the end be illusory. As Frank Kermode puts it, both world and book may be "hopelessly plural, endlessly disappointing; we stand alone before them, aware that they may be narratives only because of our impudent intervention, and susceptible of interpretation only by our hermetic tricks." If this is the case, our sole hope and pleasure "is in the perception of a momentary radiance, before the door of disappointment is finally shut on us."[40] What we call "History" could well be a mere succession of happenings without connection, purpose, or goal other than the interpretations we impose on them, the arbitrary nature of which only serves to mock us with the capriciousness of our existence.

Learning Again to Take Our Bearings

For all their differences, the divergent interpretations of the modern world offered by Fukuyama and Kermode put different versions of the question posed in the introduction: Where, then, do we stand? At the end of history, either triumphant, confident, and in control, able to see all the worlds in an instant, or alone, helpless, and disoriented, mired in our parochial particularities? Our attempt to answer this question will be conditioned by the fact that, as the poet Wallace Stevens observes, "we live in the description of a place and not in the place itself."[41] In other words, all human beings inhabit the world in terms of some sort of imaginative depiction of how that world is ordered and how they are related to it. By itself the end of history, narrated so differently by Fukuyama and Kermode, does not point unambiguously in one direction or the other, but is susceptible to rival interpretations that seem to be little more than expressions of taste and personal preference, having no compelling connection to the world of time and space.

The conclusion that human beings are historical all the way through cannot help but be a counsel of despair for those who had placed their faith in the projects of the modern world. This despair, expressed in the absolute relativism and romantic nihilism of postmodern thought, is but the inverted image of modernity's arrogance. The possibility that human beings may not be gods after all is a discovery that weighs heavy upon many, for once the picture of an eternal, ahistorical truth has been exposed as a chimera, they still assess the everyday world "from the perspective of eternity—static and changeless as the printed word is when compared with the spoken. So we think of ourselves as being left with 'only' the realities and Being that are disclosed

40. Kermode, *Genesis of Secrecy*, 145.
41. Stevens, letter to Henry Church, April 4, 1945, *Letters*, 494.

in time, and left 'only' with history."[42] Indeed, for far too many in our world of aimless production and conspicuous consumption, there is finally no history, no memory, no past or future, only the nothingness from which we can try to rescue the present moment and perhaps hope to snatch the next moment as well.[43] Dietrich Bonhoeffer concludes, perhaps with a touch of sad irony, "Nothingness binds itself to us and nothingness puts us in its debt."[44]

Christians need not be paralyzed by this false dichotomy. There are no good reasons (only residual habits of mind and their associated neuroses) to be forced into choosing between the illusion of being able to comprehend the whole in one glance and the despair of stumbling blindly along in the encircling gloom. Instead we may transcend the circumstances and preoccupations of the present by discovering something of how we came to be the way we are. We do this by examining where we have come from and where we believe we are headed. Though we cannot get "outside" our time, we can take our bearings within history and seek to discern the contours of its temporal meter and rhythms.[45] There are no theories that can supply the necessary perspective, though they may assist us along the way. As Augustine understood when he sat down to compose *The City of God*, only the writing of a certain kind of narrative history can provide the church with what it needs to follow the course of events that led to its current state.[46]

As I have already indicated, there was a time when Christians took their interpretive bearings from the practices cultivated by and constitutive of the church as the body of Christ, which also proclaimed the end of history. These practices embodied a specific shared way of interpreting human life as it is lived in relation to God and to the world about them. And the church did this not for itself alone but for the sake of the nations, for the diverse meanings of this peculiar term *God* are far from self-evident. They could be learned only by observing what this community did, not only when it was involved in explicit theological reflection (though this was important) but also when it gathered to worship, teach, and exchange gifts, and then dispersed so that it could offer itself as a living sacrifice, sharing in and bearing witness to the irruption of God's regime in the world.[47] Such sacrifice involved the particular ways this community used the same range of goods and endured the same sorts of hardships that all suffer in this age.

42. Poteat, *Philosophical Daybook*, 65.
43. Bonhoeffer, *Ethics*, 128.
44. Bonhoeffer, *Ethics*, 120, my translation.
45. Lash, *Theology on the Way to Emmaus*, 65.
46. See MacIntyre, *After Virtue*, 113; Milbank, *Theology and Social Theory*, 71.
47. Williams, *On Christian Theology*, xii.

These Christians knew that the kingdom of God consists not in talk but in power (1 Cor. 4:20) and that the divine presence and activity are principally manifested not in words or ideas (though these do have an important role to play) but in and through our participation in a social regime of power consisting of activities, habits, and relationships that over time bind women and men to Christ and thus to each other in much the same way as a person's extremities are attached to her or his body. In this context faith is not primarily a matter of what goes on "inside" isolated individuals but has everything to do with what happens to our bodies and what we do with our bodies—eating and drinking, enjoying the company of friends, marrying and giving in marriage, having children and burying parents, making and using signs, acquiring and disposing of property, producing and exchanging goods, enduring the normal hardships of human life and suffering at the hands of enemies, and above all, bearing witness before the fallen powers of this age to the wisdom of God in its richness and diversity (Eph. 3:10).

Christians in an earlier era knew, then, that the world happens to us—addresses us, summoning us to respond—only as embodied beings. The body is integral to Christian life, language, and witness, constituting the site where temporal events, the making and use of signs (both linguistic and liturgical), and a social grammar of communication, production, and exchange intersect to form the irreducible sinews of human existence. From this standpoint the world that happens to bodies does not consist of lumps of inert "stuff" waiting for us to impose our self-selected valuations on it. We inhabit the world, understand it, are affected by it, and act upon it only as an embodied complex of signs, the meaning of which is never self-evident. In the constantly shifting interactions between events, signs, and networks of communication, individual action and social situation can never be isolated from each other; their respective contributions to this complex are thoroughly contingent (without being arbitrary) and constantly modifying each other.[48]

With the dismembering of the church, however, Christian bodies are at the mercy of secular regimes of power. Faith is no longer intrinsically related to the social exchanges that occur only between physical bodies in connection with the mediation of signs and texts that have their material origin in these same bodies.[49] Abstract notions such as "conscience," "individual belief," and "sensibility" now fill the role once played by ecclesial practices. All talk of redemption, forgiveness, and reconciliation is confined to the interior life of the individual, with no intrinsic connection to the unfolding of history,

---

48. Milbank, *Theology and Social Theory*, 71; cf. Certeau, *Mystic Fable*, 80–81; Boyle, *Who Are We Now?*, 59–60, 155, 226, 228, 241.

49. Clapp, *Border Crossings*, 97.

the sacramental life and theological language of the church, or the social and political structures of this world. As a result, Christians regularly embrace a range of moral positions and live lives that are increasingly indistinguishable from those of non-Christians.[50]

In its present condition the church has little to offer for the healing of the nations. Indeed, it can barely help itself, ensnared in what I call the Schlesinger Bind. In his insightful biography of Reinhold Niebuhr, Richard Fox observes that many of those who admired Niebuhr's work nonetheless wondered with Harvard professor and presidential adviser Arthur Schlesinger Jr. whether "the part about God and sin was really necessary."[51] Niebuhr no doubt would have answered with an emphatic and unequivocal yes, but the ambivalence surrounding the theological underpinnings of his thought is a by-product of a general tendency on the part of many churches, particularly in North America, to see the gospel as essentially the capstone of human experience, capable of being translated virtually without remainder into terminology that is not explicitly Christian or even theological. As one astute observer puts it, this tendency is nicely expressed in the conclusion to many a sermon, "And perhaps Jesus said it best . . ."[52]

The challenge confronting the church in these circumstances is analogous to the epistemological crises that have occupied the attention of philosophers of science for several decades now. Such a crisis occurs when anomalies arise within a basic research project that resist all attempts to deal with them. The problem, says Joseph Rouse, "is not that scientists do not know what to believe; scientists are professionally accustomed to uncertainty of *that* sort. It is that they are no longer quite sure how to proceed: What investigations are worth undertaking, which supposed facts are unreliable artifacts, what concepts or models are useful guides for their theoretical or experimental manipulations?"[53] While crises of this sort seldom if ever collapse completely the intelligibility of a field of activities and achievements, they do blur its shape and direction, such that practitioners become disoriented, unable to place their own work within it. They recognize the need to try a different approach, another set of techniques or new instrumentation, but what sense these things would make is no longer clear.

In like manner the problem for the body of Christ is not that we do not know precisely what to believe, say, or do when confronted with new or puzzling circumstances. Men and women down through the centuries have

---

50. Asad, *Genealogies of Religion*, 39, 79.
51. Fox, *Reinhold Niebuhr*, 225.
52. Copenhaver, Robinson, and Willimon, *Good News in Exile*, 9.
53. Rouse, *Knowledge and Power*, 33–34 (emphasis original).

known that human beings must deal with such ambiguity countless times throughout their lives. Indeed it is a perennial aspect of Christian life and thought as well. "The Christian engaged at the frontier with politics, art or science," writes Rowan Williams, "will frequently find that he or she *will not know what to say.*" This is a time of real testing for the viability and flexibility of the church's tradition, as Christians struggle to discover whether there is any sense in which the other languages we are working with can be faithfully incorporated in our theology.[54]

The difficulty is rather that the shared practices, judgments, and institutions that once allowed Christians to interact with the world about them and engage in meaningful transactions with one another have eroded to the point that we no longer know how to proceed. The uncertainty, however, is not limited to a single field or enterprise, as with an epistemological crisis in science. It affects virtually every aspect of Christ's body; its members, sundered from one another, are disoriented, unable to locate the coherence and meaning of their lives within a common frame of reference that lends significance to their shared existence. In such circumstances the contention that world and book may be hopelessly plural, and history endlessly disappointing, appears to many to be increasingly plausible.

Though we might be tempted, Christians would be foolish to follow the lead of self-described postmodernists who discern nothing in the universe but chaos and call it carnival. The holophobia that feeds such tendencies reflects the pessimism of a generation of intellectuals whose hopes in the triumph of the institutions of modernity—cultural, social, political, scientific, and economic—over the ills of humankind proved ill founded.[55] As Cornel West has observed, the postmodern disclosing and debunking of the binary oppositions in the Western philosophical tradition are "interesting yet impotent bourgeois attacks on the forms of thought and categories of a 'dead' tradition, a tradition that stipulates the lineage and sustains the very life of these deconstructions." These attacks are symbiotic with their object of criticism, remaining alive only as long as they give life to their enemy.[56] Such behavior is a type of neurosis, and those who suffer from it exhibit a characteristically neurotic compulsion to repeat a particular emotional stimulus—in this case, the parricidal act of shattering bourgeois identity. They are unable to accept the loss of their past (namely, the emancipatory project of modernity) and thus subscribe to a view of the present—as an endlessly repeated moment of consumption—that excuses them from having to consider time as anything

---

54. Williams, *On Christian Theology*, 38–39 (emphasis original).
55. Eagleton, *Illusions of Postmodernism*, 4–5.
56. West, "Ethics and Action in Fredric Jameson's Marxist Hermeneutic," 138.

other than one damn thing after another.[57] They too greedily devour what past generations have produced but produce little or nothing to sustain future generations.

Nicholas Boyle traces the postmodern compulsion to the writings of Martin Heidegger, whom he calls the first systematic philosopher of the post-bourgeois age. Heidegger failed in the task he set himself, to construct a philosophy of historical time, because he did not take adequate account of the process of consumption, which in this regard takes place in the form of the reception of a historical tradition. In particular, he cut his links to the most extensive corpus of thought on the relation of Being and historicity that the Western world has to offer: Catholic Christology and ecclesiology. Inherent in both of these doctrines is a theme neglected throughout Heidegger's thought: bodies—that is, "the natural and risen body of the incarnate Lord, and the bodies of the faithful, sexually generated, destined to die, and sustained in life by their participation in the economic nexus. How these bodies have become or are to become the Mystical Body, the temples of the Spirit, is the question in theological anthropology Heidegger decided in 1919 not to answer."[58]

Neurotic postmodernists, by contrast, fail to take adequate account of the process of production, by which we hand convictions and virtues on to the next generation. Their respective accounts detach the activities of thinking and writing and the formation of identity from the socioeconomic reality of purposive work, and so in the end from a followable history. Once we learn how to see ourselves as both consumers and producers existing in the world in bodily form, however, "thought and writing and identity can again be related to historical time. To produce for others is to make a future, and to consume what others have produced for us is to receive a past."[59]

I am particularly interested in the claim that the activities of production and making, reception and consumption, constitute the substance of our bodily relationship to past and future. In other words, who we are and what we are to be about in the world become concrete and visible to us in an act of historical interpretation, "in the words by which a past given to us is related to a future of our own making." The church's interpretive art opens the way for our understanding of and participation in the unfolding of time as history.[60]

At the heart of these practices is memory, which is the wellspring of both personal and communal identity and the means by which we constitute ourselves as identifiable subjects with a coherent and continuing personal narrative.

57. Boyle, *Who Are We Now?*, 318.
58. Boyle, *Who Are We Now?*, 318, 226.
59. Boyle, *Who Are We Now?*, 318.
60. Boyle, *Who Are We Now?*, 318.

It is only through memory that we learn that character *and* situation, self *and* other, are made and therefore not immutable. The concepts of person and community are but abstract indices denoting actual lived continuities that *are* memory, capable of generating at any particular point in time an almost infinite range of moves. Because of this power, men and women are not trapped and confined in the present moment but can locate it as the invention of temporal processes and actions, allowing them to transcend the limitations to which the here and now would restrict us.

Following as Interpretive Activity

Linking interpretation to memory does not mean that what was said and done in the past provides formulas that we can draw on to decipher an infinite variety of historical and social contexts through the application of deductive logic. As heir to the Aristotelian tradition of practical reasoning, hermeneutics needs to unravel the complex and confusing contingencies of human existence and to account for the ever-changing nature of social regimes and their distinctive ways of regulating bodies. In our present circumstances our interpretive efforts must come to terms with a world that is fashioned around, on the one hand, the state's claim to exclusive political sovereignty, a claim that is grounded principally on the possession and use of coercive force, and on the other, evolving patterns of capital accumulation and modes of social regulation that have reconstituted production and consumption as a series of discrete functions with no principle of continuity save that which is exercised solely in accordance with the global market.[61] The challenge to theology, then, is to show how the church's interpretive venture, grounded in its generative memory, enables us to say in these circumstances that the world is followable, that it can be truthfully narrated as having been spoken into existence by God, provided that our habits of mind have been properly trained and provisioned.

To understand something of what it means to claim that the happenings of the world are followable, consider what is involved in following the action in a game of skill and chance such as baseball.[62] The skills that are needed to keep track of the game at any given moment, to see which moves in certain situations would most likely lead to a good outcome, to know how each pitch, hit, out, and inning contributes to the final outcome, cannot be reduced to knowing the rules. Someone who has never seen a baseball game could obtain a copy of the rulebook and memorize it and still not have the slightest

---

61. Boyle, *Who Are We Now?*, 28; Budde, *(Magic) Kingdom of God*, 19–26.
62. Much of what follows is from Gallie, *Philosophy and the Historical Understanding.*

notion of how to follow the action on the field. We must first be attentive to the teleological character of baseball if we are to track the progressions of the game as it moves inexorably toward its mandated, though as yet unresolved, conclusion. In the sense I am using here, then, following is a form of attentiveness that is ordered to a telos, an end.

There are, of course, various levels of skill in following a baseball game, from the casual fan who knows the difference between balls and strikes, ground-outs and home runs, but not much more, to the expert who can explain to less knowledgeable spectators the ins and outs of tactics and strategies—the placement of players in the field, why one reliever rather than another was brought in from the bullpen—and even predict which team is more likely to win the game. Explanations of this sort are best while one is viewing an actual game, making clear to novices not only why the manager pinch-hit for this player or intentionally walked that one but also pointing out what could have been done differently in this situation and why it might have made more sense. One thus cultivates a grasp of the point and purpose of the game, what counts as winning or losing, whether a particular game was played well or poorly, and a host of other considerations.

Following a baseball game also demands that one have an intrinsic interest in the way the game develops "play by play." Unlike a gambler, for example, who need not know how to follow in detail the game on which he bets, since his interest rests solely in the final score, followers have a stake in the outcome—in the case of a ball game, which team wins or loses. The stakes are raised when those who are following the action are also participants in the game. The attentiveness that is cultivated by players immediately engages their action on the field, and therefore it constitutes the game in ways that not even the most knowledgeable spectators in the stands are able to do. "Only followers are in a position to judge the truth about the game," writes James McClendon, "and part of that truth is whether one is a player or only a spectator."[63]

Though one may be a skillful spectator, there will always be a difference between those who sit along the baselines and those who are "doers of the word, and not merely hearers" (James 1:22). With reference to the mission of the church, this level of following is called discipleship, which, beginning with conversion, consists of taking the way of Jesus as one's own.[64] We should not take the analogy too far, for in the matter of whether life or death has the final word, there are ultimately no spectators. The church learns how to "follow the game" to serve as sacrament of God's will and wisdom for the whole of

63. McClendon, *Witness*, 356.
64. McClendon, *Witness*, 356.

creation. The members of Christ's body thus are summoned to learn how to attend to the work of God in Jesus's life, death, and resurrection for the sake of a world that can see but not understand, hear but not comprehend. Through the admittedly imperfect activity and communion of these disciples, men and women are confronted time and again with the words and works of Jesus and thus are given the opportunity to discover who and what they have become in the economy of this fallen age so that they might reclaim who and what they are called to be in the household of God's creative and redemptive activity.

Following the Apocalypse

The activity of following the action on a ball field begins with the obvious yet necessary assumption that it is in fact a baseball game that is being played and not some other sport. The interpretive art of Christian pilgrimage that provides the church with the ability to follow the rhythms and progressions of a world that is fallen and yet cherished by its Creator also begins with certain assumptions, starting with the hermeneutical stance narrated in New Testament texts and spelled out in the early church's *regula fidei*, or rule of faith,[65] and its historic creeds. This interpretive surmise both emerges from and leads back to the church's constitutive practices as a distinctive way of interpreting the world, both as it has been and now is and as it will be in the end. The point of engagement between these two times intruded into the world in and through one Jewish man, an itinerant rabbi who spent his days pursuing a way of life that moved inexorably toward confrontation and violence. His life was cut short by a peculiar alliance between the mightiest and most efficient empire the world had ever known and those whom this imperial power had selected to administer the affairs of his own people.

The execution of Jesus did not, however, bring his story to an end. His followers testified to his mysterious triumph over death, signaling the divine vindication of all that he had said and accomplished during his lifetime. His resurrection from the dead decisively established him as the center from which all things on earth and under heaven move and toward which they return. Creation had crossed a threshold that signaled the advent of a state of affairs that is represented in the New Testament by apocalyptic motifs and symbols. Though it has often been misinterpreted, the imagery of the sun being darkened and stars falling from the heavens serves primarily to accentuate the disruptive character of the divine presence and activity, in

65. Cf. Blowers, "*Regula Fidei* and the Narrative Character of Early Christian Faith," 199–228.

particular its conflict with powers that enslave the whole of creation. The divine activity in this conflict is decisive, displaying for all to see the warp and woof of the cosmos.

As a consequence of the uniting of the reality of God and the reality of the world in Jesus Christ,[66] the church audaciously claims that the meaning of every human action and affection, the significance of every movement of history, the veracity of every assertion, the wisdom of every construal of human experience, the reasonableness of every assumption of how human beings should relate to each other and the world of which they are inextricably a part, yea, even the movement of the sun and other stars, can in the final analysis be truthfully assessed only in connection with the brief but intense flurry of events that swirled around this one Jewish man and the band of followers he gathered around him. Through the living sacrifice of his disciples down through the centuries, the risen Christ continues to call into question the dominant practices, relations, and habits of the age, and thus the reworking of life and language is a never-ending task for the church.[67] The church can therefore never be truly "at home" in a fallen world but exists in this time between the two ages as a pilgrim city.

McClendon unpacks this interpretive stance in his discussion of the "baptist vision,"[68] which he defines as "shared awareness of the present Christian community as the primitive community and the eschatological community. In a motto, the church now is the primitive church and the church on judgment day; the obedience and liberty of the followers of Jesus of Nazareth is our liberty, our obedience, till time's end." To clarify the sense of the copulative "is" in these phrases, McClendon draws an analogy to the Catholic doctrine of the Eucharist: "There the bread (and wine) upon the altar, when consecrated, *is* the body (and blood) of Christ. Not 'represents' or 'symbolizes,' but *is*. No lesser word will do. In the force of that 'is' lies the power, the distinctive emphasis, of the Catholic doctrine. . . . Now compare the claim made by the baptist vision: The church now *is* the primitive church; *we* are Jesus' followers; the commands are addressed directly to *us*." The "is" in the baptist vision "is mystical and immediate; it might be better understood by the artist and poet than by the metaphysician or dogmatist."[69]

McClendon is surely right when he says that the sort of imagination typically cultivated by artists and poets is needed to attend truthfully to the intersection of past and future. That said, he fails to describe adequately the

---

66. Bonhoeffer, *Ethics*, 54–55.
67. Williams, *Wound of Knowledge*, 1.
68. McClendon, *Ethics*, 18–19, 33.
69. McClendon, *Ethics*, 30–31 (emphasis original).

imaginative surmise that ties together the various constitutive practices of the church into an interpretation of human life lived in relation to God.[70] The chief liabilities of this baptist vision lie in part with the univocal force he attributes to the "is" in the proposition "the church now is the primitive church and the church on judgment day" and with his claim that the "is" articulated by this hermeneutical principle is "mystical and immediate." The challenge of following Christ in our time and place is a question that cannot be resolved simply by identifying ourselves directly with those called by Jesus during his lifetime. Our situation is not identical to that of the first disciples, and we must attend to the difference between the two times if we are to be faithful to the commands of Christ. Moreover, those who were in the company of the Lord during the days of his earthly existence "belong to the word of God and thus to the proclamation of the word. In preaching we hear not only Jesus's answer to a disciple's question, which could also be our own question. Rather, question and answer together must be proclaimed as the word of scripture." At the same time, says Bonhoeffer, eliminating obedience to Christ's commands would wrongly annul a straightforward understanding of the commandments. We are therefore presented with a real dilemma: simple obedience to the word of Scripture is necessary for the followers of Christ if cheap grace is to be avoided, but Scripture would be misconstrued "if we were to act and follow as if we were contemporaries of the biblical disciples."[71]

In spite of these missteps, McClendon gives us our first clue for how to deal with this part of the problem in his appeal to the real presence in the Catholic understanding of the Eucharist.[72] First, Christ's real presence in the eucharistic feast is indeed a mystery, but it is not immediate, for the sign of bread and wine mediates his presence, his self-communication, to the church now. Indeed, given our fallen, failing, as-yet-unresurrected bodies and our current powers of bodily communication, the presence of the risen Lord, the communication of his resurrected body, requires sacramental mediation. The reality of the resurrection and the world to come can only appear in this age in the form of a sign. If the future were ontologically commensurate with present history, it would no longer be future, and Christ's presence with us would no longer be sacramental, for we could then see him "face to face" (1 Cor. 13:12).

Considered in this context, the Eucharist is the presence of Jesus of Nazareth's raised body insofar as it can communicate with and be communicated to our mortal bodies. This understanding of the real presence is predicated on

---

70. See Williams, *On Christian Theology*, xii.
71. Bonhoeffer, *Discipleship*, 82.
72. In what follows I am indebted to Turner, *Faith, Reason and the Existence of God*, 63–67.

the conviction that the resurrection radicalized and intensified Jesus's bodiliness. In his *premortem* existence Jesus's presence, his ability to communicate, to interact intelligibly with others, was limited by his mortality. When he was raised from the dead, he was released from those limitations, and thus when he ate fish with his disciples in the upper room, he was more present to them, not less. The resurrection freed him from the constraints of mortal existence while at the same time allowing him to be involved in it.[73] In this sense he is thus more bodily present to us now in the sign of the Eucharist than before his death. But this presence also involves a real absence, because as he was, we are. In short, Christ both "is" and "is not" present in the Eucharist.

This leads us to a second point. Christ is not locally present in the same sense that the bread and wine, the material sign of Christ's presence, are. According to Thomas Aquinas, "Christ's body is not in this sacrament in the same way as a body is in a place, which by its dimensions is commensurate with the place; but in a special manner which is proper to this sacrament. Hence we say that Christ's body is upon many altars, not as in different places, but 'sacramentally': and thereby we do not understand that Christ is there only as in a sign, although a sacrament is a kind of sign; but that Christ's body is here after a fashion proper to this sacrament." It is important not to confuse the material reality of the signifier and the formal character of the sign in its function as signifying. The force of the qualifier "real" is therefore not that of being materially in that place (*localiter*), because in its formal character the sign signifies Christ's body and blood precisely insofar as they are also "absent," the latter term defined by contrast to the material presence of the sign itself. Only the material sign is locally present, not the risen Christ, who, after all, is in heaven, seated at the right hand of the Father.[74]

On this much Thomas and those who reject the real bodily presence of Christ in the eucharistic celebration agree. Ulrich Zwingli, for example, writes, "Observe, therefore, what a monstrosity of speech this is: I believe that I eat the sensible and bodily flesh. For if it is bodily, there is no need of faith, for it is perceived by sense; and things perceived by sense have no need of faith, for by sense they are perceived to be perfectly sure."[75] The difference comes when Thomas asserts that the locally present sign *becomes* the body and blood of Christ, whereas for Zwingli he is present only in our commemoration of him, not in reality. This means, ironically, that the bread and wine become for Zwingli the unequivocal sign of Christ's real absence, such that the sign completely displaces what is signified, whereas for Thomas they form the

73. Williams, *Resurrection*, 106.
74. Aquinas, *Summa theologica* III.75.1; cf. III.58.1.
75. Zwingli, *Commentary on True and False Religion*, 213–14.

"sesquiguous" sign of both his real presence and his eschatological absence. The same one who walked along the shores of the Sea of Galilee and is now at the right hand of the Father is truly, really, bodily "there" in the Eucharist, but not as he was two thousand years ago, nor as he is now and will be seen by us in the kingdom, "face to face." He is "there," instead, sacramentally.

The sesquiguous meaning of the copulative "is" in the eucharistic liturgy applies also to the church's interpretive surmise. Because the world to come has intruded into the middle of history in the life and passion of Jesus, the past now lives on, and the future is already present. At the same time, the incursion of the new creation in the life, death, and resurrection of Jesus of Nazareth, extending through the bodies of those who are united to one another in him, remains to be consummated. Christ's followers have thus had to deal with a unique and unanticipated set of circumstances, because they exist at the point of intersection between these two ages. Past and future are at hand in the only way that the biblical past (which apart from the sovereign act of God is irretrievable) and the apocalyptic future (appearing in the midst of the regularities by which the fallen world holds together) can be present—in the form of a sign (namely, the church itself), which, as Vatican II put it, is the mysterious sign of union with God and of unity among humankind.[76]

We can therefore say that there is a sense in which the church now *is* the primitive disciple band and the church on judgment day, but we must also say *pace* McClendon that the time we now inhabit is *not* that of Jesus and the Twelve, and because we still pursue a modus vivendi with a world living under the sentence of sin and death, it is also *not* that of the messianic age. This dialectic of "is" and "is not," in which neither the affirmation nor the negation has preeminence, gives rise to the interpretive challenge with which the church must always contend. Like those first disciples, we find ourselves hard-pressed between competing allegiances. Jesus claims our total faithfulness as the one who reveals the Father, and he will tolerate no competitors or rivals for the requirements of the kingdom. He summons us to the freedom of obedience, however, in the midst of a world over which rebellion and death still exert their power. We still await the day of the Lord, and the members of his body must continue to proclaim the reality of the cross until he comes in glory (Mark 13:26; 1 Cor. 11:26).

Unlike for Jesus's first followers, the world with which we have to contend is not identical to that of first-century Galilee, Samaria, and Judea. Given the contingencies of creaturely existence, simple obedience cannot be reduced to identifying ourselves directly with those called by Jesus during his lifetime,

76. *Lumen Gentium*, 1.

or with any other point in history. As with each generation of Christians seeking to obey the summons of Jesus to follow him, we must take up the question of how we best narrate the intrusion of the age to come into the distinctive circumstances of our own time and place. To do this we must take into account the dismembering of the church as that set of bodily practices that allows human beings to live truthfully and faithfully in the world before God, a process that must be examined in conjunction with the emergence, development, and demise of the social project of Christendom.

Some will no doubt disagree, insisting instead that a cultural or institutional synthesis between the body of Christ and society analogous to the one that once distinguished the *corpus Christianum* can and should be salvaged. Others recognize the futility of such a salvage operation and look for ways to translate the Christian hope of salvation into a social grammar that is acceptable to the regime composed of state and global market. Scripture and tradition point us in a different direction. As the followers of him who "suffered outside the city gate in order to sanctify the people by his own blood" (Heb. 13:12), the members of Christ's earthly-historical body constitute a company of nomads, on pilgrimage to the messianic kingdom. We linger for a time in the circumstances in which we find ourselves, making a home for ourselves "as in a foreign land, living in tents" (11:9). Under the figure of living in tents, then, we look to the form of life the Jews developed in exile and diaspora for our initial understanding of the church's interpretive practices. Before we can examine the dismembering of Christ's ecclesial body, then, we must first explore the historical currents that caught up the early followers of Jesus in the apocalyptic action of the God of Israel.

3

CAUGHT UP IN THE APOCALYPSE

God's Incursion into the World in Israel and Christ

There was a time when the church was very powerful—in the time when the early Christians rejoiced at being deemed worthy to suffer for what they believed. . . . Whenever the early Christians entered a town, the people in power became disturbed and immediately sought to convict the Christians for being "disturbers of the peace" and "outside agitators." But the Christians pressed on, in the conviction that they were "a colony of heaven," called on to obey God rather than man.

Martin Luther King Jr., *Letter from Birmingham Jail*

In Graham Greene's novel *The Power and the Glory*, a nameless "whiskey priest" does not immediately flee to safety in the aftermath of an anticlerical revolution in Mexico, as his fellow priests have done, but stays behind performing the duties of his office. He finally tries to escape but is arrested after delaying one more time to hear the confession of a dying man. Once in custody, he gently debates the police lieutenant who has pursued him for months, telling him that he, the officer, is not fighting against a dissolute cleric unworthy of martyrdom, but against God. The officer, looking to shift the focus of the conversation, asks him why he, "of all people," remained behind when the others fled. The priest replies, "Once I asked myself that. The fact

| 51

is, a man isn't presented suddenly with two courses to follow: one good and the other bad. He gets caught up."[1]

Greene's whiskey priest reminds us that our usual ways of engaging the world are not formed by choosing beliefs and dispositions for which we have good evidence or rational warrants, but by getting caught up in activities and judgments that provide the basic constraints on what human beings in a particular time and place can reasonably do and say together. The allegiance we pledge to God, country, or kin; our settled habits of acting and speaking; our imaginative grasp on the world; the modes of reasoning we employ; and especially the loves that shape and direct our lives are never the product of autonomous individuals choosing a worldview in response to some sort of disengaged study of reality. These begin to develop as we are, quite literally, born into sets of relationships and historical events. Though our convictions, habits, and affections can change, it invariably occurs only when certain relationships and events catch and hold us within their nets. When that happens, we typically say that we have undergone a conversion of some sort.[2]

Getting caught up in a peculiar way of living and thinking, which I describe as the art of pilgrimage, accurately describes the process that has constituted the body of Christ from its inception. A group of Galilean Jewish peasants unexpectedly found themselves "pulled into walking the path that Jesus walks, into the messianic event."[3] This event is narrated in the New Testament as the *apocalypse* of the long-awaited eschatological reign of God, the eruption of "God's justice and salvation on earth" before the rulers and authorities of this age.[4] Christ's life, death, and resurrection plunged these women and men into the midst of the divine struggle with and triumph over temporal powers and principalities that have long sought to usurp God's sovereign authority over creation. A new and distinctive set of allegiances, beliefs, dispositions, and loves irrupted in the middle of a world subject to the rule of death and sin, proclaiming the good news to all creatures that, in the end as in the beginning, God will be all in all, and creation will be liberated from its bondage to decay, as life rather than death will have the final word.

The incursion of God into the world, however, did not appear out of a social or historical vacuum. The early followers of Jesus believed themselves to be "the first-fruits of restored Israel and . . . heir of all those confessions by which Israel had classically defined itself."[5] Gentile believers, engrafted

1. Greene, *Power and the Glory*, 190–95.
2. Long, *Goodness of God*, 37.
3. Bonhoeffer, *Letters and Papers from Prison*, 480.
4. Trocmé, *Jesus and the Nonviolent Revolution*, 38.
5. Meyer, *Early Christians*, 43.

by their baptism into the covenants and commonwealth of Israel by Christ's passion and resurrection, shared in God's blessing of Abraham and Sarah and in Israel's calling to be a priestly kingdom, to bless all the families of the earth (Eph. 2:11–14; see also Gen. 12:1–3; Exod. 19:6). Caught up in a reconfigured Jewish story, the early Christian community recapitulated the nomadic life of the people Israel, with the same kinds of trials and temptations, now under the sign of the cross.

Jesus's ministry was decisively shaped by his reading of the Scriptures, and that reading was performatively set within Jewish practices and institutions of first-century Galilee and Judea. Everything that he said, did, and suffered in connection with his company of followers not only summed up Israel's sojourn with God but also anticipated what the chosen people would become in the future through God's apocalyptic action. The biblical events and ideas that shaped Jesus's self-understanding and ministry can therefore not be described as mere "husks" to be discarded once the kernel has been extracted. Though it is certainly the case, as Henri de Lubac so eloquently puts it, that "Jesus causes them to burst forth or, if you prefer, sublimates them and unifies them by making them converge upon himself," these ideas and images do so only insofar as they retain their original references to historical facts and realities: "These realities, in the context of which Jesus places himself and which he thereby transforms, are sown all through the history of Israel and constitute the very object of Israel's expectations."[6]

The redemptive activity of God initially breaks into the world through the events and practices that constitute Israel as a particular people and nation. Human beings learn about this God not first of all through an abstract set of divine attributes but by the fact that he is "the God of *this* community with its particular, socially distinctive features." The unutterable name of the God of Israel is disclosed "as part of the process whereby a community takes cognizance of its own distinctive identity." This community fashions an understanding of who this God is "by asking what it is that constitutes *itself.*"[7] A truthful understanding of God comes to be in and through the existence of this people who supply tangible signs of God's redemptive activity in the world. "The circumcised body of Israel is," writes Michael Wyschogrod, "the dark, carnal presence through which the redemption makes its way in history. Salvation is of the Jews because the flesh of Israel is the abode of the divine presence in the world. It is the carnal anchor that God has sunk into the soil of creation."[8] The story of the apocalypse of God in Jesus Christ and his

6. De Lubac, *Scripture in the Tradition*, 7–8.
7. Williams, *On Christian Theology*, 134–35 (emphasis original).
8. Wyschogrod, *Body of Faith*, 256.

pilgrim people can be truthfully narrated only in connection with the story of Israel as God's chosen people.

Reconnecting the Christian story with the people of Israel—both canonical Israel, whose story is narrated in the Old Testament, and living Israel (that is, the Jewish people)—will not be an easy task, for the construction of Christendom in its manifold forms over the centuries was largely undertaken apart from God's chosen nation. But it is an essential task nevertheless, for as Willie Jennings contends, "Christianity and Christian theology are unintelligible without Israel." God's chosen people make up the interpretive horizon in terms of which we must not only understand the constitution of the people of God but also find the resources to imagine the possibilities of rerootedness and life-giving newness.[9] We must first learn, as Bonhoeffer writes in one of his prison letters, to read the New Testament in light of the Old,[10] but we must also do so in connection with the living root from which we must continue to draw spiritual nourishment (Rom. 11:17–24).

Putting matters this way is theologically sound, but I recognize that it may raise some questions, the first of which is the troublesome specter of expropriative supersessionism, the belief that the church replaced Israel as the chosen people of God within the economy of redemption. Rosemary Radford Ruether, in an abrupt manner, voices this concern in the form of a question: "Is it possible to say 'Jesus is Messiah' without, implicitly or explicitly, saying at the same time, 'and the Jews be damned'?"[11] While I reject what seems to be Ruether's implied answer to that question, I also acknowledge that the narration of the story of Israel I offer is not one that Jews would claim as their own.

That said, we simply cannot ignore the New Testament's proclamation that in Christ God has chosen to lead human beings into radically new modes of living that no longer take as constitutive "beliefs and practices once held or practiced." The way the early church fathers regularly interpreted Israel's Scriptures, says John David Dawson, "extends without supplanting the former Jewish meanings—that the spirit does not undermine but instead draws out the fullest meaning of the letter; the letter must remain in the spirit because the spirit is the letter fully realized."[12] Jewish theologian David Novak states that Christians cannot escape every implication of the charge of supersessionism nor should seek to do so, because supersessionism as such need not denigrate Judaism or seek to replace Israel as God's chosen people. Christianity

---

9. Jennings, *Christian Imagination*, 251.
10. Bonhoeffer, *Letters and Papers from Prison*, 367.
11. Ruether, *Faith and Fratricide*, 246.
12. Dawson, *Christian Figural Reading*, 217.

can look happily to its Jewish origins "and still learn of those origins from living Jews," says Novak, and at the same time affirm that "God has not annulled his everlasting covenant with the Jewish people, neither past nor present nor future. Jews can expect no more than that from Christians, and Christians probably cannot concede any more to Judaism. For if Christianity does not regard itself as going beyond Judaism, why should Christians not become Jews?"[13]

A second concern with this approach to Israel's Scriptures has to do with centuries-long historical debates about how much we can actually know about many of the persons and events narrated in the Old Testament. Was there, for example, really an "exodus" from slavery in Egypt? Was David (assuming he even existed) actually a king whose realm matched the scope described in 2 Samuel, or was he just a local warlord? When were the accounts of these and other events written? Were they written around the time they occurred and then later edited, or were they written many centuries later? In what follows I sidestep taking a position in these debates, not only because of their contested nature but, more importantly, because what matters is how Jews of the first century may have understood and told this story, setting the context for the advent of Jesus of Nazareth and the claims that his followers made about him.

Our mothers and fathers in those early centuries sought to live out—imperfectly, to be sure—the evangelical summons, inherited from the story told by their Jewish forebears, to live in tension with a fallen world. The reason for living in tension with the wider social world, then and now, is to separate believers not from the human race as such, but from all communities and kinships whose boundaries fall short of the human race, past, present, and future.[14] The tension derives from a sense of anticipation that matters cannot and will not be left by God as they are. The sources of this tension are not limited to overt conflict and antagonism. Tension is also generated through partial fulfillments, as seen, for example, in the civil rights movement of the 1960s, such that the sense of anticipation in the future flows through the plenitude and power of what comes before it.

Thankfully there have been many along the way who have not forgotten that to follow the crucified Lord of life and to live as artisans of the age to come required that they live in tension with the present order of things. These witnesses, many of whom were martyrs for the faith, are not simply figures from the past, but sisters and brothers who, having been caught up in

13. Novak, "Edith Stein, Apostate Saint," 17.
14. Williams, *On Christian Theology*, 228, 233.

the path Christ walked and having exemplified for us the ways that the art of pilgrimage interacts with the challenges and opportunities of particular times and places, continue to "accompany us in the mystery of the communion of saints."[15] For the most part, however, the desire to fit in, to belong, has proved hard to resist, particularly when, one after another, the earthly regimes offered opportunities that seemed too good to too many to pass up. Far too often we have succumbed to the temptation to live as others do, endeavoring not to be what we were called in the Spirit to be—sojourners making our way to the city that is to come—but rather allowing ourselves to be those who not only make peace with the earthly city but cannibalize our biblical and theological heritage in vain efforts to prop up the *civitas terrena* in spite of Augustine's contention that it is constitutionally unjust, in that it fails to give God his due.[16]

Reading the New Testament in Light of the Old

When Jesus came onto the scene announcing the drawing-near of God's messianic reign (Mark 1:14–15), the Jewish people had been laboring for centuries to make sense of what had happened to them following their expulsion from the promised land in the sixth century BCE. The covenants that God had made with their ancestors seemed remote, their promises largely unfulfilled. And yet, surprisingly, the Jewish people did not abandon the ways of their forebears. Instead, they reconfigured old practices and institutions and devised new ones that would allow them to cope with the harsh realities of exile and dispersion while remaining faithful to the God of Abraham and Sarah, Moses and Miriam, Deborah and David, Jeremiah and Huldah.

Jewish life in the first century CE was permeated with tensions and ambiguities. In their synagogues and the Jerusalem temple the Jews worshiped the God of their ancestors, professing with the psalmist that "the LORD, the Most High, is awesome, a great king over all the earth" (Ps. 47:2), whose dominion over the creation admits no rivals and no partners. And yet everywhere they looked in their daily lives, they saw something very different. A vast array of worldly powers and authorities claimed privileges and prerogatives the Jews reserved for God and God's rule alone. According to the poet Virgil, for example, fate had "set no limits, space or time" to the Romans, granting them "empire without end."[17] These principalities challenged divine sovereignty

---

15. Francis, *Address of His Holiness Pope Francis to the Pilgrimage from El Salvador*.
16. Augustine, *City of God* 19.21.
17. Virgil, *Aeneid* 1.333–34.

at virtually every turn, claiming that the constellation of institutions, events, and peoples over which they presided was the true, real, and rational order of things, and there was no choice but to act in accordance with it.

Jews, whether in foreign lands or in the occupied land of their ancestors, found themselves hard-pressed between competing demands on their allegiance. There was the exclusive and all-encompassing claim of the God of Abraham, the God of Isaac, and the God of Jacob on them: "Hear, O Israel: The LORD is our God, the LORD alone. You shall love the LORD your God with all your heart, and with all your soul, and with all your might" (Deut. 6:4–5). This confession was not an abstract idea about what God was like, but "always a polemical statement directed outwards against the pagan nations."[18] Jewish teachings about monotheism, election, covenant, holiness, idolatry, and the ways they presupposed one another were "a shorthand way of articulating the points of pressure, tension and conflict between different actual communities, specifically, Jews and pagans."[19] Beliefs were not incidental to their common life but were like threads in a finely woven garment which, once removed from that piece of clothing, soon lose all pattern and texture.

Jews' loyalty to the God of their ancestors took the precarious form of following a way of living that distinguished them from the ways of the peoples in whose midst they lived, affecting every aspect of life. Jews were not only faced with the daily necessities of building houses, planting gardens, marrying and giving in marriage, and raising sons and daughters; most had to go about these matters while dwelling as aliens in foreign lands. Moreover, they were also charged by God to work for the common good of the place where they lived, for as Jeremiah had written to exiles in Babylon, they were to seek the peace of the city where God had sent them, praying to the Lord on its behalf, for in its welfare they would find their welfare (Jer. 29:7).

Over the centuries, then, diaspora Jewish communities large and small cultivated the difficult and precarious art of living between competing interests and demands on their loyalty. They worked diligently to forge forms of life befitting their status as the people chosen by God to serve the peoples of the earth as a priestly kingdom and a holy nation, while at the same time formulating a viable modus vivendi with the established ways of their hosts. The practices, habits, convictions, and institutions that they developed as the constitutive elements of this art of diasporic politics gave shape and direction to their lives and enabled them to remain faithful to God while they dwelt in foreign lands.

18. Wright, *Who Was Jesus?*, 49.
19. Wright, *Climax of the Covenant*, 122.

At the foundation of their art was the practice of attending to their present circumstances under the sign of their past, in terms of an ongoing history with God that they were convinced was not over and done with. Gathering together on the Sabbath in local synagogues, and whenever possible on festival days in Jerusalem, the Jewish people developed modes of reasoning about the world on the basis of a common set of texts that had grown out of their ancestors' experience with God. It was largely out of this need to learn time and again in new circumstances what it meant to be God's in-between people that the biblical canon gradually took shape. And these lessons were painful on more than a few occasions, as the Jewish people were compelled to suffer, as Wyschogrod puts it, "for the sanctification of God's name."[20] And suffer all too often they did, like "a tempest-battered ship lurching to windward first and then to lee."[21] *Israel* was thus a fitting name for them, for throughout their history they were compelled to strive with God and other human beings, and only in the striving did they flourish (Gen. 32:28).

This story began when a man and a woman, without a single heir, left their ancestral home to journey toward an unknown place and an uncertain future. By all appearances Abraham and Sarah were destined for a life of anonymity as nomads in the land of Canaan. One would never have guessed that they would be the forebears of that people through whom all the other families of the earth would be blessed. And yet, writes Gerhard Lohfink, this is the way the God of Israel works, beginning "in a small way, at one single place in the world. There must be a place, visible, tangible, where the salvation of the world can begin: that is, where the world becomes what it is supposed to be according to God's plan. Beginning at that place, the new thing can spread abroad, but not through persuasion, not through indoctrination, not through violence. Everyone must have the opportunity to come and see. All must have the chance to behold and test this new thing."[22]

More was afoot than just the beginning of yet one more ancient people group. The grammar and vocabulary of Genesis suggest that in Abraham, Sarah, and their progeny, God begins the work of re-creating the *imago Dei* in humanity. When the Lord summons Abraham and says that in him and his descendants all the families of the earth shall be blessed (Gen. 12:3), the rebellion and resulting curse that holds all creation in its sway begin to be reversed. The blessing of Adam and Eve at creation and the divine command to "be fruitful and multiply, and fill the earth and subdue it; and have dominion over the fish of the sea and over the birds of the air and over every living thing

---

20. Wyschogrod, *Body of Faith*, 24. Cf. Aquinas, *Summa theologica* I.13.8 ad 1.
21. Dante, *Purgatory* 32.116–17.
22. Lohfink, *Does God Need the Church?*, 27.

that moves upon the earth" (1:28) reappear in connection with the promise made to Abraham, Sarah, and their offspring. At major turning points in their story—the initial summons, the making of the covenant, and the sacrifice of Isaac (12:2–3; 17:2, 6, 8; 22:16–18)—the language of blessing, of multiplying and being fruitful, is transferred to them and their descendants, albeit with two significant changes. The command ("be fruitful . . .") becomes a promise ("I shall make you fruitful . . ."), and possession of the land of Canaan takes the place of Adam's dominion over all the earth.[23]

From the faithfulness of this couple, fragile and fallible though it was, a small group of people emerged over the course of several generations. As the life-giving breath of God animating this people encountered the sweltering winds of human rebellion and death, storm clouds began to boil up on the horizon. The first faint rumbling of thunder came wafting across the arid wasteland of a fallen world when their descendants, now a small group of prospering herdsmen, suffered under the brutal hand of oppression and slavery in Egypt. But the God who had made a covenant with their ancestors heard their cries and delivered them from their bondage "with a mighty hand and an outstretched arm, with a terrifying display of power, and with signs and wonders" (Deut. 26:8). Once they were out of Egypt, this God led them to a mountain, where he identified himself by a strange name, which, following Gregory of Nyssa, I would render as "he who is sought,"[24] or which we shall paraphrase as "he who is known only on the journey."[25]

There is no fact in Jewish teaching more significant, writes Wyschogrod, than the recognition that the God of Israel has a proper name. Tradition surrounded this name with endless mystery, "so that it became an ineffable name because it celebrated the most terrible of all recognitions, the personality of God."[26] This and other forms of address for God are not generic concepts for the divine, but personal names that enabled the Jewish people to attend truthfully to the One who rescued them from their captivity in Egypt. With these names they recognized that God had freely and truly identified himself *by* and *with* them.[27] The Creator of the heavens and the earth had bound himself to one particular portion of his handiwork, not for its own sake alone but for the sake of all the nations of the earth.

23. Wright, *Jesus and the Victory of God*, 262–63.
24. Gregory of Nyssa, *Commentary on the Song of Songs*, homily 6, cited in de Lubac, *Mystery of the Supernatural*, 200.
25. See McClendon, *Ethics*, 187; McClendon, *Doctrine*, 285.
26. Wyschogrod, *Body of Faith*, 91.
27. See Jenson, *Triune God*, 46–50, 59–60.

Under Moses's leadership, the people entered into covenant with their deliverer at Mount Sinai, where they received the Torah, a life-conferring gift of salvation closely aligned with their deliverance from bondage. Indeed, it was essential, since no society can long exist without a determinate social order articulated by a network of laws that direct human actions and relationships to their proper, just ends.[28] The Torah specified the political form that the community was to take once they reached the promised land, orchestrated around the command to worship the LORD alone, with every aspect of life oriented to the God of Abraham, the God of Isaac, and the God of Jacob.

Following the travails that occurred in connection with this assembly, the people resumed their journey toward an uncertain future and an unknown place, with only the judgments, witnesses, and decrees of the nascent Torah to hold their fragile band together. At the culmination of their prolonged trek through the wilderness, the tribes of the LORD finally entered the land promised to the offspring of Abraham and Sarah. This aspect of the story is crucial, for the existence of Israel as God's peculiar people was fundamentally mediated not only by the Torah but also through the land. Possessing the land was necessary if they were to follow the order of life God had established in the Torah; possessing Torah was necessary if they were to flourish on the land that was God's gift to them and to their descendants forever. The promised land was the material cause of the LORD's kingly rule over Israel,[29] forming together with Torah and the people of Israel an indissoluble triad.

Situated at the junction of Europe, Asia, and Africa, this particular piece of real estate, like the people themselves, occupied an in-between place. From the rise of the great ancient civilizations in Egypt, Asia, Asia Minor, and Europe until today, most of the great empires of the world have fought for control of this land. Hittites, Egyptians, Philistines, Assyrians, Babylonians, Persians, Greeks, Romans, Muslims, Crusaders, Europeans, Americans, and others have sought to control this tiny corridor between three continents. There are few places on this planet more suitable for a people whose raison d'être demanded that they come into contact with the nations of the world.

In the early years of their existence in the promised land, the tribes of Israel eschewed any sort of central ruling authority. The absence of a king or similar figure represents a significant development. Monarchs whose sovereignty was secured by divine decree ruled the nations all around them. In Mesopotamia, Egypt, and Canaan, the institutions of kingship and centralized rule were woven by sacred epic into the fabric of reality from the beginning of time.

28. Lohfink, *Does God Need the Church?*, 74–88.
29. O'Donovan, *Desire of the Nations*, 41.

Obedience to the gods and obedience to the king were inextricably related. The tribes of the LORD, however, were to be the exception to this rule. The distinctiveness of early Israel's regime is set forth in exemplary fashion in the story of Gideon, an early charismatic figure who led a small band of warriors to victory against one of their perennial enemies, the Midianites. Elders from a handful of tribes, impressed with Gideon's courage and ingenuity in battle, saw him as someone who could provide stability and security to a loose-knit collection of peoples struggling to survive in a harsh and unforgiving land. And so, in keeping with the practice of the nations and peoples around them, the "men of Israel" offered him the opportunity to establish a dynastic monarchy for himself and his sons. But Gideon emphatically declined their offer, declaring instead that neither he nor his sons, but only the LORD, would rule over Israel (Judg. 6:11–8:23).

Though the notion of divine kingship does not by itself explicitly *denote* a specific political realm, it does by *connotation* suggest the existence of a people who profess allegiance as subjects of that king. The reality of God's reign gains traction in the political world of tribes, monarchies, and empires through the actual gathering-together of a people that give their allegiance to him as his loyal subjects and through whom the world would be confronted by his exclusive claim upon it.[30] God's claim to sovereign rule over all creation thus found historical expression as a distinct *regime* in the covenant concluded at Sinai between Israel and the God of their ancestors, who would forever be their king ruling over a kingdom (*malkuth*) unlike that of any earthly king (Exod. 19:6).

The reality of God's kingship engaged the characters and events of history through a people whose life together displayed, albeit imperfectly, the significant political features of divine sovereignty. The tribes of Israel—in their actions and relationships, their memories and expectations, their achievements and failures—constituted both the enduring form and content of this regime. As a result, though the events of the exodus took place before the Sinai assembly was convened, they derived their lasting significance from what subsequently took place in the wilderness and then in the land promised to Abraham and Sarah. Deliverance from slavery "does not happen for its own sake; it is not solipsistic. A departure simply for the sake of departure would be absurd. The Exodus brought the people out of Egypt in order to bring them into a new society."[31]

Over time, however, Israel succumbed to the temptation that to survive they must become like the other nations. The elders of the various tribes

---

30. Wright, *New Testament and the People of God*, 307.
31. Lohfink, *Does God Need the Church?*, 74–75.

implored Samuel to appoint for them a king, a request that he greeted with dismay. In a subsequent prayer the prophet was told by God, "Listen to the voice of the people in all that they say to you; for they have not rejected you, but they have rejected me from being king over them. Just as they have done to me, from the day I brought them up out of Egypt to this day, forsaking me and serving other gods, so also they are doing to you" (1 Sam. 8:4–8). Thus began a turbulent and tragic experiment with the ways and means of ancient monarchies: "warrior and soldier, judge and prophet, diviner and elder, captain of fifty and dignitary, counselor and skillful magician and expert enchanter" (Isa. 3:2–3).

The covenant was handed over to a regime that had formerly been regarded as antithetical to the covenant's constitution at Sinai, perhaps under the belief that Israel could accommodate the institutions, offices, and practices of human kingship while remaining true to its identity as God's priestly people. During this period the prophets played a key role, serving as the advocates and interpreters of God's sovereignty over against the pretensions of the royal and priestly families in the kingdoms of Israel and Judah. They were not solitary religious geniuses who set themselves over against the institutionalized power of canonical texts, dogmatic traditions, priestly hierarchies, and rote liturgies. Instead they kept alive in Israel the constitutive memory of divine kingship, and also helped to refine the picture of the God they served and of their own status as the chosen people. "Thus says the LORD," they repeated time and again, preserving the identity of Israel's only true sovereign, who demands justice from those in power, acts on behalf of the poor and oppressed, and invites all to make their way toward that future country where all shall "sit under their own vines and under their own fig trees, and no one shall make them afraid; for the mouth of the LORD of hosts has spoken" (Mic. 4:4).

The experiment in monarchy, though it lasted in one form or another for more than four centuries, was ultimately a failure, the labors of the prophets notwithstanding. The kingdoms of Israel and Judah fell to Assyria and Babylon, their populations slaughtered, deported, or left destitute while outsiders from all over the region poured into the social vacuum that was created. Virtually all the significant markers of Israel's covenant relationship with God—possession of the land, the Davidic dynasty, the temple in Jerusalem—disappeared, trampled underfoot by imperial armies that asserted their sovereignty over all the earth. And yet, remarkably, though the God of Israel's ancestors had abandoned them to their enemies, he did not dissolve the covenant with them, and their existence as a people, with their self-identity in the most important respects intact, did not come to an end. The chosen people survived against all odds, and at times they even flourished. Why this happened demands an explanation of some sort, particularly if the status of the church as the nomadic people of God is connected in some significant way to these events.

Following the Rhythms of History and Creation

What could possibly have persuaded the "dry bones" of Israel to continue to believe in the reality of God and their covenant relation? Were their hopes anything more than an exercise in collective self-deception? According to Friedrich Nietzsche, it was only during the time of its kings that Israel stood in a right and natural relationship to all things. Israel's depiction of God "was the expression of a consciousness of power, of joy in oneself, of hope for oneself: through him victory and welfare were expected; through him nature was trusted to give what the people expected—above all, rain." The people, in their cultic festivals, expressed this affirmation of themselves, of their power and nobility, through offerings of gratitude "for the great destinies which raised them to the top" and for "the annual cycle of the seasons and to all good fortune in stock farming and agriculture." But with their eviction from the land, says Nietzsche, these expressions of vitality, confidence, and joy were taken away. "The old god was no longer able to do what he once could do," Nietzsche concludes. "They should have let him go."[32]

Nietzsche's reading of the situation cannot be dismissed out of hand, so why did the remnant not let the old god go? It would seem that during this time the faith of Israel was rooted in the recognition of discontinuity, and the tension that recognition generated gave rise to a new accounting of what was to come. This refigured narrative "challenges and contradicts a consciousness of land loss and expulsion as false consciousness," writes Walter Brueggemann, "because the power of anticipation rooted in the speech of God overwhelms the power of expulsion." Out of the recognition of discontinuity and the sense of anticipation it initiates, the story continues.[33]

The exilic and postexilic prophets who renarrated this story stated that in these times that were out of joint, God was saying to the faithful, "When you call upon me and come and pray to me, I will hear you. When you search for me, you will find me; if you seek me with all your heart, I will let you find me, says the LORD, and I will restore your fortunes and gather you from all the nations and all the places where I have driven you, says the LORD, and I will bring you back to the place from which I sent you into exile" (Jer. 29:12–14). As the years, decades, and centuries went by, the long-awaited "return of the

32. Nietzsche, *Antichrist*, 594.
33. Brueggemann, *Land*, 15–16.

LORD to Zion" in power did not occur (Isa. 52:8), and yet the Jews did not abandon their ancestral heritage, as so many clans, tribes, peoples, and nations in similar circumstances had done, and as one might expect. They would not let the God of their ancestors go.

The exiles continued to affirm that God had plans for their welfare, to give them a future with hope (Jer. 29:11), in large part because of the way they learned to narrate their journey through time as a followable story with a beginning, a middle, and an end.[34] Drawing on the writings of their ancestors, they developed a form of attentiveness to the constantly shifting interrelation of bodies, both human and nonhuman, that constitute what we have come to think of as history.[35] They learned to see the temporal rhythms of human life as embedded within overlapping layers that were moving incessantly toward some sort of resolution, an *eschaton*. Of these layers, the most obvious are the regular and reliable patterns of the physical world: sunrise and sunset, new moon and full moon, wet, hot seasons and dry, cool seasons, times to sow and to harvest, and so on. The psalmist thus writes:

> You have made the moon to mark the seasons;
>   the sun knows its time for setting.
> You make darkness, and it is night,
>   when all the animals of the forest come creeping out.
> The young lions roar for their prey,
>   seeking their food from God.
> When the sun rises, they withdraw
>   and lie down in their dens.
> People go out to their work
>   and to their labor until the evening. (Ps. 104:19–23)

Note that the author does not regard human existence as essentially separate from the world around it, but as immersed in its recurring patterns.

Of course, Israel's Canaanite, Egyptian, and Mesopotamian neighbors also had forms of attentiveness to these regularities of "nature," as we are now wont to label the nonhuman world. These societies typically regarded these patterns as deities who guaranteed the established order and stability of the world. The veneration of them as the guarantors of continuity and return against the ever-present threat to the fragility of the established regime

34. Though many contend that these sorts of grand interpretive schemes are no longer credible, they make a far more grand, far more totalizing claim than any of the stories that have supposedly been unthroned ever made. Like an unwelcome houseguest, metanarrative may have been tossed out the front door, but it almost immediately slipped in the back.

35. Boyle, *Who Are We Now?*, 226.

served as the social basis for regulating day-to-day life within these ancient kingdoms. Indeed, says Robert Jenson, the gods "*are* Continuity and Return," their identity and authority vested in the persistence of a beginning whose continuing stability needed to be protected against the vagaries of time and fortune.[36] The modes of power and knowledge fostered around the worship of these gods served to organize both time and space as a predictable field of operations subject to the institutions of monarchy and priesthood, palace and temple. Therefore, these deities that are inhabitants of the world and of history became for Israel figures of alienation, dependency, and oppression.[37]

In Israel, by contrast, a distinctive temporal rhythm for dealing with these patterns developed, orchestrated around the number seven. This rhythm of life and work wove together the regularities of the material world, cultic observance, and social order around an institution unique to Israel: the Sabbath. Through this day of rest that cuts at regular intervals into life, writes Lohfink, "God draws the people out of its work every week anew, so that it cannot lose itself in the world and work. It is to shape the world through its work, of course, but not to enslave itself to the world and its gods."[38] When observed in exile and diaspora, this aspect of the art of living between competing claims provided the Jewish people with the means to live faithfully both within and above a world that routinely succumbs to the process and products of its own labor. Without such a practice, writes Abraham Heschel, Jewish and gentile women and men alike eventually fall victim to the works of their hands, "as if the forces we had conquered have conquered us."[39]

In *Creation and Fall* Bonhoeffer echoes Heschel's observation, stating that human freedom and the mandate to rule creation in Genesis 1 do not signify that we are free from nature: "On the contrary, this freedom to rule includes being bound to the creatures who are ruled. The ground and the animals over which I am lord constitute the world in which I live, without which I cease to be." With the fall, however, this connection to the earth is lost, and with it our mandate to rule. We do not rule, we are ruled, as our desire to master the earth becomes the power by which it seizes hold of us and holds us in thrall.[40]

The major agricultural festivals detailed in the Old Testament were also structured around this pattern of seven, again with the aim of setting the Israelites apart from their Canaanite neighbors. The Feast of Unleavened Bread was to last for seven days, followed by seven weeks of seven days, leading up

36. Jenson, *Triune God*, 67 (emphasis original).
37. McCabe, *God Matters*, 42.
38. Lohfink, *Does God Need the Church?*, 82.
39. Heschel, *Sabbath*, 27.
40. Bonhoeffer, *Creation and Fall*, 66–67.

to the Festival of Weeks (Exod. 34:18–22). "The purpose of this is clear," writes Lohfink, "precisely where the Canaanite world of the gods held its strongest position—in the fruitfulness of the fields, in rain and harvest—Israel set itself apart, giving itself a different festival rhythm and thus also in this field, so sensitive for an agricultural people, giving all honor to [the LORD]."[41] Through these festivals God reconfigured a social world that was originally set up to perpetuate what had always been.

The markers that these recurring patterns of seven introduced into the unfolding of time were not limited to clearly sequestered "cultic" observances and rituals but played a significant role in organizing the type of social relations that should exist among members. It was not just the single year that was subjected to God's rule by being divided into weeks, each ending with the Sabbath. The passing of years was also divided up into sabbatical intervals. Every seventh year the social world was to be reconstituted, as debts were forgiven and slaves set free. And in the Year of Jubilee, which came after seven sets of seven years, any land sold to pay debts was to be returned to its original owner (Deut. 15:1–5, 12–15, 17; cf. Lev. 25:1–55).[42]

Through these practices and habits, the regularities of nature interacted with other, less regular and more complex rhythms—in particular, the rhythms of the physical and psychological development of human beings from birth to old age and then death, and the rhythms of the development of the social sinews that composed the political, economic, and cultural structures and relationships that existed within and between nations and peoples. Situated like all other peoples in the middle of these complex rhythms, exilic Jews identified a coherence and purposefulness in things that moved toward a kind of closure or cadence in the form of a "gathering together" of the created order.[43] They realized that the rhythms and progressions of human history, the constantly transforming social positions and political hierarchies, closed down certain possibilities and opened up others, the realization of which might or might not take place in the manner they anticipated. Once these possibilities unfolded, the whole process moved on to pose new progressions. Only by taking account of time in this manner, then, did they learn who they were, how things came to be the way they were, and the range of possibilities in the future.

From Israel's vantage point, this history was not cyclical or, strictly speaking, linear. The coming to be and passing away of time was instead marked by a dynamic field of equilibrium and tension, repetition and innovation, recapitulation and resolution embodied within and between these overlapping natural and

---

41. Lohfink, *Does God Need the Church?*, 81.
42. Lohfink, *Does God Need the Church?*, 82.
43. Begbie, *Theology, Music and Time*, 37–68.

social strata. The "tensed" quality of temporal interrelations between natural and human bodies, arising out of antagonism or a state of incompleteness, meant that matters would not be left as they were at any given moment. The people found themselves drawn toward the future, with an expectation that the various possibilities for completion—for example, the establishment of harmonious and just relations between parties formerly involved in conflict—would somehow be resolved and the truth of their existence would be disclosed, but also with the understanding that the particulars of any resolution, closure, and disclosure would generate in turn further tensions, progressions, and possibilities.

To speak of history as followable, therefore, is to invoke a particular metanarrative about time. Israel's story (which took form in the developing canon of the Bible) was ordered around God's mighty acts and righteous judgments, coalescing over time into a complex pattern of expectation, tension, delay, and resolution leading to further anticipation and tension. This pattern was traced back to the beginning of things, when God's peaceable intentions for creation were disrupted by humankind's desire for mastery over themselves and the garden in which they lived. The natural unity of the human race, grounded in the image of God, was torn asunder by the attempt to usurp God's prerogative as Creator and Sovereign. "Whereas God is working continually in the world to the effect that all should come together into unity," writes de Lubac, "by this sin which is the work of man, 'the one nature was shattered into a thousand pieces' and humanity which ought to constitute a harmonious whole, in which 'mine' and 'thine' would be no contradiction, is turned into a multitude of individuals, as numerous as the sands of the seashore, all of whom show violently discordant inclinations."[44] This shattering of primal unity, depicted so powerfully by Adam and Eve's effort to blame someone or something else for their disobedience, gives rise to division and death, fratricide and idolatry, filling the earth with violence (Gen. 1:26–28; 3:4–6, 12–13; 6:11). As Fyodor Dostoevsky puts it in "The Dream of a Ridiculous Man," "Oh, I don't know, I can't remember, but soon, very soon the first blood was shed: they were shocked and horrified, and they began to separate and to shun one another. They formed alliances, but it was one against another. Recriminations began, reproaches. They came to know shame, and they made shame into a virtue. The conception of honor was born, and every alliance raised its own standard. . . . A struggle began for separation, for isolation, for personality, for mine and thine."[45] In short, history had devolved into "a complex network of human denial and deceit."[46]

44. De Lubac, *Catholicism*, 33–34.
45. Dostoevsky, "Dream of a Ridiculous Man," 316–17.
46. Burrell and Malits, *Original Peace*, 15.

The disruption of God's intended end for creation resulted in the dispersal of the nations (Gen. 11:1–9). But God did not abdicate divine sovereignty over a fragmented and antagonistic world or abandon it to utter futility. Time and again God intruded into humankind's self-devised plans and strategies, with the chosen people as the principal point of divine incursion. The blessing of Abraham and Sarah and the summons to follow God to a new land, where they would become the progenitors of a people through whom God would bless all the families of the earth, thus sounded the first notes of the divine counterpoint to humankind's unconstrained lust for mastery and usurpation of power.[47]

The existence of the Jewish people, says Wyschogrod, is the earthly abode of God, "among or in whom God dwells." It is vital, therefore, that this people live ethically, and when they do not, God severely punishes them. Nevertheless, sin does not drive God out of the world completely, for that would happen only with "the destruction of the Jewish people." Wyschogrod then makes the surprising claim that Adolf Hitler understood this: "He knew that it was insufficient to cancel the teachings of Jewish morality and to substitute for it the new moral order of the superman. It was not only Jewish values that needed to be eradicated but Jews had to be murdered."[48]

The recurring pattern of equilibrium, dissonance, recapitulation, innovation, and resolution, ever giving rise to new waves of temporal development, is deeply embedded in Israel's narration of history. Called to be a "peculiar people,"[49] whose blessing at the hands of God would be extended to all the families of the earth, Israel nonetheless wanted to serve their God the way other nations served theirs. This motif recurs throughout Scripture: the complaints of the Hebrews as they left Egypt and made their way to Sinai; their initial refusal to enter the promised land following the making of the covenant out of fear of giants and fortified cities; the constant worship of idols during the period of the judges, which left the people perpetually subject to the rule of Canaanite kings; the request to have their own king during the time of the prophet Samuel, so that they might be like all the other nations; the seductive trap of trusting in the horses and chariots of unreliable allies during the time of the divided monarchy. Time and again Israel did evil in the sight of the LORD, repeatedly exchanging their birthright as God's chosen people for the tepid and idolatrous pottage of temporal security and welfare.

As a result of their disobedience (which is consistently linked in Scripture with the worship of idols), Israel was caught up in habits and institutions that led to its expulsion from the land of promise and dispersion among the

47. Augustine, *City of God* 1.pref., 30; 14.28; 19.14.
48. Wyschogrod, *Body of Faith*, 223.
49. Deut. 14:2 (KJV); cf. Deut. 26:18; Titus 2:14; 1 Pet. 2:9.

nations.[50] But even then the frenzied nature of their existence in exile did not come to an end. Those who returned to the land in the days of King Cyrus of Persia continued to languish under the oppressive rule of foreign powers, thus perpetuating the exile of slavery. Their God had not yet returned triumphantly to Zion to redeem Israel as promised by the prophets (Isa. 52:7–8, 10; Ezek. 43:1–9). With Joel they cried out: "Have pity, O LORD, upon your people! Do not hand over your possession to shame, that foreign nations should rule over them" (2:17).[51]

The Rise of Apocalyptic

In spite of the disappointment and hardship of exilic life, the Jewish people were still by and large persuaded that God's redemptive work with and through them had not been arrested by their hard-heartedness. When in the past they cried out to God in repentance, the LORD had heard their cry and acted in their behalf. Manna was provided in the wilderness; judges were raised up to deliver the people from their enemies; a man after God's own heart was anointed as king; Jerusalem was graciously spared when threatened with seemingly overwhelming force. With each provisional fulfillment the original promise was elaborated or augmented, often in surprising and yet coherent ways. Each partial resolution created an expectation and hope for something more, thus expanding the content and range of the original promise. "As successive hopes find fulfilment," writes Anthony Thiselton, "a tradition of 'effective history,' or 'history of effects' . . . emerges in which horizons of promise become enlarged and filled with new content."[52]

The gradual return of Jews to the promised land, fragmentary and under the dominion of foreign rulers though it may have been, was regarded by some as just such a partial fulfillment of the promised ingathering of Israel. But it was evident that a complete return had not occurred and that the dispersion continued. In these circumstances the dry bones of Israel and Judah were compelled to make a critical hermeneutical judgment. In the minds of many, "the promise of a nation righteous and true and peaceful had eventually either to be spoken as an *eschatological* promise or to be forgotten."[53] The God of their ancestors either had utterly abandoned them or, in the course of handing them over to their enemies, had begun "a new thing" in their midst (Isa. 43:19), a work that

50. Lohfink, *Does God Need the Church?*, 90.
51. Translated by Wolff, *Joel and Amos*, 39.
52. Thiselton, *Interpreting God and the Postmodern Self*, 150–51.
53. Jenson, *Triune God*, 69.

eluded human planning and calculation and would culminate in the rescue and restoration of Israel and the extension of God's blessing to all nations.

Later biblical authors gave voice to the second option, refiguring the story of God's presence and activity (formerly vested in Davidic palace and Solomonic temple) in radical terms. They envisioned the realization of God's promises within an *apocalyptic* transposition of the rhythms and hierarchies that ordered creaturely life.[54] A new covenant with the chosen people was in the works: "It will not be like the covenant that I made with their ancestors when I took them by the hand to bring them out of the land of Egypt—a covenant that they broke, though I was their husband, says the LORD" (Jer. 31:32). This new thing would not merely add new works to old, enlarging and expanding upon the motifs that formerly distinguished the historical vectors of their life with God, but would transcend the old works' modes of continuity.[55]

Many Jews began, over a period of centuries, to look for signs of the radical restructuring of the patterns around which nature and history unfold and cohere.[56] The initial strains of this hope were sounded during the seventh century BCE, as a new intensity in the eschatological visions of judgment and restoration began to emerge within the ranks of the prophets. Jeremiah tells the inhabitants of Jerusalem and Judah:

> I looked on the earth, and lo, it was waste and void;
> and to the heavens, and they had no light. . . .
> I looked, and lo, the fruitful land was a desert,
> and all its cities were laid in ruins
> before the LORD, before his fierce anger.
> For thus says the LORD: The whole land shall be a desolation; yet I will not make a full end. (4:23, 26–27)

The whole cosmos, and not just the people of Israel and their immediate enemies, now stood beneath God's sovereign judgment. "For the day of the LORD is near against all the nations," says Obadiah.

> As you have done, it shall be done to you;
> your deeds shall return on your own head. . . .
> But on Mount Zion there shall be those that escape,
> and it shall be holy;
> and the house of Jacob shall take possession of those who dispossessed
> them. (vv. 15, 17)

54. Jenson, *Triune God*, 70.
55. Jenson, *Triune God*, 69.
56. Jenson, *Triune God*, 69.

Redactors of the prophetic books then elaborated on this theme of a radical transfiguration of the continuities by which time and space are ordered. In the book of Isaiah we read that though the "earth lies polluted under its inhabitants . . . [who] have transgressed laws, violated the statutes, broken the everlasting covenant," the time is coming when God will "create new heavens and a new earth; the former things shall not be remembered or come to mind." On that day the powers in heaven and rulers on earth will "be gathered together like prisoners in a pit; they will be shut up in a prison, and after many days they will be punished," while the peoples of the earth who will be invited to a feast dwell on God's mountain, where they will find "rich food filled with marrow, [and] well-aged wines strained clear." At that time the LORD will destroy "the shroud that is cast over all peoples, the sheet that is spread over all nations; he will swallow up death forever" (24:5; 65:17; 24:21–22; 25:6–8; cf. Ezek. 38–39).

In the books of Zechariah and Daniel the earlier prophetic oracles that speak of cosmic judgment and redemption coalesce into fully developed apocalypses depicting a form of the world that is commensurate with the hope of God's promise to Israel. For that reason, the world to come appears in this age only in image and figure, not as event. In Zechariah's "night visions," a patrol sent by God reports that the world remains unchanged and that any prospect for the redemption of Jerusalem depends on God's intervention. The prophet then sees that the powers or "horns" that scattered Judah and Israel will be struck down, allowing Jerusalem to be reestablished, protected by a wall of fire that is the glory of God's own presence in the city. Two "anointed ones" unite those who have returned to the city in anticipation of God's Spirit filling the earth. As a result of God's action, "Many nations shall join themselves to the LORD on that day, and shall be my people"; and God will dwell in their midst (1:7–21; 2:11; 4:1–4, 10–14; 6:1–8). In Daniel it is the opposition of these nations to Israel and God that is detailed, with their fate decided by the coming of "one like a son of man." Following the decisive battle between the forces aligned against God and those powers who fight for the LORD, the defeat of death implied in other portions of Scripture is explicitly described in terms of resurrection (12:1–3).[57]

Since the present ordering of the cosmos could not contain the promise and prospect of these events, apocalypses announced that this order would at some point come to an end, thus making time and space for a new heaven and a new earth to appear. The time of creation was subdivided into the exile of the present age (*olam hazeh*), when the wicked flourished and God's

57. Jenson, *Triune God*, 70–71.

people suffered the rule of idolatrous powers that claimed for themselves what belongs to God alone, and the age to come (*olam haba*), when all creatures would witness the restoration of God's sovereignty, the defeat of sin and death, and the vindication of Israel and righteous gentiles. Extraordinary phenomena—eclipses, earthquakes, and floods—were used as portents of this transposition, for only such language could do justice to the dreadful events that would accompany such momentous events.[58]

The apocalyptic grammar that is subsequently taken up in the New Testament establishes "an indispensable theological vocabulary" for describing the world and our participation in it, and does so "with relentless formative reference to the sovereign God of the gospel of salvation in Jesus Christ." While the apocalyptic discourse of the biblical witness is a difficult grammar to learn and sustain, it is "uniquely adequate both to announce the full scope, depth, and radicality of the gospel of God, and to bespeak the actual and manifest contradiction of that gospel by the actuality of the times in which we live."[59] In this capacity, apocalyptic images and narratives of the New Testament function, as James Stewart puts it, not as inessential scaffolding that we may take down once we have reconstructed their "meaning," but as "the very substance of the faith."[60]

Far from predicting the imminent destruction of time and space, of "history" itself, then, the apocalyptic imagination preserves and intensifies the sense of expectation, delay, tension, and eventual resolution that pervades Israel's attentive following of creation's movements. The biblical writers hold in generative tension the motifs of the nearness *and* the deferment of God's reign and regime—that is, the "is" and "is not" of apocalyptic thought. We thus find throughout these writings a pronounced sense of exigency and longing for the day of the LORD compounded by exhortations to patience that tacitly acknowledge that God does delay. "There is, in other words," writes Jeremy Begbie, "an appeal both to God's righteousness—God's justice will eventually prevail—and to God's sovereignty—his righteousness will prevail at his own appointed time. Neither element need be suppressed in favour of the other."[61]

The promised land continued to figure prominently within the apocalyptic transposition of the rhythms that order the world. Pledged by God to Abraham, Sarah, and their descendants (Gen. 12:7), the land—signified by the temple—formed an indissoluble triad with the Torah and Israel's status

58. Wright, *New Testament and the People of God*, 299.
59. Ziegler, *Militant Grace*, 19, 26.
60. Stewart, "On a Neglected Emphasis in New Testament Theology," 300.
61. Begbie, *Theology, Music and Time*, 119.

as God's chosen people. Israel had possessed the "Holy Land," in whole or in part, from Joshua to Josiah, a time span of more than five hundred years. It is therefore not surprising that in exile the desire to return to the land was the cornerstone of Jewish hopes:

> By the rivers of Babylon—
>> there we sat down and there we wept
>> when we remembered Zion.
>
> . . . .
>
> If I forget you, O Jerusalem,
>> let my right hand wither!
> Let my tongue cling to the roof of my mouth,
>> if I do not remember you,
> if I do not set Jerusalem
>> above my highest joy. (Ps. 137:1, 5–6)

In the early years of the exile Jews were sustained by this powerful memory and by the hope that God would soon gather the exiles and return them to this land.[62] As the months and years turned into decades and centuries, however, the land continued to languish under the domination of foreign rulers. Its rich yield, its fruit and its good gifts, went to foreign kings whom God had set over the Jews (Neh. 9:36–37). In addition, pagan institutions were established, often in or around Jerusalem, which had become the focal point of the land of promise. And though there is disagreement among scholars regarding the amount of taxation levied by the gentile rulers on the Jews who had returned to Judea and Galilee, virtually all agree that making a living from the land was at best extremely difficult.[63]

With the memory of shared space growing ever more remote and the hope of return seemingly infinitely deferred, many believed that only a radical reordering of the regularities by which the world coheres could possibly vindicate this memory and hope. Jewish apocalyptic writings were in part a response to the shared memory of life together in the Holy Land and to the hope that one day the people would return and live there once again "under their own vines and under their own fig trees," where "no one [would] make them afraid" (Mic. 4:4). In his prayer for the people, the figure of Daniel cries out: "Incline your ear, O my God, and hear. Open your eyes and look at our desolation and the city that bears your name. We do not present our supplication before you on the ground of our righteousness, but on the ground

---

62. See Boyarin, *Radical Jew*, 245.
63. See Sanders, *Judaism*, 168–69.

of your great mercies. O Lord, hear; O Lord, forgive; O Lord, listen and act and do not delay! For your own sake, O my God, because your city and your people bear your name!" (Dan. 9:18–19). And when God would finally act to redeem his people, he would restore the land and cleanse the temple, the rule of the kings of this world would be shattered, the mountain of the LORD's house would fill the whole earth, and God's rule would encompass all peoples (Dan. 2:35; 7:14; cf. Mic. 4:1).

Another development within postexilic Judaism's refigured reading of time as history, appearing in close proximity with the rise of apocalyptic forms of reasoning, was a host of vaguely defined and often conflicting messianic expectations. Though there was no one accepted understanding of the Messiah, the various movements that spoke in these terms did tend to share an expectation that Israel's long history and suffering would finally reach its goal. The coming king who would be the agent through whom God would accomplish the great restoration of Israel would also cleanse the Holy Land promised to their ancestors. The messianic ruler became for some "the focal point of the dream of national liberty."[64]

The initial impetus for the messianic idea had been the struggle between the proponents of monarchical unification of the tribes of Israel and those who continued to represent the case for divine kingship. This crisis led eventually to the prophetic designation of the human king of Israel, the one who follows the LORD (cf. 1 Sam. 12:14), as the anointed of the LORD, *mashiach YHWH*.[65] Heightened expectations were invested in a new king from the line of David who would be "Wonderful Counselor, Mighty God, Everlasting Father, Prince of Peace," establishing justice and righteousness forever, such that even nature's own predatory predilections would be pacified (Isa. 9:6; 11:6–9). Jenson contends that in one way or another these predications "burden the coming one with expectations this age cannot accommodate."[66]

There is one final and inescapable step in this radical transposition of the temporal patterns that presently order heaven and earth. "Everlasting and universally encompassing righteousness and peace, eternal and universal love, and these as characters of a reality transcendent to 'this age,'" says Jenson, "can only be predicates of God himself." The content of Israel's apocalyptic hope is only possible through a participation in God's own reality, described by the Greek fathers as "deification." But such a conclusion is not possible

64. Wright, *Jesus and the Victory of God*, 483.
65. Buber, *Kingship of God*, 162.
66. Jenson, *Triune God*, 84.

strictly within the context of the Old Testament, for without a resurrection, "hope for deification would be intolerable hubris."[67]

Jesus as the Apocalypse of God

According to developing eschatological sensibilities, God does not leave the world to its brokenness and violence but intrudes upon the immanent causal sequences of history with portents of judgment and redemption. The Jewish people found themselves time and again in between a God intent on judging a wayward world and a rebellious creation. As the psalmist puts it, "Our God comes and does not keep silence, before him is a devouring fire, and a mighty tempest all around him. He calls to the heavens above and to the earth, that he may judge his people: 'Gather to me my faithful ones, who made a covenant with me by sacrifice!'" (Ps. 50:3–5). As they had been for centuries, the people of Israel were to be the chosen "body" through which the decisive divine activity would take place and reclaim God's rightful dominion over a world presently ruled by death and sin.

It is from this social and historical soil that Jesus of Nazareth emerged, proclaiming to his fellow Israelites, "The time is fulfilled, and the kingdom of God has come near; repent, and believe in the good news" (Mark 1:15; cf. Matt. 4:17). Through his life, death, and resurrection, God's messianic rule promised to Abraham and Sarah's offspring becomes a present reality in connection with the day-to-day concerns and celebrations of life. Over against the forces and powers that had governed the course and content of life in the ancient world virtually uncontested, Jesus inaugurates an alternative pattern of communal life, a distinctive set of personal habits and relations, and a different story that offers a different way to make sense of all things on earth and under heaven. The meaning of all other figures, events, and institutions no longer resides in themselves. They are now derivative signs, the significance of which can be followed only in their relationship to this one Jewish man and the body politic of the church, over which he rules as head.

The New Testament witness to the messianic event is by no means uniform, as evidenced by its literary and theological diversity, but the distinctive motifs of apocalyptic thought nonetheless figure prominently in virtually every book. Owing to what God accomplishes in Christ, the world has crossed a

---

67. Jenson, *Triune God*, 71. And yet, Jenson argues, voices within postcanonical Judaism did affirm deification materially if not formally in its description of the life of the blessed in the age to come, when "the righteous [will] sit with their crowns on their heads enjoying the effulgence of the *Shekinah*." b. Berakhot 17a, cited in Jenson, *Triune God*, 71n55.

decisive threshold with the triumph of God over death and sin. At the same time, however, all creation awaits the final transfiguration of heaven and earth. The necessities of eating, drinking, marrying and giving in marriage, having children, burying parents, acquiring and disposing of property, and producing and exchanging goods continue as before. The biblical writers thus locate the whole of creation in a period of time in which two ages and two social orders overlap. There is the present age, over which the authorities and powers exercise dominion but which will ultimately pass away, and the age of God's everlasting reign, when all creatures will witness God's triumph over sin and death and the vindication of the righteous in Israel and among the nations.

To follow the coming of God's everlasting rule in connection with events in the present, the Gospel authors refined the literary technique of foreshortening, introduced in the Old Testament by the book of Daniel. Foreshortening compresses the time between what is near at hand and the last things, putting them into immediate juxtaposition. In chapter 7, for example, the author, writing sometime in the middle of the second century BCE during the Maccabean revolt, adopts the sixth-century perspective of the character of Daniel to describe past events (the conquests of Alexander the Great and the rise of Hellenistic kingdoms in the Middle East in the fourth century, culminating with the rule of the tyrant Antiochus IV in the second) in connection with God's imminent judgment on these kingdoms (the "present" of Daniel's readers) and the establishment of the everlasting kingdom of the Son of Man (the eschatological backdrop against which all these events are depicted).

Through skillful use of foreshortening, things that have already occurred, things that will occur shortly, and things to be revealed at the end of the age are blended together with the "present" of the author, not in an effort to deceive his readers by surreptitiously claiming the *ex eventu* authority of a past hero of Israel, but to fashion a trioptic awareness: (1) the memory of Daniel and his friends struggling to survive in Babylon during the exile, providing the narrative standpoint for the passage; (2) a depiction of how everything on earth and under heaven will eventually end up with the coming of the Son of Man, whose reign will be everlasting; and (3) how both of these impinge upon the times and tasks of the Jews during the Maccabean revolt (the "present" of the book's intended readers).[68]

The same procedure is used in the thirteenth chapter of the Gospel of Mark, the so-called Little Apocalypse. In this extended discourse (which is rare in Mark), Jesus warns about the impending destruction of the temple in Jerusalem. When questioned about the timing of these events by his inner

68. McClendon, *Doctrine*, 94.

circle of disciples, Jesus gives what appears to be a confusing answer. He begins by stating that there is coming a time of persecution for his followers leading up to the consummation of this age, as they will be brought before governors, kings, and synagogues to testify about him. Jesus then ties these tribulations to allusions about the coming destruction of Jerusalem, which will bring with it terrible suffering and give rise to false messiahs and prophets (vv. 5–23). He then speaks in explicitly apocalyptic terms about the sun being darkened and the stars falling from the heavens as harbingers of the final coming of the Son of Man in clouds of glory (an image drawn from Dan. 7) to gather the elect from the four corners of the earth (Mark 13:24–27). Finally, he counsels his disciples to learn the lesson of the fig tree and to recognize from the signs that "all these things" will occur within this generation, but that no one but the Father knows the day or hour these things will occur. Jesus concludes with a short parable summoning his disciples to stay awake, to remain alert (vv. 28–37).

If the author of Mark wrote these verses sometime between 60 and 70 CE (or even later), then it would seem that Jesus was mistaken about the timing of these events, if not completely incoherent. The end of the age had not occurred during the generation of Jesus's listeners, and the fall of Jerusalem either had already taken place or was imminent. And yet the evangelist sets these words down with no apparent discomfort. This fact leads McClendon to argue that Mark had skillfully adopted the standpoint of the pre-Easter disciples for his narrative. All the events depicted in this chapter, "the spread of the gospel, the suffering of the missionaries, the destruction of Jerusalem, the coming of false Messiahs, and the apocalyptic last coming of the Son of man were from the time standpoint of the first disciples future events." Through the technique of foreshortening, Mark has fashioned attentive awareness to "(1) what Jesus had once said and done (the 'present' of Mark's narrative), (2) how everything would end up (the long future), and (3) how both of these impinged upon the 'present' needs and tasks of the Marcan church (the 'present' of Mark's readers)."[69]

These disciples served as a tangible sign that God had not left the world to its own futility but invited all to share now in the well-being of the city that is to come (Heb. 13:14). The innumerable transactions that constituted the common life of these early Christians were caught up in the exchange that God in the incarnation made with the *oikonomia* of the world, a term that derived from words meaning "house" (*oikos*) and "law" (*nomos*) and that in its most comprehensive sense denoted the regulation of the household that is

69. McClendon, *Doctrine*, 94.

creation itself. In the words of Athanasius, the Word of God assumed a body capable of death so that that body, "participating in the Word who is above all, might be sufficient for death on behalf of all, and through the indwelling Word would remain incorruptible, and so corruption might henceforth cease from all by the grace of the resurrection." This exchange was accomplished not through some sort of legal or monetary transaction but through the union of the immortal Son with human nature, clothing it with incorruption in the promise of the resurrection: "And now the very corruption of death no longer holds ground against human beings because of the indwelling Word, in them through the one body."[70]

The Eucharist was the *res et sacramentum*, the reality and the sign performed by the church that, more than any other, made present this exchange of charity between God and humankind whenever and wherever Jesus's followers were gathered together in his name. Paul declares, "Because there is one bread, we who are many are one body, for we all partake of the one bread" (1 Cor. 10:17). Time and again the eucharistic liturgy makes the church what it is, *re-membered* as Christ's true body, with each participant connected not only to Christ, who is the head of the body, but to one another as in a natural body. Every time believers gather around the table of their Lord, the things of this world—including its modes of accumulating, consuming, and exchanging material goods and services—are turned toward God. This meal positions all other realities, because it makes a present reality "the moment of *ultimate exchange* between God and humanity that Christians cannot but claim to be the basis for all other exchanges."[71] The Eucharist thus becomes the paradigm for these other exchanges.

The life that Jesus lived with his followers thus marked the beginning of the recapitulation of all things, setting before a rebellious cosmos the decisive sign in terms of which all other relationships and exchanges that compose humankind's common life are to be parsed. As a consequence of this one Jewish man's life, the prevailing order of time and space is turned upside down in classic apocalyptic fashion, including the normal distribution of material goods. The Gospel of Luke thus proclaims in Mary's song of praise and thanksgiving that

> [God] has shown strength with his arm;
>   he has scattered the proud in the thoughts of their hearts.
> He has brought down the powerful from their thrones,
>   and lifted up the lowly;

70. Athanasius, *On the Incarnation* 9.
71. Long, *Goodness of God*, 236 (emphasis original).

> he has filled the hungry with good things,
>> and sent the rich away empty. (Luke 1:51–53)

Though no one economic regime can claim to be adequate for every time and place, Jesus cultivates with his band of disciples a distinct and concrete mode of life together. The inaugural sermon of Jesus, recorded in the fourth chapter of the Gospel of Luke, is a case in point. Instead of using the phrase "the kingdom of God is at hand; repent and believe in the good news" to introduce the period of Jesus's public ministry, as Matthew and Mark do, Luke places Jesus in the synagogue in his hometown of Nazareth, where he reads a passage from Isaiah 61 that he then turns upon himself and his forthcoming ministry:

> The Spirit of the Lord is upon me,
>> because he has anointed me
>>> to bring good news to the poor.
> He has sent me to proclaim release to the captives
>> and recovery of sight to the blind,
>>> to let the oppressed go free,
>> to proclaim the year of the Lord's favor. (Luke 4:18–19)

After reading, he sits down and declares that this Scripture has this very day been fulfilled in their hearing. This passage not only is explicitly messianic but also conceives of that expectation in expressly social terms. Jesus's first-century Jewish audience would have heard this passage as a reference to the fulfillment of the Year of Jubilee and as suggesting, in the context of his ministry, that the coming of the kingdom would, as a part of the restoration of Israel, bring about a new regime of accumulation and exchange among the elect in line with Jubilee provisions for releasing slaves, forgiving debts, and redistributing land to those who had lost it due to economic exigencies.[72]

Jesus's proclamation is confirmed by other texts in the Lukan corpus. In Luke's version of the Beatitudes, Jesus says, "Blessed are you who are poor. . . . Blessed are you who are hungry now" (6:20–21), emphasizing the beneficence of God's apocalyptic reign for those who suffer from want. Later in the same Gospel, at the conclusion of a crucial passage in which Jesus tells the crowds that they must take up the cross and follow him to be his disciples, he says to them, "None of you can become my disciple if you do not give up all your possessions" (14:33). And following the exchange with the rich ruler in

---

72. Yoder, *Politics of Jesus*, 11, 29.

Jerusalem, Jesus tells his followers that those who have left house and family for the sake of the kingdom will receive back much more in this age; and in the age to come, eternal life (18:29–30).

Similar practices are detailed in the Acts of the Apostles. Following Peter's Pentecost sermon and the release of Peter and John, for example, we read that the believers had all things in common (*ēn autois hapanta koina*) and that they would sell their possessions and goods and distribute the proceeds "as any had need" (2:44–45; 4:32, 34–35). In 1 Corinthians 11 Paul argues that believers are dying because they have failed to "discern the body," each going ahead with his own meal (*to idion deipnon*). Paul's choice of words here parallels that of a statement in Acts 4, where Luke writes that "no one claimed private ownership of any possessions, but everything they owned was held in common," in Greek, *oude heis ti tōn hyparchontōn autō elegen idion einai all ēn autois hapanta koina* (v. 32). The contrast is that of the faithful life, where all things are held in common, with the life they have left behind, in which one could treat one's possessions as private.[73]

The first Christians attended to this radical restructuring of human existence, which at its heart involved a transfer of allegiances and a transformation of conduct, with great seriousness. The author of the Epistle to the Colossians, in an exhortation to his readers not to lie to one another, reminds them that they "have stripped off the old human with its practices and have clothed [themselves] with the new human, which is being renewed in knowledge according to the image of its creator. In that renewal there is no longer Greek and Jew, circumcised and uncircumcised, barbarian, Scythian, slave and free; but Christ is all and in all!" (Col. 3:9–11 alt.). The transition from the old society (exemplified by Rome) into the vanguard community of the new creation involved "a change of rulers, a turning away from the gods and demons of Gentile society and an entry into the Church as the space of Christ's lordship." To guide this transition, says Lohfink,

> probably as early as the second century the candidates for baptism each had to produce a guarantor who would attest the sincerity of their conversion. They had to take part in a three-year baptismal catechesis that carefully educated them in Jewish-Christian discernment and the form of life demanded by faith. The ancient Church took it for granted that the Christian life of the baptismal candidates would not come of itself, but had to be learned. It was also assumed that evil is powerful and that every inch of the reign of God had to be fought for.[74]

73. Long, *Goodness of God*, 237.
74. Lohfink, *Does God Need the Church?*, 211.

Caught Up in the Spirit

The inauguration of God's apocalyptic reign in the ministry, passion, and triumph of Jesus proved to be so disruptive to established regimes that the re-organization of human existence became a never-ending task for his followers. It took centuries to develop relatively adequate ways of saying what needed to be said about the sense and direction of his life, death, and resurrection. They discovered, for example, new uses had to be put to the word *God*. Without jeopardizing the mystery and simplicity of God, they determined after years of deliberation that the only way to do justice to all that Jesus did and suffered was to speak of him as the incarnate Word of God. In the words of Ignatius of Antioch, Christ "is the mouth . . . by which the Father has truly spoken."[75] In the person of Jesus, God joined the divine nature to the day-to-day realities of human existence in order to re-create its shattered bone and severed sinew. Without effacing the difference between the speaker and the word spoken, the church was convinced that it was *God* who appeared in the particular events and circumstances of this man's life and worked to gather together what had been dispersed by humankind's disobedience.

The church's conviction that God's address and agency took flesh in a particular person who lived at a certain time and place and who said and did and suffered certain things did not cancel or set aside the particularities of Jesus's own history. On the contrary, so crucial were the events of his life that the only appropriate form in which the truth about him could ultimately be told was that of a story. But as pivotal as his personal story was, it was not sufficient to confess that the Son entered fully into time and history and in so doing perfectly fulfilled the will of the Father. The mere fact of God's self-identification with humanity through the incarnation made no particular difference to the lives of others. Hans Urs von Balthasar observes, "In that light his life is still only one existence among others; and if it is no more it can only be, even in its highest perfection, a (perhaps unattainable) moral example for others living before and after him."[76]

By itself, then, the story of this one man's life, as remarkable as it was, remains extrinsically related to the lives of those who came after his earthly ministry. The question is, therefore, What does *that* life of faithfulness to God, *that* death willingly accepted, *that* triumph over death, have to do with *this* life that each man and woman must now live? And so when the church down through the centuries struggled with what to make of this continuously

---

75. Ignatius of Antioch, *Epistle to the Romans* 8. Williams paraphrases Ignatius's statement here as "he is himself 'what the Father says.'" Williams, *Wound of Knowledge*, 19.

76. Balthasar, *Theology of History*, 79.

unfolding drama, they concluded that they could not stop with the confession of Jesus as God's own utterance, for to do so would reduce his story "to the status of an *anecdote*: a tale without enduring or universal significance."[77] If all those who live in a different time and place, who do and endure things in circumstances that are marked by their own distinctive particularity and contingency, are to grasp the significance of Jesus, they must learn how to narrate their own lives as both distinct from and, at the same time, a continuation of his story. This happens only as the universal efficacy attributed to Christ's concrete historical existence is performatively extended to and displayed in every time and place, so that it becomes the immediate norm of every human being's singular existence.

It is the work of the Holy Spirit to orchestrate time and again in the ever-changing circumstances of creaturely existence the divine polyphony of life,[78] which takes form in what Augustine calls the whole Christ, *totus Christus*, consisting of both head and body,[79] mediated through gathered Christian communities throughout the globe. The Spirit's labor is an ongoing, never-ending endeavor, because times and circumstances change. New characters, social settings, and historical events are constantly being incorporated within the ebb and flow of time around its center. The meaning of this process is therefore never fixed but continues to unfold in the style of a historical drama that is never over and done with. The unity of this drama's story line resides not in the sameness of its performance but in timely and faithful transpositions of the rhythms and progressions of human acting and relating that God had decisively set in motion with the call of Abraham and Sarah, which reached its decisive moment in the suffering and resurrection of Jesus.

This connection between Israel and Jesus needs to be constantly reiterated, because the church is perpetually tempted to see Jesus and his followers as having left completely behind all the crucial elements of Israel's story—the Torah, the land, the temple, the rites, and the holy days. There is, to be sure, a good deal of ambivalence in the New Testament with respect to these things, as witnessed in the tension in some of Paul's statements about the works of the law (Rom. 3:28; Gal. 3:11) and Jesus's proclamation that not one letter or letter stroke will pass away from the Torah until "all is accomplished" (Matt. 5:18). Another prominent example is found in the various ways the temple figures into the story of Jesus and the early church. On the one hand, the announcement of the birth of John the Baptist occurs in the temple (Luke 1:8–20); Jesus's parents present him in the temple soon after

---

77. Lash, *Easter in Ordinary*, 282 (emphasis original).
78. See Bonhoeffer, *Letters and Papers from Prison*, 393–94.
79. Augustine, "First Homily on First John," 261.

his birth "according to the law of Moses" (2:22); the only story about Jesus between his birth and the beginning of his public ministry occurs in the temple (2:41–50); Jesus sees to it that the temple tax is paid (Matt. 17:25) and refers to the temple as God's house that needs to be cleansed of the money changers (Matt. 21:12–13; John 2:14–17); and the conclusion to Luke's Gospel states that after the resurrection and ascension of Jesus, the disciples returned to Jerusalem and "were continually in the temple blessing God" (Luke 24:53). On the other hand, Jesus states that something greater than the temple is in the world, with the implication that it is inextricably associated with him (Matt. 12:6); that the temple complex will in the not-too-distant future be laid waste (Mark 13:2); and that his body will be the new temple that will be destroyed and then raised in three days (John 2:19).

A similar ambiguity regarding the temple, and Jerusalem and the promised land more generally, can be discerned in other New Testament writings. In the Acts of the Apostles, for example, the disciples continue to worship in the temple regularly (2:46). At the same time, however, the promised land functions in the narrative as a point of dispersion for the gospel, that the gospel might reach "to the ends of the earth" (1:8). In the Epistles it is the body of Christ that is described as God's temple (1 Cor. 3:16; 2 Cor. 6:16; Eph. 2:21–22; 1 Pet. 2:11), "a dwelling place for God as visible as the Temple in Jerusalem, but nomadic, on pilgrimage."[80] Hebrews alludes to the temple in Jerusalem as a "parable" (*parabolē*) of the present age and a "mere copy" of the heavenly sanctuary or age to come (9:8–9, 24). And in the final vision in the Revelation of John, the new Jerusalem, whose dimensions seem to encompass the whole earth, has no temple, "for its temple is the Lord God the Almighty and the Lamb" (21:22; cf. 21:16).

It is clear that these markers of Jewish identity no longer serve the same function that they did within Second Commonwealth Judaism. The Torah is reinterpreted christologically, attesting to the disclosure of the righteousness of God in the faithfulness of Christ (Rom. 3:21). National, ethnic, and geo- graphical boundaries are also radically reconfigured by the advent of the messianic age. As Frederick Bauerschmidt puts it, the "Spirit-filled commu- nity, dispersed throughout the world, enacting again the story of Jesus in a multitude of places, telling his story in alien tongues, creates sacred 'spaces' in which the land of promise appears not as 'this soil' but as 'this people.'"[81] Or as N. T. Wright characterizes the change, "Jesus and the church together are the new Temple; the world . . . is the new Land."[82]

---

80. Bauerschmidt, "Walking in the Pilgrim City," 506.
81. Bauerschmidt, "Walking in the Pilgrim City," 507.
82. Wright, *New Testament and the People of God*, 366n31.

At the same time, however, these pivotal aspects of Jewish life and language are not discarded as useless husks, but as Paul states in Romans 9–11, they continue to stand, in all their particularity, as permanent figures and types within it, without which the story of Jesus and the church cannot be truthfully narrated.[83] As noted above, the blessing of Adam and Eve at creation and the divine command to be fruitful and multiply and have dominion over the earth are recapitulated in the promise of offspring and land made to Abraham. But just as the world was not abandoned when God entered into covenant with Israel, neither are Israel and its key symbols left behind with the fulfillment of that covenant in the life, death, and resurrection of Christ and the creation of the church.

Caught Up in the Messianic Suffering

In continuity, then, with all that God has accomplished in and through Israel, the Spirit gathers together a people from every tribe and nation, language, and culture (Rev. 5:9) to be the living members of the body of Christ. This community exists not for its own sake but for the sake of a world that even in its violence and rebellion God has never stopped cherishing. The followers of Jesus are constituted, as the tribes of Israel had been before them, as an in-between people, this time as the vanguard of the messianic age in the midst of the present world. This constitution puts this fragile and fallible community squarely at the meeting point between the two ages, where life is never boring, frequently precarious, and at times positively dangerous. "For while we live," Paul writes to the saints in Corinth, "we are always being given up to death for Jesus' sake, so that the life of Jesus may be made visible in our mortal flesh" (2 Cor. 4:11). The members of the body of Christ thus do not simply find themselves passive bystanders to the events of a fallen world. The Spirit receives the offering of their bodies (Rom. 12:1) as a living sacrifice to extend that pivotal point of exchange—fashioned initially by Jesus's life, death, and resurrection—between a world destined to pass away and one that will endure forever.

The New Testament authors use a variety of apocalyptic images to drive this point home. As we have already seen, Paul regularly divides the time of creation into two ages. There is the present age, when the wicked flourish and God's people languish under the rule of idolatrous powers that claim for themselves what belongs to God alone. And there is the age to come, when all creation will witness the restoration of God's sovereignty, see the vindication

83. Bauerschmidt, "Walking in the Pilgrim City," 507.

of Israel and the righteous among the gentiles, and celebrate the blessings of a new heaven and a new earth, where death will have been vanquished and where neither the sound of weeping nor the cry of distress will be heard. In Christ, Paul argues, this new creation has already been manifested: "So if anyone is in Christ, there is *a new creation*: everything old has passed away; see, everything has become new!" (2 Cor. 5:17, emphasis added).

Apocalyptic imagery of this sort is not confined to the Pauline correspondence but can be found in Jesus's own teaching and preaching as well. In Mark's Gospel, for example, Jesus tells his disciples, "Truly I tell you, there is no one who has left house or brothers or sisters or mother or father or children or fields, for my sake and for the sake of the good news, who will not receive a hundredfold now in this age—houses, brothers and sisters, mothers and children, and fields, *with persecutions*—and in the age to come eternal life" (Mark 10:29–30, emphasis added). Not only does the image of two ages appear prominently in this passage but also the recognition that belonging to Christ's circle of friends brings with it two things: a foretaste of the blessings of the messianic age in the form of shared practices and resources *and* the sort of trouble that comes with belonging to a group that refuses to play by the established rules of the game.

The members of Christ's body could thus expect to bear the enmity that the present age harbors for the ways of the world to come. "Blessed are those who are persecuted for righteousness' sake," says Jesus, "for theirs is the kingdom of heaven. Blessed are you when people revile you and persecute you and utter all kinds of evil against you falsely on my account" (Matt. 5:10–11). Paul likewise commends the saints in Thessalonica, because they became imitators of the apostles and of the Lord: "For in spite of persecution you received the word with joy inspired by the Holy Spirit, so that you became an example to all the believers in Macedonia and in Achaia" (1 Thess. 1:6–7). And in 1 Thessalonians Paul also reminds his readers, "For you, brothers and sisters, became imitators of the churches of God in Christ Jesus that are in Judea, for you suffered the same things from your own compatriots as they did from the Jews" (2:14).

The conflict of God's rule with the established authorities and powers that culminated in Jesus's crucifixion at the hands of the Jewish and Roman authorities is thus recapitulated time and again by his followers, for all the world to see. In the New Testament the cross is not an abstract symbol of the ambiguity of history or of humankind's finite freedom. It signifies instead the concrete and decisive contraction of time between the two ages, and as such it entails several interwoven layers of meaning. The cross was, first of all, a free act of sacrifice offered by Jesus to God for the sake of God's people, and ultimately for all creation. Paul thus writes in the salutation of his Letter to the Galatians that the Lord Jesus Christ "gave himself for our sins to set us free from the present evil age, according to the will of our God and Father" (1:3–4). But even at this basic level the cross did not stand by itself but was seen as the culmination of a life lived wholly out of obedience to God. As Paul reminds us in the great christological hymn recorded in his letter to the Philippians, Jesus "humbled himself and became obedient to the point of death—even death on a cross" (2:8).

In a variety of ways, then, Scripture describes Jesus's crucifixion as necessary. In the story of the two disciples making their way to Emmaus, for example, the risen Lord appears to them and says to them, "Was it not necessary that the Messiah should suffer these things and then enter into his glory?" (Luke 24:26). The necessity of his death had nothing to do with satisfying some sense of penal justice on God's part. Nowhere in the New Testament do we find depicted a courtroom scene in which God the Father is the righteous judge, Christ the defendant, and his suffering and death a penalty paid. The cross is necessary because of the kind of world we have made for ourselves, a world bent not toward God but toward violence and death. Crucifixion is what happens to human beings when they are faithful to God rather than the rulers of the present age. Atonement occurs in turn because of God's faithfulness to Jesus. Paul thus regards the cross as a triumph over the rulers and powers of this present age (Col. 2:15; cf. 2 Cor. 2:14). By accepting his death, Jesus demonstrated that he was free from the rebellious deceptions of a world that thinks that the creature rather than the Creator determines the order and end of all things.

In this aspect the cross was a unique and unrepeatable event, for with Christ "everything—absolutely everything—had, of course, been already given."[84] It was not merely a heroic example of how we ought to live and perhaps die for our fellow human beings, but the decisive moment in time when God's life-and-death struggle for the destiny of creation was decisively joined. But the cross is also the central figure for our participation in the life of Christ, which is a communal life of faithfulness to the God who breaks into the humanly contrived order of things with the peace of the city that is to come. It is in this sense that Paul introduces the great christological hymn in Philippians with the admonition, "Let the same mind be in you that was in Christ Jesus" (2:5). The Epistle to the Hebrews declares in like manner that it was fitting that

> God, for whom and through whom all things exist, in bringing many children to glory, should make the pioneer of their salvation perfect through sufferings.

84. De Lubac, *Scripture in the Tradition*, 6.

. . . Since, therefore, the children share flesh and blood, [Christ] himself likewise shared the same things, so that through death he might destroy the one who has the power of death, that is, the devil, and free those who all their lives were held in slavery by the fear of death. (2:10, 14–15)

Therefore Jesus also suffered outside the city gate in order to sanctify the people by his own blood. Let us then go to him outside the camp and bear the abuse he endured. (13:12–13)

The cross thus also serves as a synecdoche in early Christian writings, signifying a life lived wholly out of obedience to God, and in that capacity it names a pattern of atonement to be repeated by the communal body of Christ. As Paul asserts in Romans, the righteousness of God is revealed through the faith of Christ for our own life of faith (Rom. 1:17; 3:26). The apocalyptic fault line formed by the meeting of the two ages, decisively established by the events of Jesus's life, now cuts straight through each and every member of Christ's body. His followers constitute the temporal intersection between Pentecost and parousia within which all creation is now set. In this "tensed" interval, Christians become in Christ the righteousness of God (2 Cor. 5:21), embodying sacramentally the healing of the whole of creation.

And since in God life, not death, has the final word for creation, God's vindication of the way of Christ signified by the cross was disclosed in the resurrection. With the ascension of the risen Lord to the right hand of God, the early Christians declared that the world had definitively crossed the threshold into the age to come. The rulers and authorities of this present age, though not directly acknowledging Christ's lordship, had been decisively defeated and brought under his sovereignty, and thus they were the unwitting servants of God's final (though still future) triumph. The practices and habits that bound together this motley mob of misfits and malcontents in a new style of life were a tangible sign to the world that God's everlasting reign, which had drawn near in all that Jesus did and suffered, was now making its way to the ends of the earth in the power of the Holy Spirit. "The church is God's new will and purpose for humanity," says Bonhoeffer. "God's will is always directed toward the concrete, historical human being. But this means that it begins to be implemented *in history*. God's will must become visible and comprehensible at some point in history."[85]

The visibility of this fellowship was crucial, for though the triumph of God over death signaled that this new era was at hand, the early Christians also quickly discovered that the "end" was not yet. Paul's description of the

---

85. Bonhoeffer, Sanctorum Communio, 141 (emphasis added).

church as living between the times typifies the struggle of the New Testament authors to find appropriate ways to depict this overlap between two ages and two social orders, for in appearance most things went on pretty much as they had before. Babies were born and the elderly buried, goods were bought and sold, the priests and scribes continued to gather at the temple, the Romans looked to expand their empire, and death still exercised its terrible dominion over the created order. The summons of Jesus in the Sermon on the Mount for his followers to be salt and light (Matt. 5:13–16) draws metaphorically upon two different senses of the body to drive home the same point: that the members of the body were to manifest the coming reign and regime of God to a world that had not completely disappeared but was destined to wither away.

The church, caught up in the apocalyptic action of God (a fact celebrated in eucharistic gatherings and lived out in a life of communal solidarity and hospitality to the stranger), thus bore witness to the world that the end toward which all creation is moving is not determined by those whom this age calls powerful, but by the one who gathers together all things in heaven and on earth in the crucified Messiah of Israel (Eph. 1:10). God's messianic rule established the goal toward which all things tend, and it also set the limits for the exercise of power by all worldly authorities. In and through this small group of people everything in the created order, all life, was "immediately confronted with a claim that is non-negotiable in the sense that in the end God will irrefutably be—God."[86] The mission of the church was not merely to communicate information about him to anyone who would listen, but to put the bodies of its members on the line between the two ages on behalf of him who lived and died for the sake of the world.

The Fading of Apocalyptic Attentiveness and the Re-expansion of Time

The New Testament's emphasis on the imminence of the apocalyptic day of the Lord was preserved to varying degrees well into the patristic era, as seen, for example, in the fathers' understanding of all that is involved in Christ's cosmic triumph over death, the devil, and sin.[87] Augustine, to cite but one example, cautions his readers against those who say that there will be no more persecutions of the church until the time of the antichrist.[88] But as the centuries wore on, the apocalyptic compression of time that captivated the imagination of the early church gradually faded into the background, and the vivid

86. McClendon, *Doctrine*, 66.
87. See Florovsky, "Empire and Desert," 133–59.
88. Augustine, *City of God* 18.52.

sense of expectation generated by this view of things was relaxed. Believers' sense of history "re-expanded," and the *eschaton* was projected further and further into the future "and thus into insignificance."[89] The keen awareness of living in the tension between the "is" and the "is not" gradually faded, and the demarcation between church and world (and the corresponding line that passes through the soul of each Christian[90]) grew more and more opaque.

With the fading of the apocalyptic tension that so characterized the life and witness of the early church, Christians increasingly made themselves "at home" in the present world. As Martin Buber puts it, the "Christian cosmos arises; and this was so real for every mediaeval Christian that all who read [Dante's] *Divina Commedia* made in spirit the journey to the nethermost spiral of hell and stepped over Lucifer's back, through purgatory, to the heaven of the Trinity, not as an expedition into lands as yet unknown, but as a crossing of regions already fully mapped."[91] Buber paints here with too broad a brush, but the portrait he creates rightly directs our attention to momentous changes in the ways Christians came to be caught up in the world that have become visible only in retrospect. It is to the story of these changes we now turn.

89. McClendon, *Doctrine*, 90.
90. McClendon, *Ethics*, 17.
91. Buber, *Between Man and Man*, 153.

4

LET US BE LIKE THE NATIONS

Becoming Entangled in the Ways of the World

The children of the world are consistent too—so I say they will soak up everything you can offer, take your job away from you, and then denounce you as a decrepit wreck. Finally, they'll ignore you entirely. It's your own fault. The Book I gave you should have been enough for you. Now you'll just have to take the consequences for your meddling.

Walter M. Miller Jr., *A Canticle for Leibowitz*

In her book *Bystanders*, Victoria Barnett identifies some of the factors that "fostered passivity and complicity in Nazi Germany and in other countries"[1] in the lives of ordinary people during this most odious of episodes in human history. By "ordinary people" she is referring not to prominent members of the Nazi Party or to the soldiers of the Waffen-SS (Schutzstaffel) who operated the concentration and death camps. Instead, she has in mind those people who sought to go about their daily lives while one of the most sinister regimes the world has ever known committed unspeakable atrocities all about them. They might have been ordinary people, but their behavior was anything but ordinary. It was instead grotesque and freakish.[2]

1. Barnett, *Bystanders*, xvi.
2. O'Connor, "Some Aspects of the Grotesque in Southern Fiction."

Barnett contrasts these bystanders to the handful of people who worked to rescue the victims of the Nazi regime. She notes in particular that the differences between the rescuers and those who went about their daily lives without attending to the great evil taking place all around them were not noticeable prior to 1933, the year that Adolf Hitler came to power in Germany. "In social and historical circumstances that demanded little of them personally," she writes, "the two groups were indistinguishable from one another. After 1933, however, these good citizens begin to move in opposite directions."[3] The question, therefore, is what factors led bystanders and rescuers to take diametrically opposed paths.

According to Barnett, studies show that strongly held religious feelings and beliefs were *not* significant factors for distinguishing bystanders from most rescuers. When interviewed, less than 30 percent of Polish rescuers cited religious conviction as a motive, and in Italy and Denmark, where there was significant activity against Hitler's "Final Solution," religious factors evidently did not play a major role. The principal difference was that rescuers found it difficult "to remain passively on the sidelines under a system like Nazism. Their natural tendency was to help its victims and resist the dictatorship's demands upon them." Barnett contends in particular that those who worked to rescue the victims of the Third Reich were distinguished from bystanders by a certain type of *vision*. This vision was of a different kind of society and of themselves as citizens of that alternative society. It compelled them to be attentive, to see that they had "a personal stake in what was happening around them."[4]

Bystanders, by contrast, were generally people who were principally concerned about themselves. Those who averted their gaze from the evil going on around them were those whose lives had always revolved around their own needs: "Even those who had qualms about what was happening under Nazism chose to remain silent. They evaded the intentionality that is the prerequisite for rescue or resistance. . . . They denied any connection between their own lives and what was taking place around them." They accepted the persecution of the Jews as an unpleasant but unchangeable reality and arranged their lives, psyches, and ethics accordingly, so that they did not have to deal with what was going on there. When asked after the war about these events, the good citizens of these towns claimed that they were *machtlos*, powerless to do anything about their situation, paralyzed by fear and the threat of retribution (though relatively little harm typically came to those in villages who did refuse to comply with Nazi policies).[5]

3. Barnett, *Bystanders*, 159.
4. Barnett, *Bystanders*, 30, 158, 159, 172.
5. Barnett, *Bystanders*, 5–8, 159.

Two of the factors cited by Barnett to account for the inaction of the bystanders, when taken together, shed light on our inquiry into the dismembering of the church as the body of Christ. The first has to do with her observation that in social and historical circumstances that demanded little of them personally, the two groups were indistinguishable from each other. The existence of the Christian had become coextensive with, and thus indistinguishable from, that of the typical citizen of the nation-state. The second is the claim of bystanders, including many Christians, that they were powerless to resist the evil in their midst. They literally knew no other power, no other disciplined form of life, than that regulated by the rulers and authorities of this age.

As I noted in the last chapter, the early followers of Jesus, having been caught up in the apocalypse of God, embodied before the world a distinctive pattern of life together, constituted by an alternative set of habits and relations, and embodied a different story in terms of which to follow the rhythms and progressions of history. God fashioned from the resources of diverse times and places a transformative social grammar for catching a glimpse of truth's beauty. Through their participation in the body of Christ, these women and men bore witness that the meaning of all other figures, events, and institutions could be discerned only in relationship to the one in whom God's own speech took flesh. The reorganization of human life and language inaugurated by the life and passion of Jesus, a project embodied in and mediated by the practices and institutions of the church, including modes of material exchange, became a never-ending task.

The mission undertaken by these artisans of the age to come was "not to exist 'in itself' but to be the 'sacrament,' the *epiphany*, of the new creation." Their shared practices established the performative links between, on the one hand, day-to-day life in a world where people eat and drink, marry and give in marriage, have children and bury parents, acquire and dispose of property, exchange goods, and the like, and on the other, the resurrection and the world to come. The body of Christ embodied this new social dimension into the world, its practices not just the *means* but also the *media* of grace. In and through these activities the church learned of its calling, received the power of the Spirit to fulfill it, and became "the sacrament, in Christ, of the new creation; the sacrament, in Christ, of the Kingdom."[6]

The process of getting caught up in new or different forms of life and thought, however, can and does work the other way as well. The tribes of Israel had been gathered from among the nations to be a "peculiar people"

6. Schmemann, *Church, World, Mission*, 136–37 (emphasis original).

so that the world might know the will, wisdom, and blessing of God. They did not always relish their peculiarity, however, but often wanted to serve their God the way other nations served theirs. "Let us be like the nations," they declared to the prophets, and thus they found themselves entangled in a series of events that led, according to the prophets, to their exile and dispersion (Ezek. 20:21; cf. 1 Sam. 8:5, 20). The story of God's chosen people, who repeatedly responded to the divine summons by reproducing the disobedience and rebellion of the fall, is in important respects one of being caught up in the worship of necessity that is idolatry. The catastrophe of the fall of the monarchy, the destruction of Jerusalem, and the exile did not, however, spell the end of the covenant relationship. A faithful God instead folded these events back into the saving history of the chosen people, allowing them in their affliction to "recognize their guilt and turn back to God, thus correcting the direction they [were] going. The crisis of the people of God would then be one of the reasons why God's cause does not fail, but instead goes forward as a history of salvation." The end of David's monarchic regime led "to a rebirth of the people of God," thus making the exile and diaspora parts of "a *saving* history and a step into the future."[7]

Like Israel before it, the church became ensnared in a similar pattern of divine call, rebellion, and judgment. It exchanged its peculiar portion in the promises of God to Israel, bequeathed in the messianic event of Jesus Christ, for a share in a new sort of regime for the earthly city, one in which the church hierarchy shares power and authority with secular rulers. The aim of those who led the way was in many respects a noble one: to help liberate creation from the dominion of death and darkness and make it new before God by the power of the Holy Spirit. But what they set into motion contributed instead to the dismembering of the church as the bodily presence of Christ in the world, leaving its scattered members at the mercy of powers and authorities that now no longer even bother to give lip service to the God of Abraham and Sarah.

The body of Christ is now caught up in a powerful disciplinary regime that subdivides social space into discrete spheres—political, economic, civic, cultural, religious, and domestic. This process of differentiation functions effectively to domesticate, marginalize, and exploit the church's traditional regime of life and language. We find ourselves, like Israel, refugees and exiles in a strange land, where we are compelled to "serve other gods made by human hands, objects of wood and stone that neither see, nor hear, nor eat, nor smell" (Deut. 4:28). If we are persuaded, as participants in the covenants

7. Lohfink, *Does God Need the Church?*, 105 (emphasis original).

of promise, that in spite of what has happened our life with God has not come to an end, then we must once again find our bearings and discover something of how we came to be in this situation. What happened to the church, where it now stands, and what we may hope for it in the future must therefore be parsed in terms of Israel's story, for the events of Israel's history with God are types (*typoi*) intended to instruct the church in precisely this task (1 Cor. 10:6, 11). But which is the most adequate type?

Peculiarity and Conformity

In *The End of the Church*, Ephraim Radner advances a bold and controversial claim: the post-Reformation church, governed by a separative logic that contradicts Christ's mandate that the members of Christ's body should love each other in a way that relies on the other in visible unity, has been abandoned by God. This willful refusal to maintain the bonds of ecclesial unity, especially a common eucharistic communion, has prompted God to withdraw the Spirit from the church, thus condemning it to destruction and death. Radner formulates his thesis on the basis of a typological reading of the story of divided monarchy in the Old Testament. Due to this division, Israel was eventually abandoned by God to its enemies and forced to endure war and an exile that in some respects has never ended. And as with all good figural readings of the Old Testament, Radner connects this reading to the person and work of Christ, who mediates the figure of Israel to the church, including his acceptance of complete divine abandonment on the cross.[8]

There is much to commend in Radner's figural reading of the present situation, above all his recognition that the present status of the church must be construed typologically in terms of Israel's canonical story. He is also correct in pointing out that there has been a centuries-long contradiction of ecclesial love and a separative logic at work in a willfully divided church. Among different Protestant denominations in particular there is a persistent and pervasive tendency to pit variegated aspects of Christian life and thought against one another: Bible versus tradition, personal experience versus ecclesiastical authority, feeling versus intellect, spontaneity versus liturgy, discipleship versus doctrine, evangelism versus spiritual formation, apostolic office versus apostolic teaching, and so forth. Virtually nonexistent is any confession of the sin of denominational self-sufficiency. The sort of humility that is generous enough to accept correction from other traditions, or a generosity humble

8. Radner, *End of the Church*.

enough to accept that each tradition must recognize its place within and dependence on the Catholic church, is seldom in evidence.[9]

In the final analysis, however, the specific features of Radner's figural reading do not adequately account for the dismembered state of the church, particularly its diachronic dimensions. The failure of charity that currently divides the body of Christ must be traced in large part to a new love that long ago seduced it with promises that this false suitor had no intention of keeping. The seeds of the separative logic that germinated during the sixteenth and seventeenth centuries and blossomed with the rise of the modern world were in fact sown centuries earlier, when the church joined forces with the rulers and authorities of the present age to govern the *saeculum*. As the church became increasingly at home in the world, the task of forming the Christian body, both communal and individual (with the exception of cloistered and mendicant communities), was ceded incrementally to the secular authorities and institutions, resulting in a minimalist ethics that effectively adapted the social mission of the church so that it could accommodate the habits and relations of the secular regime. When that sphere began to fragment in the late Middle Ages, the division of the church, first into separate denominations and then into isolated monads, was for all practical purposes a foregone conclusion.

The problematic nature of Radner's spiritual reading of the Old Testament lies in his selection of the division of David and Solomon's kingdom as the principal figure for interpreting the state of the post-Reformation church. At first glance the typological resemblance between a divided kingdom and a divided church seems ready-made. But positing the division of the kingdom as the source of Israel's disobedience and failure of steadfast love (*chesed*) obscures the plain sense of the text, on which sound spiritual exegesis necessarily depends. Both Torah and the Prophets link the idolatry and rebellion that led to Israel's destruction and exile not to the division of the united monarchy (an institution that certain prophets had doubts about from the outset) but to the usurpations of monarchic practices and institutions in both north and south. Hosea is thus typical when he says,

> Israel has spurned the good;
>> the enemy shall pursue him.
> They made kings, but not through me;
>> they set up princes, but without my knowledge.

9. I am indebted to Schlabach, "Correction of the Augustinians," 74, for this way of putting the matter. "Catholic church" here is not limited to the Roman Catholic church, but as I said in the introduction, I am skeptical of the idea of the small-*c* catholic church.

> With their silver and gold they made idols
>> for their own destruction. (8:3–4)

And therefore, says Amos to the inhabitants of the kingdom of Israel,

> you have built houses of hewn stone,
>> but you shall not live in them;
> you have planted pleasant vineyards,
>> but you shall not drink their wine. (5:11)

When the elders of the tribes of Israel first approached the prophet Samuel about appointing for them a king, they evidently envisioned the institution of the monarchy as a reliable locus of stability and prosperity: "We are determined to have a king over us, so that we also may be like other nations, and that our king may govern us and go out before us and fight our battles" (1 Sam. 8:19–20). Their desire to be like other nations was not a preference based on a carefully calculated typology of political regimes. It was instead the expression of a desire for the sort of stability and security that was associated with the gods of the other nations, an idolatrous longing that, as Samuel and then Nathan sought to make clear from the beginning (1 Sam. 8:7–9; 2 Sam. 7:4–7), ran counter to the mission first set before Abraham and Sarah.

It is the shift to a monarchic regime, setting into motion the forces that ultimately led Israel into exile, and not its subsequent division along tribal lines, that offers the most instructive *typos* in the Old Testament for figuring the dismembered state of the body of Christ in this time after Christendom. We must take care, however, not to perpetuate a caricature or promote a blanket condemnation of what is often referred to as "Constantinianism." The question of whether it is even accurate to refer to the changes that took place beginning in the first half of the fourth century CE as the Constantinian shift is widely debated. Many in the patristic era celebrated the first "Christian emperor" as a sign of divine providence, pronouncing his reign an extension of Christ's heavenly kingdom. Eusebius of Caesarea compares Constantine favorably to Moses in the dispensation of salvation, seeing him as leading his people from the captivity of persecution.[10] And closer to our own time, Charles Cochrane has called him the "architect (to a very great extent) of the Middle Ages."[11] To such minds Constantine's "conversion" marked the beginning of the *corpus Christianum*. Recent scholarship generally takes a more restrained approach. Sociologist Rodney Stark, for example, contends

---

10. Eusebius, *History of the Church* 9.9.5–6; Eusebius, *Life of Constantine* 1.12.
11. Cochrane, *Christianity and Classical Culture*, 211.

that Constantine's turn to Christianity was an expedient response to the exponential growth of the church during the latter half of the third century.[12] Historian Averil Cameron concurs with Stark, arguing that "Constantine marks a convenient but not an all-important landmark" in the spread of Christianity within the empire.[13]

It is imprecise, moreover, in certain respects to speak of Constantinianism as though the relations between church and secular rulers that developed during the Middle Ages and that eventually led to the fracturing of the church as an institution in the sixteenth century were the direct design and result of Constantine's efforts, or as though, at the very least, the essentials of those relations were firmly in place by the end of the fourth century. A series of changes following the time of Constantine kept the situation fluid, beginning with the collapse of the empire in the West in the fifth and sixth centuries and the rise of Germanic kingdoms that replaced the imperial regime. Moreover, a line of thinking in both Jewish and Christian circles, going back to at least Philo, had already accorded the emperor a significant place within God's providential rule of history. According to R. A. Markus, Melito of Sardis states that the unification of the *orbis Romanus* under imperial rule was providentially geared to the propagation of the gospel.[14] And no lesser a figure than Origen provides the classical formulation of this theme in his polemic against Celsus. By reducing the many nations of the earth to one rule, God was preparing the nations for Christ's teaching by easing the way of the apostles.[15]

Finally, though the many institutional arrangements of Christendom did not achieve what its first proponents set out to accomplish—to liberate creation from the dominion of death and darkness and to make it new before God by the power of the Holy Spirit—neither did they completely abandon the understanding of history embodied in the life and ministry of Jesus and in the early church. As the ill-fated shift from tribal confederacy to monarchy in Israel did not take place without serving an important role in unfolding the divine ordering of creation, the history of this phase in the life of the church also served a similar purpose. The patristic and medieval church cultivated practices and principles that retained something of the early church's regulation of everyday life. The "higher level of morality asked of the clergy, the international character of the hierarchy, the visibility of the hierarchy in opposition to the princes, the gradual moral education of barbarians into

12. Stark, *Rise of Christianity*, 5, 10.
13. Cameron, *Christianity and the Rhetoric of Empire*, 13.
14. Markus, *Saeculum*, 47–48.
15. Origen, *Contra Celsum* 2.30.

monogamy and legality, foreign missions, apocalypticism and mysticism . . . preserved an awareness, however distorted and polluted, of the strangeness of God's people in a rebellious world."[16]

That said, we must nonetheless recognize that though Constantine's "conversion" was not the sole or perhaps even the single most important cause of the changes that took place, the new social status subsequently enjoyed by the church, followed a few decades later by official recognition as the true *pietatis* of Rome during the reign of Theodosius I (379–95), would not have come about as it did were it not for Constantine's toleration of and personal identification with the church. The emperor's change of heart set into motion a series of events that would contribute materially to the dismemberment of the church as Christ's true body.

Those who downplay the significance of the first "Christian" emperor frequently overcompensate for past indiscretions on the part of church figures and secular historians alike. Constantine's conversion played a key role in the rapidly changing circumstances of the church with respect to its status and mission and thus with regard to its relationship to the world about it.

Citizens of Another Commonwealth

As I have noted above, early Christians regularly referred to themselves as a company of fellow travelers garnered from every tribe and language and people and nation to populate a city on pilgrimage. Some might find this terminology confusing, accustomed as we are to a very different account of what constitutes the respective realms of politics and religion. In the modern world "politics" is reserved for the practice of statecraft, while religion is something that individuals do in the solitude of their "inner self," an interior disposition of the soul toward that which transcends the physical world and which thus has no direct bearing on their public lives. But in classical antiquity "city" functioned as the principal trope denoting the shared practices, habits, and relationships that enable women and men to flourish in accordance with their highest good. Politics was the art of human community, the end of which was living well, and political institutions were a means to this end, supporting and sustaining those tasks that direct the community's members toward that highest good.[17]

The community of Jesus's followers deliberately cast itself as a body politic when it referred to itself as an *ekklēsia*, a Hellenistic term for the assembly of

16. Yoder, *Royal Priesthood*, 58.
17. Aristotle, *Politics* 3.9; Cicero, *De re publica* 1.25.39.

those holding rights and privileges of citizenship. When the church adopted this term for their association, rather than that of the ancient guilds or civic clubs, it was claiming the status of a public assembly of the social whole. The goods and activities of this particular body politic, however, were not those of the Greek *polis* or the Roman *imperium*. On the contrary, the assembly of God's messianic regime ordered the life of its members in ways that called into question virtually every social, political, and economic convention of its time. The church retained the classical telos of politics, which is the good life, and the practices and institutions of social life were likewise understood to be means to this end. But it gave the practice of politics new content— namely, "the art of achieving the common good through participation in the divine life of God."[18]

By its existence as a political community, the church called into question the dominant political assumptions and social categories of that time and place. It regarded the builders of earthly kingdoms and empires with a wary eye, because they invariably laid claim to an authority that belonged to God alone. Rome saw itself as "*the City*, a permanent and 'eternal' City, *Urbs aeterna*, and an ultimate City also. In a sense, it claimed for itself an 'eschatological dimension.' It posed as an ultimate solution of the human problem." The empire proclaimed itself a universal commonwealth, embodying the decisive expression of "humanity" and offering to all over whom it exercised author- ity the only lasting and genuine peace, the *pax Romana*. As such it claimed to be omnicompetent over human affairs and thus demanded the complete and unconditional allegiance of its subjects. "The Church was a challenge to the Empire," writes Georges Florovsky, "and the Empire was a stumbling block for the Christians."[19]

Church teaching prior to the fourth century, in keeping with the Old Testa- ment and rabbinic tradition, relativized the role that the rulers and authori- ties of this world played in the unfolding of history. Their claim to be the determinative players on the stage of history was abrogated, and like the Persian king Cyrus (Isa. 44:28–45:4, 13), they were recast as supporting actors. These temporal authorities were granted the right or power of the sword (*ius* or *potestas gladii*), which they were to use to help preserve a rebellious and chaotic world until, as Paul puts it, "Christ came, so that we might be justi- fied by faith" (Gal. 3:24).[20] These authorities served this function by pursuing certain legitimate yet limited goods—for example, restraining evil through the prudent use of coercion, facilitating the production and exchange of

---

18. Baxter, "'Overall, the First Amendment Has Been Very Good for Christianity'—NOT!," 441.
19. Florovsky, "Empire and Desert," 135, 137.
20. See Field, *Liberty, Dominion, and the Two Swords*, 45–49.

material goods through the institutions of private property and markets, and in general maintaining social cohesion so that the church could proclaim the gospel unhindered.

At the same time, however, the pre-Constantinian church as a rule prohibited believers from wielding the *gladius ultor*, the avenging sword. "Shall it be lawful," Tertullian asks, "to make an occupation of the sword, when the Lord proclaims that he who uses the sword shall perish by the sword?"[21] According to Hippolytus, a soldier who converted could remain in that position, but it was forbidden for him to put a person to death or take an oath, and no catechumen or baptized Christian could become a soldier, for to do so would be to despise God.[22] Christians were to use a different weapon, described in Scripture as the sword of the Spirit, which is the word of God (Eph. 6:17). Clement of Alexandria, calling the *gladius spiritalis* (spiritual sword) the Christian's invulnerable weapon, writes: "The loud trumpet, when sounded, collects the soldiers, and proclaims war. And shall not Christ, breathing a strain of peace to the ends of the earth, gather together His own soldiers, the soldiers of peace? Well, by His blood, and by the word, He has gathered the bloodless host of peace, and assigned to them the kingdom of heaven. The trumpet of Christ is His Gospel. He hath blown it, and we have heard it."[23] For these early fathers the two "swords" did not designate complementary offices within a unified social order, one dealing with the affairs of the material world and the other with "spiritual" matters having to do with interior dispositions of the soul, as they later became, but as mutually exclusive modes of dealing with the world's evils.[24]

Toward a "Christian" Empire

When in the fourth century the empire, which had regularly ridiculed and on occasion persecuted the church, sought it out so that the body of Christ might serve the imperial household, this appeal was initially seen as a response to the gentile mission of the church, "constituted not by the church's seizing alien power, but by alien power's becoming attentive to the church." In other words, the Christendom idea initially presupposed the apocalyptic eschatology of the early church, with church and secular rule as distinct structures belonging to two distinct societies or cities: "Until the end of the patristic period this

21. Tertullian, *De corona* 11.
22. Hippolytus, *Treatise on the Apostolic Tradition*.
23. Clement of Alexandria, *Protrepticus* 11.
24. See Murray, *We Hold These Truths*, 79–81, 186–90.

vis-à-vis is constantly in evidence, and the meaning of the Christian empire as a *capitulation* to the throne of Christ is not forgotten."[25]

The Constantinian and Theodosian establishment of a "Christian" empire was therefore, in the minds of many, a confirmation and continuation of the church's missional confidence in the triumph of God over the rulers and idols of this age.[26] The body of Christ set out to exorcise the world of its demonic powers, to liberate the empire from the thralldom of the "prince of the air"—in short, to make "this world 'new' before God by the power of the Holy Spirit." The church hoped to serve the world while remaining true to its identity as the sacrament of the kingdom, "God's eschatological vehicle of passage for this world through time into the world to come." Unfortunately, it failed in the attempt, and in spite of its best intentions the blame rests largely with the church, because in the end it succumbed to the temptation to be like the other nations, endeavoring to be "not what it is but what it is not."[27] Over the long term, the church cannot serve both as sign, foretaste, and instrument of God's coming kingdom and as the spiritual form of the earthly city. By its own actions, then, the body of Christ became caught up in a series of events that would over time lead to the dismembering of its societal fellowship and the reallocation of the dissected parts to the institutions of the modern nation-state and the global market.

There were some in the fourth and fifth centuries who came to see the Constantinian settlement as something other than the "fruition of the promised kingdom of God."[28] According to Robert Wilken, John Chrysostom disabused those who were under the impression that if one became a monk he would always receive honor and respect from Christian rulers. Chrysostom insisted that there might come a time that policies would change, or unbelievers regain power (a possibility that he had personally witnessed with the ascension of Julian to the imperial throne). "Unlike Eusebius," writes Wilken, "John did not celebrate the emperor as a 'mighty victor beloved of God,' a king who had 'wiped away all tears and cleansed the world of the hatred of God.'" Unlike many of his contemporaries, he "had no conception of a Christian empire. The Church, in John's view, was 'not dependent on the good will of the rulers.'" For Chrysostom the high hopes of the previous generation had been tempered by the recent memory of martyrs.[29]

---

25. O'Donovan, *Desire of the Nations*, 195–96 (emphasis original).

26. O'Donovan, *Desire of the Nations*, 193–99; Markus, *Saeculum*, 31.

27. Guroian, *Incarnate Love*, 146.

28. Schlabach, "Correction of the Augustinians," 64.

29. Wilken, *John Chrysostom and the Jews*, 31–32. Augustine makes a similar observation about Julian in *City of God* 18.53.

For a time Augustine ascribed to the Christian emperor, and by implication to the empire itself, a central role in the history of God's redemptive work. Around the year 400, however, a radical transformation occurred in his thinking, stimulated by the Donatist theologian Tyconius.[30] Owing to God's activity in Christ, made visible to all through the church, Augustine contends, there exist in the world two distinct kinds of human society, one earthly and the other on pilgrimage to a city that is not of its own making.[31] These two societies are related eschatologically, each possessing a different faith, a different love, and a different hope.[32] While on pilgrimage in this world, calling out citizens from all nations and forming a *civitas* of aliens speaking all languages, the church is not to occupy itself with differences in the customs, laws, and institutions by which earthly peace is achieved or maintained.[33]

According to Augustine, Christians could not neglect this earthly peace, for they had to cooperate with the earthly city in pursuit of those things that belong to the mortal nature of human beings—what we eat, what we drink, what we wear. He does add one very important proviso, which is that such pursuits should "not impede the religion by which we are taught that the one supreme and true God is to be worshipped." Therein lies the problem, he writes, for it has not been possible for the church to have rules detailing its obligations to God in common with the earthly city. "It has been necessary," says Augustine, "for her to dissent from the earthly city in this regard, and to become a burden to those who think differently. Thus, she has had to bear the brunt of the anger and hatred and persecutions of her adversaries." In spite of this animosity, Christians should cultivate skills that will allow them to use prudently those earthly goods that are necessary to life in this age, directing every good act toward that alone which can truly be called peace, "a perfectly ordered and perfectly harmonious fellowship in the enjoyment of God, and of one another in God."[34]

Augustine's rejection of an *imperium Christianum* notwithstanding, the social convergence of the church and the empire continued unabated, and by the end of the fifth century it had begun to change significantly. Pope Gelasius

---

30. See Markus, *Saeculum*, 115–22. In what follows in this chapter I am indebted to Rowan Williams's insightful discussion "Politics and the Soul: A Reading of the *City of God*." Over against Hannah Arendt, Markus, and others, Williams contends that Augustine does not repudiate the public realm in this work, but is engaged instead "in a *redefinition* of the public itself, designed to show that it is life outside the Christian community which fails to be truly public, authentically political." Williams, "Politics and the Soul," 58.

31. Duo quaedam genera humanae societatis existerent. Augustine, *City of God* 14.1.

32. Augustine, *City of God* 18.54.

33. Augustine, *City of God* 19.17; see also 5.17.

34. Augustine, *City of God* 19.17.

reconfigured Augustine's *temporal* demarcation between the two cities as a *functional* distinction between royal power (*potestas*) and priestly authority. These two would rule jointly, each according to its proper office, with the weight of authority oriented toward sacerdotal *auctoritas*, because, as the pope put it in a famous letter to the emperor Anastasius, "they must answer for kings at the divine judgment. Indeed, you know, most clement Son, that though you have received the power to govern mankind, nonetheless you must bow your head to those who have charge of divine affairs and must seek from them the means of your salvation."[35] In place of the two types of society that Augustine describes allegorically as Jerusalem and Babylon,[36] sacred and civil officials were now to rule conjointly within one social order. The duality of cities, which had distinguished the present age from the age to come, became a duality of government function or office. Sacred and secular officials were now to rule cooperatively within society, with the priestly office recognized as supreme.

A second transformation occurred during the years between Charlemagne and Pope Gregory VII, the so-called Carolingian period in the late eighth to eleventh centuries. Gelasius's two "swords" were redefined in terms of the two natures of Chalcedonian Christology. Christendom as such, and not just the church, was now the one body of Christ, with the dual offices of king and bishop corresponding to the two natures—human and divine, neither confused nor separated—of Christ. Whereas in Gelasius's schema the *potestas* of king and emperor was outside the church, and all true authority resided solely within the church, now kingship and empire were fused together with the church, with the temporal ruler endowed with titles such as "Vicar of Christ" and "King and Priest." The anointing of a king acquired a sacramental significance comparable to that of baptism and ordination.[37] In this configuration the king "exercised his office of ruling wholly within the church, as a kind of lay ministry or charism." With this "change from 'world' to 'church,'" writes Oliver O'Donovan, "the last consciousness of a notional distinction between the two societies had disappeared; one could no longer say that the ruler ruled Christians *qua* civil society but not *qua* heavenly city."[38]

The nearly total erasure of the eschatological demarcation between the two cities and the expansion of the concept of Christ's body to include temporal regimes significantly altered the mission of the church as an ongoing interpretation of creaturely existence lived in relation to the triune God. The

---

35. Gelasius, "Letter Twelve to Emperor Anastasius," 174.
36. Augustine, *City of God* 15.1.
37. Kantorowicz, *King's Two Bodies*, 42–61, 318–19.
38. O'Donovan, *Desire of the Nations*, 204, 212.

contraction of the two ages that characterized the apocalyptic motifs of the New Testament and early church faded into the background. The rhythms and progressions of history once again re-expanded as the *eschaton* was projected further and further into the future. The Christian hope gradually shifted from the renewal of all things in Christ to a concern with the fate of the individual after death. In keeping with this shift of temporal focus, patristic descriptions of Christ's cosmic triumph over death, sin, and the devil were supplanted by a preoccupation with the pains of Christ in his passion, and spiritual discipline became increasingly focused on dealing with the multiplicity of affections and appetites that mark the spiritual progress of the individual believer.[39]

The Invention of the "State"

In the eleventh and twelfth centuries, yet another shift took place, this one in connection with the Investiture Controversy. According to Gerhart Ladner, Pope Gregory VII (1073–85) recognized that the Carolingian arrangement between prince and bishop was unwieldy and unworkable, because the line of demarcation between the two powers was in practice almost impossible to define: "Even though the superiority of the spiritual over the temporal was undisputed on principle, the right order between the two was not easy to maintain in the contingencies of history."[40] The result was a gradual separation of the offices of civic and ecclesiastical authorities, with kingship increasingly divested of its sacerdotal connotations. In this arrangement the popes reserved the title of Vicar of Christ for themselves, while kingship was reconceived along the lines of what was becoming the dominant conception of God's sovereignty over the earth: "As opposed to the earlier 'liturgical' kingship, the late-mediaeval kingship by 'divine right' was modeled after the Father in Heaven rather than after the Son on the Altar, and focused in a philosophy of Law rather than in the . . . physiology of the two-natured Mediator." To reinforce this separation of civil rule from the body of Christ, Innocent III decreed in "On Holy Unction" that there was a separate anointment for bishops and kings and that the royal anointing did not confer in sacramental mode the Holy Spirit.[41]

Taken cumulatively, these changes significantly modified once again the way that church and civil authorities were related in time. With the separation

---

39. Morris, *Discovery of the Individual, 1050–1200*, 70–79, 139–52.

40. Ladner, "Aspects of Medieval Thought on Church and State," 409.

41. Kantorowicz, *King's Two Bodies*, 93, 319–21; Strayer, *On the Medieval Origins of the Modern State*, 23–26.

of the crown from the human nature of Christ, a new form of political association emerged in the fifteenth century, with roots reaching back as far as the twelfth century.[42] This new political artifact was the state, a centralized form of public power that was conceived in abstraction both from those who rule and those who are ruled and that claimed supreme authority within a geographically defined space.[43] The nascent state, which was centered on a formal and abstract concept of law, claimed a sempiternity or quasi-eternal character of its own in imitation of the pilgrim city of God. The idea of the "'temporal,' which had previously indicated that the coercive force of kingship was 'temporarily' necessary while awaiting the second coming of Christ," came to signify "an autonomous sphere which pursues its own perpetuity."[44]

The embryonic state, in a bid to establish its status as an independent and sacred "body" over against and yet parallel to the status of the church as Christ's mystical body, quickly adopted ecclesial symbols and sacramental images to secure that standing. "The new territorial and proto-national state," writes Kantorowicz, "self-sufficient according to its claims and independent of the Church and the Papacy, quarried the wealth of ecclesiastical notions, which were so convenient to handle, and finally proceeded to assert itself by placing its own temporariness on a level with the sempiternity of the militant Church."[45] One vestige of this move on the part of kings to mimic the trappings of ecclesiastical authority was commandeering the language of sanctification and sacrifice, such that the theological idea of martyrdom came to be applied to dying in behalf of one's nation-state as one's earthly *patria*.[46]

In its struggle to maintain its temporal authority in light of the fragmentation of the social unity of Christendom in the West, the church responded in kind by adapting a similar conception of law. A distinction began to appear in canon law in the thirteenth century between the sacramental power (*potestas ordinis*) conferred on priests with their ordination, giving them the ability to transubstantiate the host and thereby produce the true body (the *corpus verum*) of Christ, and the power of ecclesiastical jurisdiction (*potestas jurisdictionis*) vested in the bishop. According to this distinction, the consecration of a new bishop added nothing to his priestly authority. Instead, he received jurisdictional powers to govern the mystical body of the church. Imitating these new territorial sovereignties, the church located

---

42. Strayer, *On the Medieval Origins of the Modern State*, 15–27; Spruyt, *Sovereign State and Its Competitors*, 79.

43. Skinner, *Age of Reformation*, 353; Porter, *War and the Rise of the State*, 6.

44. Cavanaugh, *Torture and Eucharist*, 216.

45. Kantorowicz, *King's Two Bodies*, 207.

46. Cavanaugh, *Torture and Eucharist*, 217.

its source not in the sacrament of the Lord's body but in formal legal concepts. Canon lawyers adopted the term *corpus mysticum* in their efforts to establish the character of the church as a legal corporation.[47] "What mattered about the term," writes Cavanaugh, "was its organic connotations and not any connection with the sacramental body of Christ. In that process . . . corporational doctrines developed by the Church were to be of major importance."[48]

The jurists' use of the term *corpus mysticum* was a legal strategy, devised to stress the juridical bonds between the church and its head, the pope. Canon lawyers, at the behest of the pontiff, appropriated the concept of the right of property as set forth in Roman and feudal law and developed it in connection with the late medieval doctrine of the church as Christ's mystical body into the theory of "the absolute and universal jurisdiction of the supreme authority, and developed it into the doctrine of the *plenitudo potestatis* of the Pope."[49] With this doctrine the popes tried to reestablish political unity under their authority, and to do so in a world where "secular control was rapidly on the rise and the political unity of Christendom was being fragmented into sovereign nation-states."[50] The doctrine of the *corpus mysticum* did increase the authority and prestige of the Roman pontiff within the Catholic church,[51] but when Boniface VIII attempted to rein in the political power of Philip the Fair of France by asserting his authority over all Christians, his capture and humiliation by Philip's troops demonstrated that it was now the lay ruler, not the pope, who could count on the primary allegiance of the people.[52]

With these changes the social bodies of the church and the developing territorial states were increasingly separated into two independent and parallel jurisdictions. Church authorities sought to meet the rising power and independence of the state by declaring their own legal and corporate power. Cavanaugh observes that "the first treatises on the church as an organization were written only in the early fourteenth century, with the purpose of establishing the church as an 'ecclesiastical kingdom' parallel to the secular polity." Though the process of transforming the church into a "spiritual" body

47. Kantorowicz, *King's Two Bodies*, 200–206.
48. Cavanaugh, *Torture and Eucharist*, 217.
49. Figgis, *Studies of Political Thought*, 4; cf. O'Donovan, *Desire of the Nations*, 206.
50. Cavanaugh, *Torture and Eucharist*, 218.
51. Again, by rendering "Catholic church" in this somewhat awkward manner, I am trying, on the one hand, to avoid endorsing what I explicitly rejected in the introduction—the faulty notion of a small-*c* catholic church—while, on the other hand, to avoid suggesting that the present-day Roman Catholic church subsumes without remainder the idea of "catholic."
52. Strayer, "Laicization of French and English Society in the Thirteenth Century," 76.

concerned solely with the private, interior life of individuals would take several more centuries to develop fully, "it was clear at this point the construction of a separate and sempiternal political space outside the church was underway."[53] When John Calvin writes two and a half centuries later that "whoever knows how to distinguish between body and soul, between this present fleeting life and that future eternal life, will without difficulty know that Christ's spiritual Kingdom and the civil jurisdiction are things completely distinct,"[54] he reproduces late medieval conceptions that were originally aimed at maintaining the waning authority of the pope over temporal powers.

These modifications to the Carolingian arrangement between the church and civil authorities in the West remained in place until shortly before the time of the Reformation, when social changes further undercut the ability of ecclesiastical authorities to limit secular power. The dominance once exercised by the ecclesiastical hierarchy over the civil rulers in medieval society was sharply inverted, as the church either gave up its separate jurisdictional authority voluntarily or was relieved of it and redefined as a purely suasive body. Its withdrawal from the political field allowed the state to become the absolute and unquestioned authority within the (often arbitrary) boundaries that defined its territory. With the loss of its independent political authority that had allowed it to demand that civil rulers account for their actions, the ability of the church to influence its social context began to erode as well. Secular rulers maneuvering to gain control of these new political entities, by contrast, proved to be far more adept at manipulating doctrinal disputes and confessional loyalties in their ascent to power.[55]

The magisterial Reformers, for all of their insights into the fallen nature of the medieval church, did not question the division of labor between ecclesiastical and civic authorities in the latter Middle Ages. By aligning their movements with particular states' claims to absolute sovereignty over the political realm, as Martin Luther did in Germany, for example, they not only shredded further the visible unity of the body of Christ (particularly in its transnational and ecumenical expression) but also effectively (though unwittingly) provided ideological props for modern politics, especially its nationalistic fervor. The immediate effect of this novel alliance of Christian piety and national allegiance was to fan the flames of national and ethnic hatred that burned out of control in what are mistakenly called the Wars of Religion.[56]

53. Cavanaugh, *Torture and Eucharist*, 219.
54. Calvin, *Institutes of the Christian Religion*, 4.20.
55. Cavanaugh, "'Fire Strong Enough to Consume the House,'" 397–420.
56. Cavanaugh, *Theopolitical Imagination*, 20–31.

The Invention of "Religion"

Structural changes in the ever-changing social regime of Christendom were accompanied by new modes of regulating the relationship between the pilgrim city of God and the earthly city, the most significant of which was the invention of "religion." Prior to the fifteenth century no one used this idea in its distinctively modern sense, having to do with the private beliefs of an individual that have little or no direct bearing on public life. When *religio* does occur in medieval writings (which is rare), it refers either to the rule or discipline of monastic life[57] or to an acquired virtue similar to that of sanctity, a habit that, in concert with other virtues, directs the faithful to know and love God: "the activity by which man gives the proper reverence to God through actions which specifically pertain to divine worship, such as sacrifice, oblations, and the like."[58] In either sense the term presupposed a context of practices embodied in the communal life of the church. As Cavanaugh puts it, "Virtuous actions do not proceed from rational principles separable from the agent's particular history; virtuous persons instead are embedded in communal practices of habituation of body and soul that give their lives direction to the good."[59]

Beginning in the fifteenth century, the doctrinal and moral convictions that had been fostered by church teaching were gradually separated from the life and language of Christ's ecclesial body and reconfigured as abstract systems of beliefs that could be embraced voluntarily by individuals about what is ultimately true and important in their lives, but without the need to participate in the worship and witness of the church. According to Peter Harrison, Nicholas of Cusa laid much of the groundwork for this transition in the first half of the fifteenth century by characterizing different modes of faith as the result of epistemic limitations of finite human beings, with a single, infinite reality standing behind the heterogeneous expressions. He thus speaks of "one religion in the multiplicity of rites." According to Harrison, it is clear that

> Cusanus does not mean one "religion" in the modern sense, for that would imply an end to the "diversity of rites." Yet neither is he using the term in the limited sense of "monastic rule." Instead, he seeks to promote the view that diverse religious customs (the accidents of "religion," if you will) conceal a true or ideal "religion." This "*una religio*" is the unattainable truth about God—the Platonic ideal of which all existing belief systems are but shadowy

57. Southern, *Western Society and the Church in the Middle Ages*, 214; Asad, *Genealogies of Religion*, 39n22.

58. Aquinas, *Summa theologica* II-II.81.2.

59. Cavanaugh, *Theopolitical Imagination*, 32.

expressions. The faithful of all nations and creeds should persevere in their particular expressions of piety in the firm belief that the one true "religion" is the basis of them all.[60]

According to Wilfred Cantwell Smith, Marsilio Ficino builds on Cusanus's Platonic speculations in his 1474 book *De Christiana religione*, positing *religio* as a human impulse or propensity common to all women and men, "the fundamental distinguishing human characteristic, innate, natural, and primary." For Ficino, *religio* names the Platonic ideal of genuine perception and worship of God, which Smith translates as "religiousness." The various historical manifestations of this predisposition, the varieties of pieties and rites that we now call religions, are all just more or less true approximations of the one true *religio* divinely implanted in the human heart.[61] That which directs us to know and love God is thus interiorized and naturalized, made a matter of an inward awareness or sublime affection orienting individuals toward the transcendent, an innate disposition essentially unrelated to any particular ecclesial context.[62]

Humanists in the sixteenth century provided a theoretical basis for the reconfiguration of Christian faith around this new concept of religion. Seeking to secure religious liberty, Guillaume Postel contended that Christianity is the name of a set of demonstrable moral truths rather than theological claims and practices that are conjoined to a particular social regime called the church. Christian truth is based on universal axioms that underlie all particular expressions of "religious belief," and he was confident that they commend themselves to all rational women and men, even the infidel, once they learn of them.[63]

The concept of religion thus came to be identified with a set of propositions rather than a virtue or set of virtues embodied in the church, gaining wide currency in Protestant circles through the writings of Ulrich Zwingli and John Calvin, both of whom use it in the titles of two of the most widely circulated books of the sixteenth century: Zwingli's *Commentary on True and False Religion* and Calvin's *Institutes of the Christian Religion*. In the early seventeenth century, writes Smith, Hugo Grotius writes in *De veritate religionis Christianae* that the Christian religion teaches, rather than simply being the true worship of God.[64] Edward Brerwood in like fashion uses this

60. Harrison, *"Religion" and the Religion in the English Enlightenment*, 12.
61. Harrison, *"Religion" and the Religion in the English Enlightenment*, 12–13; W. Smith, *Meaning and End of Religion*, 32–34.
62. Cavanaugh, *Theopolitical Imagination*, 33.
63. Skinner, *Age of Reformation*, 244–46.
64. W. Smith, *Meaning and End of Religion*, 39–40.

concept to distinguish between "four sorts of Sects of Religion"—Christianity, Mahometanism (i.e., Islam), Judaism, and paganism.[65] The plural "religions," a theoretical construct that would have been incomprehensible according to medieval usage, first appears in the writings of this period, with each tradition so designated thereby related to the others as a species of a common genus.[66]

The effect of these developments is hard to deny. Though many disagree with the contention that there is a common, universal set of truths accessible to reason apart from the Bible or the church that informs and legitimates all particular or "positive" religious beliefs, most people routinely speak of religion as a worldview or system of belief embraced by individuals. We simply assume that, for example, the notion of Christianity refers to something actual. We habitually speak of the life and faith of the church as "Christianity," and we do not see that this is an abstraction that did not exist prior to the fifteenth century.

There are, of course, those who will argue that the transformation of an ecclesially formed faith into a religious worldview unencumbered by the untidiness of the material and social world properly lets "the spiritual be the spiritual, without public interference, and the public be the secular, without private prejudice."[67] It was initially thought by the likes of Thomas Hobbes that, for the sake of the unity of the state, there had to be one religion, just as there was one ruler, or at least there should be no public dispute over such matters, lest good order and the authority of God's appointed governors be disturbed.[68] However, once "the Business of Civil Government" is clearly distinguished "from that of Religion,"[69] and Christians can be persuaded that the biblical chant "We have no king but Caesar" is no longer blameworthy, then it becomes a matter of indifference, at least in the short term, whether there be one religion or many.

What *is* essential in this concept of religion to the rise of the territorial state is the invention of the autonomous individual. According to Robert Nisbet, the state developed as a political institution through "the gradual absorption of powers and responsibilities formerly resident in other associations and by an increasing directness of relation between the sovereign authority of the State and the individual citizen."[70] The aim of this process was to free people

65. Harrison, *"Religion" and the Religion in the English Enlightenment*, 39.
66. Cavanaugh, *Theopolitical Imagination*, 33.
67. See Milbank, *Theology and Social Theory*, 10.
68. Hobbes, *Leviathan*.
69. Locke, *Letter concerning Toleration*, 26.
70. Nisbet, *Quest for Community*, 104. Included among the institutions that facilitated this transfer of political authority were the development of law courts that allowed the king to mediate disputes between noble lords and the creation of mechanisms that enabled the crown

from the authority of other forms of association, to make their lives dependent on the state alone, unencumbered by medieval guilds or moral strictures regarding economic matters. As Cavanaugh so ably phrases it, the "realization of a single, unquestioned political center would make equivalent and equal each individual before the law, thereby freeing the individual from the caprice of local custom and subloyalties which would divide them from their fellow-citizens."[71] Freed from such "caprice," one enters into an allegiance to the state that becomes the sole political association that necessarily binds the individual. When Christian faith is transvalued into "religion," it no longer is identified with the communal life and thought of the church and thus poses no intrinsic threat to the authority of the state.

Empty Time

The demise of Christendom, the emergence of the state, and the invention of religion were not the only forces working to dismember Christ's body in the post-Reformation era, leaving behind bits and pieces no longer capable of exercising discipline over the bodies of the church's members. The last 450 years have also seen the development of new regimes of accumulation, production, exchange, and consumption, accompanied by new modes of regulating human behavior to promote and perpetuate these regimes. These economic forces work in concert with the state, replacing ecclesiastical and civil authorities as the two "swords" that jointly govern the course of the body politic, though at times, like their predecessors, they vie for supremacy. Together they have accelerated the rupture of the social ligatures that bound Christians to God, to each other, and to their own physical bodies.

The exchange of material goods in Christendom prior to the rise of capitalism was situated within a social structure that sought to order such matters to certain ends—that is, to a substantive good to which all human transactions, in their capacity as signs, were to bear witness. Jesus's appropriation of the Jubilee provisions to order the day-to-day life of his followers and the holding of all things in common described in the Acts of the Apostles, though they did not become the standard for economic activity down through the centuries, served as types for the church's teaching regarding the accumulation and use of property. (The practice of holding property in common did not disappear but was kept alive by the many religious orders.) It was widely

---

to collect tax revenue directly from the populace. Strayer, *On the Medieval Origins of the Modern State*, 26–33, 61, 69.

71. Cavanaugh, *Theopolitical Imagination*, 74.

understood that "the sharing of possessions was both a sign of the Christian community's faithfulness and a form of witness to the world."[72] Getting caught up in the apocalypse of Jesus Christ invariably involved some form of the just distribution of the things needed for this life. The church could not be faithful to its calling without embodying this witness in its life, and thus practices and principles were developed that retained something of the biblical witness with respect to the use of material goods and the means of exchange (i.e., money) for that use.

For those not called to a religious life, with its renunciation of private property, it was still understood that one's rights over the use of property were not absolute. According to Catherine of Siena, God did not concentrate the temporal goods necessary for mortal life in the hands of a few, but distributed them so no one possesses all of them, such that it would be necessary for all to "practice mutual charity."[73] Three principles emerged as guidelines for the faithful in this regard. First, all property is a gift from God, and since it is impossible for that which is finite to make an adequate return to the One who is eternal and infinite, all creatures are, quite literally, eternally and infinitely indebted. Private property is to be held as a kind of patrimony to be used for the common good, especially for the poor and needy. Such an understanding, of course, conflicts with the virtually absolute right of private property that prevails in capitalist markets. Second, there was the much-maligned and poorly understood prohibition against usury. This prohibition did not forbid all charging of interest, only that which is contrary to the charity owed to one's neighbor. Third, a just wage should be paid to workers sufficient not only to support them and their families but also to contribute to the common good.[74]

In a market-driven society, however, the formal equivalence or exchange value of a good or service prevails over a use value that can only be determined according to shared judgments promulgated by a community structured around a shared conception of interest. The result is a paradoxical situation of a heterogeneity of ends (i.e., pluralism), determined solely by consumer preference, which is imposed by and secured within an increasingly homogeneous economy. The bifurcation of fact from value quickly becomes one of the most important principles of the regulatory scheme orchestrating a global marketplace (another being the credo of the "maximization of self-interest"). "Fact" is reserved for matters that belong to the public sphere as determined by "objective" (i.e., instrumental) and "rational" (self-interested) methods. The

72. Long, *Goodness of God*, 243.
73. Catherine of Siena, *Dialogue*, 38.
74. Long, *Goodness of God*, 243–46; cf. Johnson, *Fear of Beggars*, especially chap. 6, "Why Not Be a Beggar?," 181–210.

concept of values denotes what has been assigned to the ephemeral sphere of private concerns, matters of choice, and personal preference, and thus values are irrational or at best arational. As such they come into the picture only after the facts of the matter have been determined.

Religious belief is "protected" as one species of value within this mode of regulation, but only at the cost of being effectively excluded from any kind of meaningful involvement in the concerns of everyday life. In the famous words of Thomas Jefferson, "It does me no injury for my neighbour to say that there are twenty gods, or no god."[75] Such matters are shunted to the "margins," where things are no longer intrinsically good, where their public "value" is determined solely by market exchanges governed by the principles of formal equivalence and substitutability. In our socially scripted role as consumers, we are thus free to stroll among the virtual shelves of the moral and religious shopping mall and pick out whatever marginal value "takes our fancy—Buddhism, scientology, environmentalism, feminism, gay liberation, animal rights, Jehovah's Witnesses."[76]

The regulatory apparatus of neoliberalism stipulates that a substantive understanding of what constitutes a good life must be excluded from the public sphere from the start, supposedly because teleological notions are too wedded to particular beliefs and histories to be useful in the determination of what is objective and thus universal for a multicultural society.[77] Alan Gewirth, for example, contends that if we are to regard a moral principle as rationally warranted, it must be analytic, and that any conclusions that follow from the premises of such reasoning must be necessarily entailed by those premises.[78] Thick accounts of the good such as one finds in the ancient traditions of the world are therefore deemed incapable of accommodating the vast diversity of "comprehensive doctrines"[79] that human beings have embraced at one time or another. If adherents to these doctrines cannot in good conscience restrict them to the realm of the private, neither they nor their views can be permitted within a democratic social order.

There is more at work in this exclusion of comprehensive doctrines, however, than initially meets the eye. Ruling out-of-bounds all questions about what might claim our allegiance as moral agents other than the two swords of state and market effectively opens up a space over which humanity, unencumbered by such distractions, can exert its own sovereignty against the vagaries

75. Jefferson, *Notes on the State of Virginia*, query 17, "Religion," 159.
76. Boyle, *Who Are We Now?*, 80–81.
77. Long, *Divine Economy*, 3–4.
78. Gewirth, *Reason and Morality*, 63.
79. Rawls, *Political Liberalism*, 13.

of fortune. This autonomous domain of human sovereignty comes complete with its own epic metanarrative, the comprehensive scope of which, as I noted previously, was pretentiously demonstrated by Francis Fukuyama's declaration that with the triumph of capitalism over Soviet-style communism, history had come to an end. A chief feature of the modern myth is that this sphere of the purely human and rational had always been accessible to rational (i.e., calculative) thought, though for much of history access to it lay dormant, hidden under a "sacred canopy" of ancient superstition, medieval metaphysics, and ecclesiastical tyranny.[80] Max Weber was perhaps the first to renarrate this leitmotif in the world of economics, stating that the medieval church imposed an irrational form of exchange upon an uneducated and gullible populace by means of superstition, ritual, and coercion. Thankfully, the Calvinists came along to move us toward a more rational form of economics.[81]

According to the modern epic, then, "irrational religion" had for centuries hidden the true nature of the world from humanity, and only in this, the age of science, have we been able to poke holes in this canopy and see what the universe is really like. Some even argue that this desacralizing tendency could be located at the origins of Christianity but was suppressed by the imperial aspirations of priests, bishops, cardinals, and popes during the first fifteen centuries of the church's existence. Fortunately, the Reformation started a process that would reverse that corrupt trend, and then in the nineteenth and twentieth centuries Protestant theologians, in collaboration with the new science of sociology, finally succeeded in stripping away the irrational husk of ecclesial restrictions to reveal the purity of humankind's spiritual kernel. And they did indeed free spirituality from any public interference, precisely by denying it any meaningful—which is to say, critical—posture vis-à-vis the public sphere.

As the Israelites, through their distinctive way of life, narrated the coming-to-be and passing-away of persons, peoples, and places as history, the ongoing performance of the modern epic, with state and market cast as the leading players on the world's stage, projects a mythical scene against which that performance is permanently set.[82] This picture is not the traditional Christian understanding, which is shaped by figural relationships that invoke a simultaneity of past and future in the present, such that the great personages of the Christian tradition are not regarded as alien, separated by a gulf of ever-advancing time, but as contemporaries, linked to the present time by divine providence.[83] The modern epic, by contrast, imagines a linear temporal

---

80. Berger, *Sacred Canopy*.
81. Weber, *Protestant Ethic and the Spirit of Capitalism*, 118–19.
82. See Milbank, *Theology and Social Theory*, 383.
83. Anderson, *Imagined Communities*, 22–24; Cavanaugh, *Torture and Eucharist*, 222.

sequence of cause and effect that occurs within what Walter Benjamin has labeled homogeneous, empty time,[84] which is measured by the precise, immutable units of calendar and clock. In this mythical setting the past, if rightly narrated, is the guarantor of both present and future; "Hence the importance of locating distant founding fathers and founding wars (even where their antiquity must be invented)."[85]

The aim of the modern metanarrative is to fashion a synchronic sense of time so that citizen-consumers imagine themselves as contemporaries not with the great cloud of witnesses of God's chosen people down through the centuries (Heb. 12:1; cf. 11:1–40) but with all those living simultaneously within the typically arbitrary boundaries of a particular nation-state, even though none of them will ever know more than a handful over the course of their lives. This story seeks to cultivate the picture of a stable community moving perpetually out of a heroic past, through the difficulties of the present, and into an unbounded future.[86] It is no coincidence that the preoccupation with founding fathers and wars, venerated as the guarantors of continuity and return against the ever-present threat to the fragility of the established order, bears the same marks of idolatry as does the ancients' worship of their gods.

The same epic that underwrites the categorical division of facts and values tacitly posits a certain metaphysical stance stipulating that the actual is the real and the rational. What truly is—a commercial and consumerist oligopoly—begins with the choices of individuals.[87] This social order is therefore judged to be both natural and reasonable insofar as it comports with the rational choices of individuals qua consumers. Local and global markets, together with the states that both support and regulate them (the two swords of neoliberal capitalism), thus have conferred on them the appearance of being necessary, and any opposition to them should be dismissed as romantic nonsense or madness. Any association that lies outside the orbit of these sorts of transactions between abstract consumers that are contractually linked solely by the authority of the state fails, by definition, to qualify as rational and potentially represents a disruptive or obstructionist practice that must therefore be confined within strict boundaries.[88]

---

84. Benjamin, *Illuminations*, 262.

85. Cavanaugh, *Torture and Eucharist*, 223.

86. Cavanaugh, *Torture and Eucharist*, 223; Anderson, *Imagined Communities*, 24–26.

87. To paraphrase Immanuel Kant, though a capitalist society begins with individual choices, it does not follow that it all arises out of these choices. The institutions of the nation-state, the market, and civil society do all in their power to ensure that we have no choice but to choose who and what we are as human beings. Kant, *Critique of Pure Reason*, 41.

88. Budde, *(Magic) Kingdom of God*, 81; Boyle, *Who Are We Now?*, 29.

The identification of what currently exists with what is real and rational repeats a tragic pattern that recurs repeatedly in the history of Christian thought. Beginning with Eusebius's oration of praise of Constantine as a type of messianic figure in the fourth century and extending to Max Stackhouse's panegyric to the institutions of liberal capitalism,[89] what we hear are variations on a familiar theme. What previously obtained in the world is vilified as heretical, irrational, oppressive, or superstitious, while the present social arrangement is lauded as the arrival of what God had intended from the foundation of the world.

At the heart of this marketplace metaphysics is the working hypothesis of the formally equivalent (and therefore abstract) individual, whose identity no longer derives from the people, place, and time into which it was born. This peculiar notion of the unencumbered individual makes sense only in the context of the larger myth of modernity, the story of which was initially told not by economists but by the pioneers of modern political science: Thomas Hobbes, John Locke, and Jean-Jacques Rousseau. "Man was born free," as Rousseau puts it in *The Social Contract*, "but is everywhere in bondage."[90] This stands in marked contrast to the Christian story, which states that humankind was created with a natural unity that was subsequently disrupted by the secondary intrusion of violence and death into the created order. The modern epic proclaims instead the essential individuality of the human race, with each individual set against all others in what Hobbes calls the natural state of *bellum omnis contra omnem*, the war of all against all.[91] The crucial distinction between creation and fall is thus elided, and evil with all its attendant ills is no longer understood as privation, a lack, but becomes substantial and made co-natural with the good.[92] Individuals come together on the basis of a social contract, not because they are naturally social beings bound together by a common good, but to protect person and property. Near-absolute sovereignty over private property is thus woven into the fabric of social reality.

Hobbes, Locke, and Rousseau drew heavily on theological categories that had developed in the latter Middle Ages in their depiction of the human being as essentially individual. As I have noted, late medieval theology set aside trinitarian construals of divine will and understanding and replaced them with a monarchic conception of God as "a radical divine simplicity without real or formal differentiation, in which . . . a proposing 'will' is taken

---

89. Eusebius, *In Praise of the Emperor Constantine* 16.7; Stackhouse, "Public Theology and Political Theology in a Globalizing Era," 179.

90. Rousseau, *Social Contract*, 1.1.

91. Hobbes, *Leviathan*, 1.13.

92. Milbank, *Being Reconciled*, 1–25.

to stand for the substantial identity of will, essence and understanding." In addition, the patristic concept of participation in the divine life and unity as the normative understanding of the relationship between God and human beings was set aside in the late Middle Ages in favor of the language of legal covenants, thereby instituting a conception of human interaction as essentially voluntarist and contractual.[93]

The fundamental "fact" of this secular metaphysics is a novel conception of human freedom. The construction and regulation of this power, however, is not predicated on the traditional understanding of the will as rational appetite, ordered by means of the intellect to the objects of its desire.[94] It is instead, in the words of Iris Murdoch, the outward movement of the lonely will.[95] This conception of will involves the autonomous and self-determined self, its choices for either good or evil unconstrained and unmoved by anything outside the self, and thus it is essentially unrelated to the contingencies of the material world or to a prior understanding of the good. As Immanuel Kant puts it, "Every evil action must be so considered, whenever we seek its rational origin, as if the human being had fallen into it directly from the state of innocence. For whatever his previous behavior may have been, whatever the natural causes influencing him, whether they are inside or outside them, his action is yet free and not determined through any of these causes; hence the action can and must always be judged as an *original* exercise of his power of choice."[96] Choice as a formal power of movement thus becomes the paradigm of freedom, not its most obvious result, as it was previously understood.[97]

Zygmunt Bauman contends that this definition of freedom leads to a quandary for the body politic between the intrinsic desirability of free decision-making and the need to limit freedom of those who are presumed to use it to do evil: "You can trust the wise (the code name of the mighty) to do good autonomously; but you cannot trust all people to be wise." Indeed, it is the freedom to choose that "necessitates an external force *coercing* the person to do good 'for his own salvation,' 'for her own welfare,' or 'in her own interest.'" The only practical way to ensure that individual choice will have morally positive consequences is to subject that freedom to "heteronomously set standards; to cede to socially approved agencies the right to decide what is good and submit to their verdicts."[98]

---

93. Milbank, *Theology and Social Theory*, 14–15; cf. Oberman, *Harvest of Medieval Theology*, 92, 99.

94. See, for example, Aquinas, *Summa theologica* I-II.8.1.

95. Murdoch, *Sovereignty of Good*, 35.

96. Kant, *Religion within the Boundaries of Mere Reason*, 62–63 (emphasis original).

97. Burrell, *Freedom and Creation in Three Traditions*, 92.

98. Bauman, *Postmodern Ethics*, 28–30 (emphasis original).

The civil function of religion and of religious organizations within the composite modern regime of coercion and commerce is contingency management, with sacralizing the present social order as its primary responsibility.[99] This strategy at one time had a Christian veneer to it. The civic responsibility of church was to serve as the moral conscience of the community and to ameliorate human suffering inflicted on those who slipped between the cracks.[100] In such ways Christian communities help state and market accumulate much-needed "social capital"—that is, a stock of social relations and shared values without which a neoliberal social order could not function for long and which underwrite the unconstrained exercise of self-interest.[101]

As we move into the twenty-first century, corporations and governments continue to recognize the need to manage the whims of fortune, which in recent years have played havoc with the self-identity of men and women all around the globe. The demands of state, global market, and workplace have dissolved most if not all of the social relations that traditionally have defined who we are and what we should do. The transvaluation of human beings into individuals has reached the stage where people are little more than interchangeable economic units, integers of production and consumption. In the words of Václav Havel, "Individuals confirm the system, fulfil the system, make the system, *are* the system."[102] A workforce kept at optimum flexibility, however, exacts a high price in human terms. Corporate firms are therefore interested in the potential of the church and other established religious institutions to ameliorate these costs, provided that their rituals and beliefs are supportive of the firm's goals and work to deepen the loyalty and productivity of the employees.[103]

The rulers and authorities thus decree that when Christians enter the "public square," they must set aside all things connected to the particularity of the church, most especially its comprehensive doctrines. This in effect means, among other things, that our understanding of Christ and the church must be subsumed under something like a doctrine of creation in which the proper order of things can be known apart from both Christ and the church. The state, rather than the people of God gathered by the Spirit through baptism and the Lord's Supper, becomes the "city set on a hill," and the new creation that Scripture associates with the ministry of Jesus and his followers is vested

99. See Luhmann, *Religious Dogmatics and the Evolution of Societies*; cf. Geertz, *Interpretation of Cultures*, 87–125.

100. Robinson, "Making of a Post-Liberal," 16.

101. Budde and Brimlow, *Christianity Incorporated*, 19.

102. Havel, *Living in Truth*, 45 (emphasis original).

103. I return to this question in chap. 6.

in other institutions, including corporations, which mediate salvation in the form of increased choice. Congregations that want to be players in this order of things must do so as a vendor of "spirituality," the purpose of which is to render life more bearable for those who have become little more than faceless functionaries in a vast system of production and consumption.[104]

The compliment typically paid to this new order of human existence in our time and place is that it is pluralistic and multicultural, but for many this is hollow praise indeed. A silicon web has supplanted Weber's iron cage, reducing those ensnared within it to the status of mere economic units, integers of aimless production and conspicuous consumption.[105] Pluralism is a façade for the transvaluation of all practices, institutions, dispositions, and relationships into commodities that can be exchanged in the global market.[106] A pluralist regime stipulates that choice per se is the highest good, and therefore it is committed to excluding "an entire way of life postulated upon nonconsumerist conceptions of human fulfillment, and so to favor a particular vision of the human good."[107] Virtually everything else is optional with respect to the undifferentiated individuality of the market, where every thing and every body is packaged as a product to be consumed (including marriage, having children, and making friends), and the exchange value of these products is determined by their "market share"—that is, their ability to satisfy consumers. In spite of its own best intentions, pluralism cannot help but regard "particularity as icing on a basically homogeneous cake."[108] Substantive understandings of the human good, such as that traditionally embodied in the life and language of the church, are summarily classified as restrictive practices.[109]

Ecclesiastical authorities and theologians who accede to these demands in order to establish a religious concordat with capitalism in the form of a "public theology" are required to excise those aspects of Christian thought that distinguish it as an identifiable way of life—Christ as the antitype of true humanity, the church as the true *politeia*, and an eschatologically oriented understanding of history. Ironically, such accords hark back "to the style of the *ancien régime* . . . to a society in which the churches regarded themselves as the spiritual form of a material community."[110] The difference is that churches must now "package" their spiritual values in accordance with the dictates

104. See Budde and Brimlow, *Christianity Incorporated*, 27–54.
105. Berry, *What Are People For?*, 130.
106. Boyle, *Who Are We Now?*, 79.
107. Beiner, *What's the Matter with Liberalism?*, 8.
108. Fish, "Boutique Multiculturalism," 382.
109. Boyle, *Who Are We Now?*, 26.
110. Kent, *End of the Line?*, viii.

of the market, which means that they must effectively vacate the specifically Christian content of their life and language.

Under the terms of this agreement, whatever it means to be a Christian can no longer be tied to practices that constitute the church as a social body visibly, publicly manifesting the intrusion of God's apocalyptic regime into the world, but must be limited to matters of the soul, leaving the body to the authority of the powers and economic principalities of this age. Christian identity and church authority are thus disembodied, relegated to a separate sphere of private life, transvalued into "religion"—that is, habits and practices that are useful both for depicting the mysterious and invisible whole that is the body politic of the modern state and global market and also for conserving social energies in a numinous ether called "values," which at the appropriate time can be put to a "real" social use in the state's behalf.[111]

Where Do We Go from Here?

As I noted in chapter 2, the destruction of Jerusalem and the demise of the Davidic monarchy, which resulted in the exile of many Jews to strange lands where they were compelled to serve other gods while others bore the brunt of occupation in the promised land, did not bring Israel's life with God to an end. God instead folded these events back into the saving story of the chosen people, where these events serve as types (*typoi*) to instruct those who seek to love and serve God. When we ask, then, whether a similar sort of remembering of the body of Christ can take place in our time, it is encouraging to discover that, as in the time of Elijah, not every knee has bowed to the powers and principalities of this world.

There have been those who, through the centuries, did not succumb to the temptation to fold up their tents but labored to cultivate forms of life and community that would enable them to continue the journey to the new Jerusalem. The desert fathers, writes Thomas Merton, were among the first to recognize that the gospel and the politics of the present age could never combine to create a fully Christian society: "They were men who did not believe in letting themselves be passively guided and ruled by a decadent state, and who believed that there was a way of getting along without slavish dependence on accepted, conventional values." The fathers acted as they did not because they believed they were superior to others but because they saw that the world was divided between those who imposed their will on others

---

111. See Milbank, *Theology and Social Theory*, 109; cf. Putnam's famous article "Bowling Alone," 65–78.

and those who gave in and accepted the imposition of the will of those who were regarded as successful. What these hermits sought above all else, says Merton, was their true self in Christ, which meant that they rejected the false self that was constructed under compulsion of "the world."[112]

Bonhoeffer points out that it was religious orders that initially continued the struggle of the desert fathers against the cheapening of grace that came with the secularization of Christianity.[113] Saints such as Benedict, Catherine of Siena, Francis of Assisi, Teresa of Ávila, Ignatius of Loyola, Maximilian Kolbe, and Oscar Romero, to name but a few, took up the path of resisting the temptation to conform to the world. It would be a mistake, however, to assume that only a select few can follow the path of the early church. In our own time Dorothy Day, André Trocmé, Fannie Lou Hamer, Beyers Naudé, and Jean Vanier (again to mention but a few) took up the way of the cross. These saints did not, however, suddenly appear out of a vacuum, but were the products of Christian communities that "pulled [them] into the path that Jesus walks, into the messianic event."[114] These communities, in turn, were constituted around practices that formed them in the way of peace. In the next chapter I examine two of these practices, baptism and Eucharist, that are central to any hope that God might re-member us as his Son's body in the days and years to come.

112. Merton, *Wisdom of the Desert*, 5–6.
113. Bonhoeffer, *Discipleship*, 46–47.
114. Bonhoeffer, *Letters and Papers from Prison*, 480.

5

SACRAMENTAL SINEWS

The Re-membering of Christ's Body

I knew myself to be far away from you in a region of unlikeness, and I seemed to hear your voice from on high: "I am the food of the mature; grow then, and you will eat me. You will not change me into yourself like bodily food: you will be changed into me."

Augustine, *The Confessions*

I was a college freshman, attending Sunday morning services at my local church as every good Baptist is supposed to do. I spent much of the service sorting through the various thoughts and feelings that were washing over me, trying to decide which of them constituted my personal and intimate encounter with Christ. As offspring of seventeenth-century Puritan Pietism and eighteenth-century English political philosophy, most Baptists in North America have long believed that "emotional states had a special spiritual significance and that consequently certain displays of feeling were to be considered as signs of godliness." It is this aspect of our Puritan heritage that survived the collapse of Calvinism as a theological system.[1]

---

1. Campbell, *Romantic Ethic and the Spirit of Modern Consumerism*, 127.

Today many people refer to these inner movements of the soul in which the divine speech is supposedly heard as "experiences" of God. I now realize that I was trying to discern on that particular Sunday morning what qualifies as one of those experiences. Was it the warm glow in my chest? The exhilarating feelings of certitude that asserted themselves whenever I was with those of like mind? The shiver that occasionally ran up and down my spine? It occurred to me even then that I could not really distinguish what was happening "inside" me at that moment, regardless of how immediate and intense the feelings were, from the way altogether mundane events and relationships affected me. Looking back on that occasion, I now see that what I had been told to regard as sure and certain signs of a saving relationship with God were in actuality reliable evidence only of the malleability of the soul, and in particular its capacity for self-deception. They were also both instrumental to and symptomatic of my captivity to rulers and authorities who wished to keep my Christian identity a private, "spiritual" matter.

The question of what qualifies as an experience of or relationship with God is an important one for us to ask. Is it finally some inner movement of mind, will, or affection that marks our communion with the triune God? If so, we must concede this is indeed a curious state of affairs. In what other instance does what goes on strictly within one's head or heart qualify as a personal relationship? You can have a personal relationship only with somebody, because that is what it means to be a creature—to be some *body*. Our desires and affections obviously figure into these relationships, for they are part of bodily existence, such that their absence or excess is surely a cause for concern. But they do not compose the beginning, end, or substance of any relation.

Another occasion comes to mind in this regard, some fifteen years later. Some fellow graduate students and I were celebrating the Eucharist on a Tuesday morning with brothers of the Order of St. John the Evangelist, an Anglican religious order in Durham, North Carolina. I had been attending services at St. John's House several mornings a week for a few months on the recommendation of those whose insight in matters spiritual and theological I had come to trust. But prior to that morning my experience there had been everything that I had been led to expect. Most Baptist churches observe the Lord's Supper once every three months or so, for we have been taught that if we observe it too often it will not be as "meaningful." (We never restrict the frequency of hymns, prayers, Bible reading, or sermons for that reason.) And of course, from this standpoint what makes something meaningful is that it produces an intense emotional response "inside" the individual.

It did not take long for me to discover that one could sustain the kind of emotional intensity I had come to associate with communion only for so long. The novelty of participating in the elegant and elaborate liturgy gradually subsided. I soon knew when to stand and when to sit, what to say and what to do, when to sing and when to remain silent, because we celebrated the sacrament basically the same way every day. And sure enough, my initial impression of what had transpired at Eucharist that morning at St. John's House could have become the first definition in the dictionary under the word *perfunctory*. If the day had stopped there, the events of that morning would have confirmed everything that my Puritan heritage had warned me about such "popery."

The day did not end there, of course, and so I went about my business, all of which was routine. I did not think much more about what had happened that morning until late that afternoon, when I realized that what had transpired as a result of my participation in the eucharistic liturgy all those weeks had remained with me all day. The routine transactions of that day had been caught up in the mystery at the Lord's table in a way that I had not experienced before, though at the time I was quite unaware of this process. I had discovered something of what Alexander Schmemann calls the "breakthrough" of Christ the Eucharist and Eucharist the Christ "that brings us to the table in the Kingdom, raises us to heaven, and makes us partakers of the divine food."[2] The everyday exchanges of that Tuesday, in their details quite unremarkable, I now could follow as potent signs of God's beauty and power, rendered intelligible by the social grammar embodied in the eucharistic celebration. My apprenticeship in this grammar, culminating in what the Orthodox tradition calls the "liturgy after the liturgy," had finally borne a small bit of fruit.

On that Tuesday morning, now many years ago, I took an important step on the road to recovery from Gnosticism, that ancient adversary of the church's life and mission, resuscitated in recent times by the social grammar of neoliberalism, a key player in the dismembering of Christ's ecclesial body. This process of recovering the sinews that hold together the members of Christ's body involves at its heart the sacraments of baptism and Eucharist, but we must take care as we proceed. The things Jesus intended to serve as signs of our unity we, his followers, have all too often used as a club with which to beat each other over the head, sometimes literally cracking skulls wide open over doctrinal differences regarding the font and the Lord's table. Add to this dubious track record the tenacity with which Christians of different traditions hold to a variety of doctrinal views on this subject—transubstantiation, consubstantiation, spiritual presence, "just a symbol," and so on. The roots

2. Schmemann, *For the Life of the World*, 39.

of these differences extend for centuries, secured by the sweat and sometimes the blood of our respective forebears.

Nevertheless, if Christians are to begin to disentangle ourselves from the practices and institutions of nation-state, market, and a cultural ethos of surplus desire that effectively dismembered Christ's body, we must recover something of what is properly performed by those sacramental signs instituted by Christ. I say this not out of a restorationist bent of mind, nor because I believe that what takes place at, in, and through baptism and Eucharist is either magical or mechanical. Neither holiness nor wholeness can be guaranteed simply by showing up and going through the motions of any rite. It is still the case that God "cannot endure solemn assemblies with iniquity" (Isa. 1:13). Indeed, if what Paul writes to the Corinthian church about eating and drinking to our own condemnation is still in force (see 1 Cor. 11:20–34), quite the opposite effect occurs whenever we do so. Nor do the sacraments stand alone; only in concert with the other constitutive practices and institutions of the church do they function as signs and seals of all that the triune God has done, is doing, and will do in and for the world in the name of the one who was crucified on its behalf. Our present concern with the sacraments has to do rather with the distinctive social economy and grammar of the church that is enacted by these mystical signs.

Sacrament as Apocalyptic Action

The raison d'être of the church, writes Schmemann, is "not to exist 'in itself' but to be the 'sacrament,' the *epiphany*, of the new creation." Baptism and Eucharist mark the material point of entry of God's apocalyptic regime into the day-to-day life of this world, gathering together a distinctive social order in the name of Christ. These powerful signs fashion an alternative social grammar or grammar for creaturely existence over against the grammar of the world's body politic. Time and again the sacramental signs introduce this new social dimension into the world, and they are therefore not just the *means* of grace (that is, instrumentally related to grace) but also the *media* of grace, and hence integral to its operation. In and through these liturgical practices "the Church is *informed* of her cosmical and eschatological vocation, *receives* the power to fulfill it and thus truly *becomes* 'what she is': the sacrament, in Christ, of the new creation; the sacrament, in Christ, of the Kingdom."[3]

If we are to understand how liturgy fulfills this function, writes Schmemann, we must see it in line with the apocalyptic journey into the reality of

---

3. Schmemann, *Church, World, Mission*, 136–37 (emphasis added).

God's kingdom. To punctuate the telos of this journey, the Orthodox liturgy begins with a doxology: "Blessed is the Kingdom of the Father, the Son and the Holy Spirit, now and ever, and unto ages of ages." To bless the kingdom is not simply to commend it, but "to declare it to be the goal, the end of all our desires and interests, of our whole life, the supreme and ultimate value of all that exists."[4] The church is the gathering of those in whom the ultimate destination of all life has been revealed and who, with their "Amen," have cast their lot with it. This little word is the appropriate response to the declaration that the movement toward God has begun, for it is a pledge of solidarity binding us to Christ in his ascension to the Father, a gift of inestimable value that comes only from him, "for only in Him can we say Amen to God, or rather He himself is our Amen to God and the Church is an Amen to Christ."[5]

The apocalyptic character of baptism and Eucharist presupposes a correlation between a sacrament and the sign character of the material world, both as a whole and in its constituent differences. Because it is created by God, writes Robert Wilken, "matter has within itself the capacity to become a resting place of God, to become something other while remaining what it is."[6] In its capacity to act as a sign of divine things, then, matter operates at two levels, such that, as Aquinas puts it, "all sensible creatures are [also] signs of sacred things."[7] It is crucial at this point to distinguish between two distinct uses of this term *sign*. We typically speak of signs as signs *of* something, in a way analogous to how we speak of symptoms and indications—for instance, "red sky at night, sailor's delight; red sky at morning, sailor take warning." When we use *sign* in this capacity, we look for its meaning elsewhere, as we would with a sign on a highway indicating how far it is to the next town. The sign stands in, substitutes for something else, such that to ask for its meaning is to ask what this other thing is. The signified is separate and distinct from the signifier.[8]

It is in this sense of the term that many Christians, particularly from free church traditions, talk about baptism and Eucharist as "just" a sign or symbol. In this tradition, to say that something is symbolic in nature is to assert that the water, bread, and wine represent Christ's death for our act of remembrance and therefore are simply the outward expression of an interior "spiritual" experience. But one sees this use of *sign* as well in traditions that

4. Schmemann, *For the Life of the World*, 29.
5. Lash, *Believing Three Ways in One God*, 1–2.
6. Wilken, *Spirit of Early Christian Thought*, 248.
7. "Omnes . . . creaturae sensibilies sunt signa rerum sacrum" (Aquinas, *Summa theologica* III.60.2). The distinction between the sacramental character of the world and a sacrament proper is that the latter has been ordained to signify our sanctification. *Summa theologica* III.60.3.
8. McCabe, *God Matters*, 165–66.

emphasize sacramental observance. William Cavanaugh notes that in Catholic circles there are numerous attempts to see sacrament as a sign or symbol of something else. As an example, he cites the introduction to a volume on politics and liturgy that frames the relationship between the two in precisely this manner: "Since politics is the control of power in society, the ways in which liturgy uses symbols of power has [sic] much to say in forming images and concepts of power which Christian peoples bring to bear on political questions."[9] The problem with such formulations, for all their good intentions, is that they define sacramental signs as something other than, and therefore apart from, the "real world."[10]

The other way to speak of a sign is to say that it is a sign *for* something. When we ask for the meaning of a sign in this sense, writes Herbert McCabe, "we are not asking 'what is it instead of,' what is the extra thing it stands for? We are asking 'what is it *for*?' How do we use it?" In this sense we know the meaning of a sign—a word, for example—not by asking what the other thing is for which the sign stands proxy, but by learning how to use that word in new and different settings.[11] The badge of basic linguistic competence thus involves more than simply learning stock words and phrases to use in routine situations, as tourists do when they memorize a set of stock words and phrases to use in a foreign country. It is verified instead by the ability "to move from one kind of use of expression in the context of one sentence to another notably different kind of use of the same expression in the context of another and perhaps then go on to innovate by inventing a third kind of use for that very same expression in yet another sentential context."[12] On this reading, a sign is not an object or event in which some ethereal property called "meaning" has been deposited, but "a set of relationships between objects or events uniquely brought together as complexes or as concepts."[13] The meaning of a sign thus subsists in the business the sign-user transacts with it within a complex of objects, events, and persons.[14] Signs thus organize practice, enabling us to engage the world in an almost infinite series of actions: recalling previous encounters that allow us to return to and recover what we had previously encountered, forming expectations for the future, and authorizing abductive inferences that allow us to make metaphysical surmises about the nature of reality.[15]

9. Power and Schmidt, "Editorial," 9.
10. Cavanaugh, *Torture and Eucharist*, 11.
11. McCabe, *God Matters*, 166 (emphasis original).
12. MacIntyre, *Whose Justice? Which Rationality?*, 381–82.
13. Asad, *Genealogies of Religion*, 31.
14. McCabe, *God Matters*, 166.
15. Milbank, *Word Made Strange*, 99; MacIntyre, *Whose Justice? Which Rationality?*, 356.

The ability to use signs—to engage in triadic behavior, as Walker Percy calls it—pushes us across a threshold marking the difference between an animal existing in an environment and a rational animal having a world, an organized cosmos.[16] Triadic behavior *is* our freedom, the capacity to imagine and pursue a variety of rational ends. We thus can fashion the different ways we live peaceably together within the constraints of the material world (and conversely, ways of not living together peaceably). In this respect human freedom is itself a sign of God's creative activity and is, more specifically, its source and goal. Signs also constrain us, in that signifiers function only within established social complexes (hence, they serve as modes of alienation as well as communication).[17] Finally, signifier and signified interpenetrate in such a way that the former is irretrievably transformed by the latter. To know something, to encounter it in and through the auspices of its sign, becomes the preeminent mode of our habitation of a world as an ordered whole.[18]

For those in Christ the world is an ensemble of signs by virtue of having been spoken into existence by God (regardless of whether at any particular time or place somebody is able to read the world as such). For the world to be such belongs to its ontology, the sign being "not only the way to perceive and understand reality, a means of cognition, but also a means of *participation*." The people, places, events, and things we encounter in the world do not cease being what they are in their function as signs for God's creative activity. They retain their distinctive properties, their own integrity and identity. At the same time, because they are created by God, they ultimately possess no existence that is autonomous or separate from the source of their being, of who and what they are. It is the natural sign quality of the world, its tacit "sacramentality," as it were, that in part makes sacrament possible and supplies the interpretive key for understanding it as apocalyptic action. This sacramentality of the world "is the epiphany—in and through Christ—of the 'new creation,' not the creation of something 'new.' And if it reveals the 'continuity' between creation and Christ, it is because there exists, at first, a continuity between Christ and creation whose *logos*, life, and light He is."[19] As Augustine puts it, "The Son was sent where he already was, as he both came into the world and *he was in this world* (John 1:10)."[20]

Following the signs of continuity between creation and the apocalyptic activity of God in Christ takes considerable effort and discipline in the best

16. Percy, *Lost in the Cosmos*, 96.
17. McCabe, *God Matters*, 170.
18. Percy, *Lost in the Cosmos*, 103–5.
19. Schmemann, *For the Life of the World*, 139–40, 143 (emphasis original).
20. Augustine, *Trinity* 3.3 (emphasis original).

of circumstances, requiring time and space free from distraction and a community dedicated to cultivating the requisite habits and skills. In our time and place this task has only become more difficult. In virtually every corner of the globe, the bodies as well as souls of men, women, and children are being carefully trained as "individuals," interchangeable integers of consumption and production, for whom existence consists almost entirely of making choices from a range of options that are controlled by institutions they cannot see and managed by people they never meet face-to-face. Effectively sundered from meaningful points of reference beyond their self-defined wants and desires, they form an identity as persons that consists of little more than a series of consumer choices to make and a sequence of jobs from which they will be laid off.

When we are immersed in these patterns of life and thought, it is extremely difficult to recognize the ways that the powers and authorities of this age rule our lives. As Scripture itself indicates, something more than simply being in a position to see and hear what is going on around us is needed if men and women are to penetrate the social grammar of a fallen creation. In the book of Isaiah, for example, we read that King Uzziah of Judah died around the year 742 BCE (6:1). Under his rule Judah had enjoyed a rare period of stability and prosperity that it had not known since the time of Solomon, and the news of his passing surely would have been seen as a foreboding development, especially with the ascension of Tiglath-Pileser III to the throne in Nineveh. With the Assyrian menace looming on the northern horizon, it would be natural if the people of Judah and Jerusalem lamented, "What shall become of us now that our great king is dead?" Those unable to read the signs would likely see these developments as no different from hundreds of other such events that have occurred throughout history. After all, kings and kingdoms come and go. Such is the way of the world.

According to the prophet, on the other hand, the course of these events could be understood only in terms of figures provided by Israel's past. The death of the son of David became the occasion for belatedly recognizing the One in whom Israel's safety and security truly lay: "In the year that King Uzziah died, I saw the Lord sitting on a throne, high and lofty; and the hem of his robe filled the temple." As I have noted on several occasions, the image of God as Israel's only true sovereign is inextricably embedded in Israel's memory, and it is in terms of this imaginative frame of reference that Isaiah recognized his sinfulness and that of his fellow Israelites: "Woe is me! I am lost, for I am a man of unclean lips, and I live among a people of unclean lips; yet my eyes have seen the King, the LORD of hosts!" (6:1, 5).

This text does not explicitly state what had made the lips of Isaiah and his fellow Israelites unclean, but later in the book we read that in a similar situation the people had declared that because of a covenant King Hezekiah of Judah had made with Egypt, "the overwhelming scourge" would "not come" to them. Isaiah responds, "We have made lies our refuge, and in falsehood we have taken shelter" (Isa. 28:15). And in the book of Hosea we read that the northern tribes had plowed wickedness, reaped injustice, and eaten the fruit of lies because they had trusted in their military power and the multitude of their warriors (10:13). What is clear is that Isaiah links the untimely death of a powerful king to Israel's having turned away from the rule of God, a move that invariably brings with it disastrous consequences. In an ironic pronouncement, God instructs Isaiah to say to the kingdoms of Israel and Judah:

> "Keep listening, but do not comprehend;
> keep looking, but do not understand."
> Make the mind of this people dull,
>   and stop their ears,
>   and shut their eyes,
> so that they may not look with their eyes,
>   and listen with their ears,
> and comprehend with their minds,
>   and turn and be healed.

Isaiah asks, "How long?" and the dreadful reply comes back:

> Until cities lie waste
>   without inhabitant,
> and houses without people,
>   and the land is utterly desolate;
> until the LORD sends everyone far away,
>   and vast is the emptiness in the midst of the land. (6:9–12)

Lacking Isaiah's ability to recognize the signs of God's impending judgment, the people would not rightly interpret what they saw and heard going on around them until it was too late.

The inability of the inhabitants of Jerusalem in Isaiah's day to comprehend what was happening in their midst was not an isolated event in the history of Israel. When questioned about his habit of teaching in parables to those outside the inner circle of disciples, Jesus associates his work and ministry with Isaiah's vision. He says to his followers that the mystery of God's apocalyptic regime has been given to them, but to those outside everything comes in parables, so that

> they may indeed look, but not perceive,
>   and may indeed listen, but not understand;
> so that they may not turn again and be forgiven. (Mark 4:12)

Christians need to take care, however, not to see this as a charge laid against Israel alone. The inability to follow the signs of God's incursion into a world in thrall to rulers and authorities bent on establishing their authority, to hear the rhythms, the dissonances, and resolutions of the messianic regime interrupting the continuity of the world, has sadly been all too prevalent in the lives of those who have claimed to be Christ's disciples. In Mark's Gospel Jesus castigates his inner circle of followers for being unable to grasp what is going on right in front of their eyes. "Do you still not perceive or understand?" he asks them. "Are your hearts hardened? Do you have eyes, and fail to see?" (8:17–18). Significantly, the evangelist places this saying immediately before a most peculiar event in the narrative, the story of Jesus restoring the sight of a blind man in the village of Bethsaida (vv. 22–26). After Jesus lays his hands on the man's eyes the first time, his vision is restored, but only partially. "I can see people," the man tells Jesus, "but they look like trees, walking." Jesus must touch his eyes a second time before he can see everything clearly.

This story is followed immediately in Mark's Gospel by a pivotal event that takes place in Caesarea Philippi (8:27–33). While Jesus and his disciples are "on the way," *en tē hodō*,[21] he asks them, "Who do people say that I am?" After hearing that most speak of him as some sort of prophet, he then asks, "But who do you say that I am?" Peter, always the impetuous one, replies, "You are the Messiah." Jesus cautions them not to tell anyone about this and then tells them "quite openly" that the Son of Man must suffer and die at the hands of the authorities in Jerusalem and then after three days be delivered from the grave. Peter refuses to hear this from Jesus and takes him aside to rebuke him. But Jesus does not listen to Peter. Instead, he replies in the hearing of the others, "Get behind me, Satan! For you are setting your mind not on divine things but on human things."

Peter obviously perceived something in Jesus that was noteworthy. Moreover, what he did see he described in apocalyptic and, more specifically, messianic terms. But it is readily apparent from his response to Jesus's passion

---

21. This phrase is a powerful image depicting the messianic way of life. Cf. Mark 9:33; 10:17, 32, 52; Acts 9:2; 18:25–28; 19:9, 23; 22:4.

prediction that Peter did not adequately comprehend the meaning of his confession. Nor was he alone among the disciples in this inability to understand adequately all that was entailed in the life and work of this fellow from Galilee. When it came to discerning the significance of Jesus's life among them, the Twelve were like the blind man in Bethsaida after the first time Jesus touched him. They saw something extraordinary happening in and around him, but their vision was clouded, out of focus. Something more and other than simply being physically present to see and hear what was going on was needed if they were to overcome their hardness of heart and grasp the import of the people and events that swirled around Jesus.

Everything under Heaven

We too require something more and other than simply being physically present to see and hear if we are to follow the significance of all that Jesus did and suffered in relation to our own time and place. We need new habits of life and language, different ways of assessing the world in which we live our lives to recognize and respond faithfully to the signs that the world cannot decipher. We need practices that nurture the skills that transpose simple seeing into discernment and mere existing into holy habitation. Such habits are cultivated only in a company of friends through a shared participation in a social grammar in terms of which we learn how to identify, reidentify, classify, call, and respond to all the things and persons we encounter. In short, through these activities we learn to name the world as *world*—that is, as fallen and yet still cherished by its Creator. Baptism and Eucharist find their occasion and significance, then, in the reconfiguring of life according to the social grammar that God's utterance of the Word in history and his breathing-forth of the Spirit upon the church establish.

The ability to name the activities, institutions, and events going on around us, like reading marks on a page, is thus inseparable from practices that mediate the exchange of signs between persons, beginning with Christ. The sacraments in particular propel the members of Christ's body beyond the boundaries within which state and market seek to confine us by binding us together in a new political association upon which the ends of the ages have met. Hence, Paul can write, "As many of you as were baptized into Christ have clothed yourselves with Christ. There is no longer Jew or Greek, there is no longer slave or free, there is no longer male and female; for all of you are one in Christ Jesus" (Gal. 3:27–28). In similar fashion he regards the sharing of bread and wine as constitutive of Christ's body: "*Because* there is one bread, we who are many are one body, for we all partake of the one bread" (1 Cor. 10:17, emphasis added). In this body, where we are bound to him whose life, death, and resurrection ransom us from the domain of sin, death, and the devil, the raison d'être of the incarnation is disclosed for all creatures.

The effect of these sacramental signs is to take the bodies of women and men "out" of this world and relocate them "in" the world to come. In this present age that condemned Christ and in so doing condemned itself, bread and wine cannot become the body and blood of Christ, for nothing that belongs to this age can be sacralized: "In this world Christ is crucified, His body broken, and His blood shed. And we must go out of this world . . . in order to become partakers of the world to come." The true identity of the church as the body of Christ is fulfilled in that new eon that Christ inaugurated in his passion, resurrection, and ascension "and which was given to the Church on the day of Pentecost as its life, as the 'end' toward which it moves."[22]

The world to come in which the participants in the liturgy are caught up is not, however, an "other" world, different from the one God has created in Christ and reveals proleptically to the church: "It is the same world, *already* perfected in Christ, but *not yet* in us. It is our same world, redeemed and restored, in which Christ 'fills all things with Himself.'" The distinctiveness of the sacraments lies not in their being a miraculous exception to the natural order of things in creation. The absolute newness of the Christian sacrament resides in the specific *res* that the sacrament "reveals, manifests, and communicates," which is Christ and his kingdom: "The 'mysterion' of Christ reveals and fulfills the ultimate meaning and destiny of the world itself." And since the world is created and given as food for us by God (Gen. 1:29), who then makes food the medium of our communion with him, "the new life which we receive from God in His Kingdom *is Christ Himself. He is our bread*—because from the very beginning all our hunger was a hunger for Him and all our bread was but a symbol of Him, a symbol that had to become reality."[23] Caught up in the mystery of Christ, we become attentive to the beginning and end of our existence as rational creatures, an attentiveness that is both a knowing and a desiring.

When the gathered church disperses from the eucharistic feast, the freedom that is ours in Christ translates into the ability to *follow* the dramatic pattern of events that is the liberating work of God as it unfolds within history, or more precisely, *as history*. Attending to the story of the divine performance in

22. Schmemann, *For the Life of the World*, 42.
23. Schmemann, *For the Life of the World*, 42–43, 140 (emphasis original).

the material world of time and space—getting its plot, setting, and characters straight—is a crucial activity of Christian discipleship steeped in the worship of the one true God, the end of which is to participate in the divine activity and life. By means of our sacramental participation in the life and work of God, we learn how to go on and go further as a company of nomads making our way toward that city that is to come (Heb. 13:14).

When we bring bread and wine to the Lord's table, we first of all name them as the good gifts of God's creation. We can see, smell, touch, and taste what happens when, in the providence of God, seed, soil, water, air, nutrients (which until relatively recently were provided by fellow creatures of the four-legged variety), and sunlight combine in proper proportions and under the right temperatures in due season to produce grain and grapes. Dante was surely inspired when he brought the *Divine Comedy* to a conclusion by praising that love that moves the sun and other stars, for it is the movement of these celestial bodies that, among other things, gives us springtime and harvest.

Loaves of bread and bottles of wine, however, do not spring ready-made from the earth. In these products are embodied the labor of the farmers who plant, cultivate, and harvest the grain and the grapes, the expertise of those who grind the grain into flour and mix it with other ingredients to bake it into bread, and the work of those who crush the grapes and oversee the delicate process of fermentation. And we dare not forget the equipment—tractors, combines, trucks, mill grinders, mixers, ovens, conveyors, packaging—without which there would be no bread or wine, or the energy that runs the equipment and the buildings in which it is used, or the capital goods that produce the equipment, buildings, and energy, or the contributions of scientists, engineers, technicians, roughnecks, secretaries—again without whom there would be no equipment, much less the materials from which that equipment is constructed.

Our litany about the natural world is still not finished. The trucks and trains that transport the bread and wine travel on roads and tracks that must be built and maintained. And if we are to eat and drink, the transport of goods over these thoroughfares must take place with a sufficient degree of safety. And so we commission peace officers who deter bandits, detain criminal suspects, and write speeding tickets, and we establish a massive legal apparatus of jurists, lawyers, clerks, and guards to adjudicate the guilt or innocence of the accused. These products, services, and institutions are themselves predicated on a vast array of skills and techniques that are perpetuated through institutions such as public schools, technical institutes, colleges, and universities. These provisions do not appear out of the blue; they must be provided and paid for by political institutions of some type, which themselves require considerable care and feeding.

We are not done yet. When the trucks that carry the finished products arrive in our neighborhoods, they do not just dump them in the middle of the street. The bread and wine are stocked in stores, where they are neither given away nor obtained by the direct exchange of goods and services, but acquired through the medium of money, either in paper form or, more likely, through digital means. This social artifact mediates the exchange of other goods and services (and once again all that is entailed in them) for our daily fare, often between persons separated by vast distances. The workings of the global market are therefore not absent from our feast. And then there are the hands that bake the bread and pour the wine, and the kinds of relationships that seem to form and develop only when family and friends meet around the dinner table. It is not an overstatement to say that there is virtually nothing under heaven or on earth that is not tacitly signified in some way by the bread and wine that is offered to God in the liturgy.

One of the aims of the Eucharist, however, is to help us understand that the significance of these products and relationships is not straightforward. Before the bread and the cup are blessed in remembrance of the crucified and risen one, the liturgy reminds us that we live in a fallen creation, a world ruled by fear, greed, division, and desecration, where access to daily sustenance is a tool of the rulers and authorities who claim for themselves the authority that belongs to God alone. "The crucifixion of Jesus was simply the dramatic manifestation of the sort of world we have made," writes McCabe, "the showing up of the world, the unmasking of what we call, traditionally, original sin."[24] Implicit in the Eucharist, then, is an apocalyptic phenomenology, such that the world we now inhabit shows up or appears to us in distinctive sorts of ways. The relation of the church's liturgical action to the everyday concerns and activities of human beings is therefore crucial to an adequate understanding of the social grammar presupposed by the gospel. In the words of Rowan Williams, "The eucharist hints at the paradox that material things carry their fullest meaning for human minds and bodies—the meaning of God's grace and of the common life thus formed—when they are the medium of *gift*, not instruments of control or objects for accumulation."[25]

True worship is thus fashioned around an alternative regime of life and language that is the product of the gift economy of the triune God, the center

24. McCabe, *God Matters*, 23.
25. Williams, *On Christian Theology*, 218 (emphasis original).

of which is the crucified and risen Lord, and whose extent is infinite, universal, *catholic*. The attentiveness of memory, understanding, and will cultivated by this social grammar pervades and defines everything Christians do and say. False worship or idolatry, by contrast, consists in the setting of our mind and heart, loyalty and confidence, hopes and fears, on something other than the mystery revealed in the incarnation of the Son and the breathing-forth of the Spirit upon the church. When we are convinced that the present constellation of institutions, events, and persons truthfully exhibits the abiding nature of things and that we therefore have no choice but to act in accordance with it, then idolatry takes its most virulent form as the worship of necessity.[26]

This is not to say that there are no limits to the possibilities open to us as creatures, for that too would be idolatry. To be human is to be constituted and constrained in no small measure by the limits that subsist in our relationships with our fellow creatures. In this sense, limits are a sign of grace. Walter Lowe rightly suggests that the modern rejection of limits paved the way for the ironic "dialectic of Enlightenment," in which our attempts to master the world led to the would-be master's undoing. Quoting Theodor Adorno, Lowe contends that "'the principle of human domination, in becoming absolute . . . turned its point against man as the absolute object.' Hence the sense of entrapment, the 'iron cage.'"[27] To idolize and worship necessity is to regard ourselves as without alternatives when it comes to these limits, thus rendering absolute our impotence and leaving us completely enthralled to an authority at whose throne we believe we have no choice but to kneel.

Convergence on and Divergence from Christ

It is at the baptismal font and the table of the crucified and risen Lord, then, that men and women have directly and insistently to do "with the realization of the Christ-reality . . . in the contemporary world that it already embraces, owns, and inhabits. . . . The whole reality of the world has already been drawn into and is held together in Christ. History moves only from this center and toward this center."[28] God's redemptive work of gathering together the whole of creation reaches its denouement in Christ (Eph. 1:9–10, 20–23; cf. 2:11–20). In this one man's sacrifice God's judgment and re-creation of this world find concrete embodiment, establishing the definitive link between the course of history and its consummation in the messianic kingdom.

26. Lash, *Believing Three Ways in One God*, 108.
27. Lowe, "Prospects for a Postmodern Christian Theology," 21.
28. Bonhoeffer, *Ethics*, 58.

As pivotal as the incarnation is to this movement of time around Christ, however, it is not enough to say that the Son entered fully into time and history and in so doing perfectly fulfilled the will of the Father. The universal efficacy attributed to Christ's concrete historical existence by the gospel must be performatively communicated to and displayed in every time and place so that it becomes the norm of every human being's singular existence. This is the work of the Holy Spirit, repeating in nonidentical fashion the effect of the uniting of God and human, instituted in a particular time and place by Christ, within the ever-changing parameters of this world. The Spirit gathers together persons from every tribe and language, people and nation, and forges them into the earthly-historical form of the crucified and risen Christ.[29] This pilgrim community in the power of the Spirit communicates the concrete singularity of this one Jewish man to all times and every place, for "the personal in Christ can only confront the personal in the individual Christian in union with what appears to be impersonal, the church and the sacraments."[30]

The convergence and divergence of all life, all activity, in relation to the events of this one man's life unfold as history in and through the company of disciples that joins Jesus in his atoning sacrifice. The dynamics and parameters of this twofold movement are specified by the announcement in the Gospels that in his life, death, and resurrection the kingdom of God has drawn near. And though the image of the kingdom does not by itself specifically *denote* a political commonwealth, it does *connote* a distinctive conception of politics— that is, a dedicated network of social practices through which the intrusion into the world of God's apocalyptic regime is made present and visible to all. The grammar of divine kingship thus presupposes the actual formation of a people through whom the world is directly confronted by God's sovereign claim upon it.[31]

Baptism is the sign and seal of induction into this new regime, marking the transfer of allegiance from the powers of this world to the kingdom of God, and with it the passage from life to death and then to life eternal. Paul's reference to dying and rising with Christ in baptism (Rom. 6:3–4) does not refer to the "inner experience" of an unencumbered individual but to the real moment of transition from the old society into a new form of life in the company of the crucified. In baptism God creates the body of Christ and continually adds new members to it by incorporating them in Jesus's death

---

29. Buckley, "Field of Living Fire," 91.
30. Balthasar, *Theology of History*, 81.
31. Wright, *New Testament and the People of God*, 307.

and resurrection. The baptized are caught up now in the new world that is manifested with the advent of the messianic reign of God: "So if anyone is in Christ, there is a new creation: everything old has passed away; see, everything has become new!" (2 Cor. 5:17).[32]

Immersion in the baptismal waters divests us of all previous definitions of identity based on class, ethnic or national origin, gender, and family ties: "Because in the new family [of Christ] in which all are equally sons and daughters of God there need be no more national egoisms, no struggles between classes and sexes, the promise to Abraham is fulfilled and there arises in the ancient world a new thing that is fundamentally different from all ways of life in paganism."[33] Baptism's power to divest the false identities conferred on human beings by a fallen world was nowhere more aptly (if paradoxically) demonstrated than in the early days of slavery in North America, where at first whites refused to baptize those stolen from Africa because it would call into question the legitimacy of slavery. Slave owners only began allowing the gospel to be taught to the slaves when they received assurance that it would not change the outward condition of their human "property." Despite the justifications of slavery as a means of spreading the gospel and proclamations of the duty of Christian colonists to evangelize the heathen, writes Albert Raboteau, the economic profitability of the colonial planter's slaves, not their Christianization, held top priority for him. One of the principal reasons that planters refused to permit the religious instruction of their slaves, Raboteau adds, "was the fear that baptism would emancipate their slaves."[34]

Baptism thus strips off the old human with its practices and clothes us with the new human in Christ, "which is being renewed in knowledge according to the image of its creator. In that renewal there is no longer Greek and Jew, circumcised and uncircumcised, barbarian, Scythian, slave and free; but Christ is all and in all!" (Col. 3:10–11). In this new human Christians are joined not only individually to the Head who is Christ but to one another as members of one body. As the sign of induction into that people who keep company with the God of Jesus Christ, then, baptism inserts us into the way of being and acting that flows from the triune life of God. We are literally immersed into the overflowing love and genuine freedom that is the divine essence. But as Hazel Sherman points out, participation in the economy of God's work does not equal arrival. We still journey toward the city that is to come even as we share in its life and aims through the activity of the Spirit.[35]

32. Lohfink, *Does God Need the Church?*, 208–10.
33. Lohfink, *Does God Need the Church?*, 211.
34. Raboteau, *Slave Religion*, 98.
35. Sherman, "Baptized," 113.

Baptism admits us to the eucharistic feast of the pilgrim people, described in patristic and early medieval texts in terms of a threefold articulation of "the body of Christ" in the writings of Paul: the historical body of the man Jesus of Nazareth; the sacramental body (*corpus mysticum*, mystical body); and the ecclesial body (*corpus verum*, true body). The sacramental body and the ecclesial body were closely linked in these early writings, with a temporal caesura or gap between them and the historical body. This caesura separates the originating event (the life, death, and resurrection of Jesus) from the manifestation of its effects, which takes place within the liturgical complex of a visible community and secret action or "mystery."[36] Together the Eucharist and the church constitute the contemporary performance of the historical body, the unique event of Jesus. The *communio* of the gathered community and the invisible action of the sacrament forge the essential unity between past event and present community: "The 'mystical,' then, is that which 'insures the unity between two times,' and brings the Christ event into present historical time in the church body, the *corpus verum*."[37] The eucharistic celebration is the performative medium for communicating the grammar (*communicatio grammaratum*) of God's redemptive work to the followers of Christ, and with it the church's interpretive stance in the world.

The gap between Jesus's historical body and the sacramental and church bodies also serves as a warning to Christians not to see the ecclesial community of which they are a part as a simple continuation or extension of Jesus. According to Williams, "When the Church performs the eucharistic action it *is* what it is called to be: the Easter community, guilty and restored, the gathering of those whose identity is defined by their new relation to Jesus crucified and raised, who identify themselves as forgiven." The church is therefore rightly understood as Christ's body, "the place of his presence," writes Williams, "but it is entered precisely by the ritual encounter with his death and resurrection, by the 'turning around' which stops us struggling to interpret *his* story in the light of *ours* and presses us to interpret ourselves in the light of the Easter event."[38]

The emphasis in the early church was thus on the Eucharist as sacred action; the community performed the mysteries (*mysteria telein*) or did the Eucharist (*eucharistiam facere*). At stake in this performance was the church's participation in Christ's sacrificial offering. As the true body of Christ performing his will, "the eucharistic action is necessarily His action of sacrifice, and what

---

36. Certeau, *Mystic Fable*, 82–83.

37. Cavanaugh, *Torture and Eucharist*, 212. The embedded quotation is from Certeau, *Mystic Fable*, 83.

38. Williams, *Resurrection*, 58, 84 (emphasis original).

is offered must be what he offered. The consequences of His action are what he declared they would be: 'This is My Body' and 'This is My Blood.' They [the members of the early church] made the sacrament depend upon the sacrifice."[39] Paul's admonition to the Christians at Philippi to have the same mind as Christ Jesus finds its social location in this sacrament qua sacrifice: "Work out your own salvation with fear and trembling; for it is God who is at work in you, enabling you both to will and to work for his good pleasure" (Phil. 2:12–13). This statement emphasizes the social grammar fostered by the dynamic interactions between the community, the liturgy, and the presence of the risen Christ and God's apocalyptic regime.

The mysterious action of the sacraments incorporates the bodies of Jesus's followers into the messianic suffering of God, thereby signifying the end (which is both telos and *eschaton*) of all true sacrifice in the atoning death of the righteous one. In the words of Augustine, "The whole of the redeemed City—that is to say, the congregation and fellowship of the saints—is offered to God as a universal sacrifice for us through the great High Priest Who offered even Himself for us in the form of a servant, so that we might be the body of so great a Head."[40] As the dwelling place of God in this age, the members of Christ's commonwealth offer up their own bodies to become the living doorposts and lintels on which the Spirit puts the blood of the Paschal Lamb of God who takes away the sins of the world. Incarnation and atonement, reconciliation and the sharing of burdens are thereby communicated, not as abstract facts, but as the concrete *grammaratum* of individual and communal being, producing "a new kind of efficacious sacrifice of praise, self-sharing and probable attendant suffering which unites us with [Christ] in the heavenly city, and at the same time totally obliterates . . . all the contours of inside and outside which constitute human power."[41]

The performative process of repeating in every time and place the social grammar of the divine kingdom is ordered around the habits and relations of the eucharistic *anamnēsis*: "Do this in memory of me." When Christians remember Jesus around the table, it is not we who recall him through an act of memory. As numerous biblical and liturgical studies have demonstrated, the liturgy brings the sacrifice of Jesus before God in such a way that it is presently operative by its effects within the ecclesial body.[42] Through its act of

---

39. Dix, *Shape of the Liturgy*, 12, 245–46.
40. Augustine, *City of God* 10.6.
41. Milbank, *Word Made Strange*, 151.
42. Dix, *Shape of the Liturgy*, 245; see also Dahl, *Jesus in the Memory of the Early Church*, 11–29; Jeremias, *Eucharistic Words of Jesus*, 237–55; Wainwright, *Eucharist and Eschatology*, 64–68; Chenderlin, *"Do This as My Memorial"*; Capes, "Lord's Table," 199–209.

thanksgiving (the root meaning of "Eucharist"), the church "offers its thanks, its communal sacrifice, its giving itself away, its losing control in order to be faithful and obedient to the God 'who so loved the world that he gave his only begotten Son' to the end that all who believe in him should not perish but have everlasting life." This is how Christians are *re-membered* by God to the risen Christ and to one another and become the true body of Christ.[43] The pattern of friendships that characterizes life together in the company of Jesus's disciples is above all else a eucharistic achievement, for it is in the course of friends sharing the divine food that the Spirit re-members them as the body of Christ.[44]

The church so constituted offers to the world the social grammar of the new creation—the peaceable relationships, the reconciling patterns of conduct, *and* the tribulations—introduced into the midst of the old by the sacrifice of Christ. The unfolding of history in anticipation and refusal of the reality of God taking flesh in the world is tangibly manifested through the habits and relations of Christ's ecclesial body to the rulers and powers of this present age (Eph. 3:10; cf. Gen. 12:3; Matt. 25:31–46). Without the bodily participation of the church in what God has accomplished (and continues to accomplish) in Christ's offering, the meaning of the incarnation, the enfleshment of God's own self-expression, is effectively reduced to an anecdote about another time and place.

This work of the Spirit is an ongoing, never-ending endeavor, because times and circumstances change. New characters, social settings, and historical events are constantly being incorporated within the temporal ebb and flow of creation around its christological center. The meaning of this process is therefore never fixed or formulaic, but continues to unfold in the style of a historical drama, the performance of which is never over and done with. The ways that the sacramental grammar of Christ's body incorporates those of African descent in the United States, for example, will differ in certain respects from those operative with other persons and groups. The unity of this drama's story line resides not in the sameness of its performance, but in timely transpositions of the patterns of human acting and relating decisively enacted by the life and passion of Jesus.

The dramatic unity wrought by these practices should therefore not be misread as uniformity. The Holy Spirit particularizes the universality of the new humanity in Christ by constituting the church as a community of differences.[45] Incorporated into this community through the sacraments, women and men

---

43. H. Smith, *Where Two or Three Are Gathered*, 64–65.
44. Lehmann, *Ethics in a Christian Context*, 65.
45. Buckley, "Field of Living Fire," 91.

receive the gifts of the Spirit, which determine the distinctive singularity of personal existence in the body politic of Christ. Within this community neither the whole nor the members are simply functions of the other, and so collectivism and individualism are ruled out from the start. Differentiation is not for its own sake, to be consumed as yet one more commodity, but so that all might share in one calling—to be for the sake of the world sign, foretaste, and herald of the destiny of all things in God's new creation.

From Apocalyptic Action to Sacred Spectacle

Baptism and Eucharist bind Christians together with the risen Christ in a distinctive type of political commonwealth, creating the standpoint that enables us to interpret other social formations through comparisons with its own social grammar.[46] The advent of this other city led many in the Roman Empire to look upon the followers of Christ as a subversive presence within their society.[47] They were regarded as self-righteous and fanatical, worshipers of a capricious deity, atheists, the enemy of humankind and a just social order. What was it about the church that so upset the Romans? If the essence of the gospel as understood by the early church consisted principally in a private transaction between God and the individual, and thus had little or nothing to do with the commitments, claims, and corruptions of the public realm, what could possibly have led Rome to classify this new movement as an illicit political society?

Perhaps imperial officials were just mistaken about the message of those early followers of Jesus. That explanation, however, does not stand up to scrutiny. Our ecclesial forebears could have taken refuge under a provision in Roman law that allowed for the establishment of a *cultus privatus* dedicated to the pursuit of personal piety and otherworldly salvation, but they did not do so.[48] Instead they proclaimed allegiance to Christ and his kingdom in a manner that required its members to renounce loyalty to Caesar. It would appear that they deliberately provoked Roman customs and conventions with a social, this-worldly alternative to the empire that incorporated elements of its host culture while remaining a distinct polity. It was this fact that led Rome to label Christianity a seditious and revolutionary movement: "The life and teachings of Jesus led to the formation of a new community of people . . . [that] had

46. Milbank, *Theology and Social Theory*, 388.

47. Wright, *New Testament and the People of God*, 350.

48. Westerhoff, "Fashioning Christians in Our Day," 280; Wright, *New Testament and the People of God*, 350, 355.

begun to look like a separate people or nation, but without its own land or traditions to legitimate its unusual customs."[49]

Rome was suspicious of the early church because the gospel as it was embraced and proclaimed by the first Christians did not primarily have to do with the communication of information on how to experience salvation within the self (more on this Gnostic misconception below), but with the judgment and transfiguration of the world, or as Scripture puts it, the re-capitulation of all things in heaven and on earth in Christ (Eph. 1:10). To be sure, the very notion of gospel, of good news, denoted a message, but it was always a message about "what we have heard, what we have seen with our eyes, what we have looked at and touched with our hands" (1 John 1:1). The gospel as it was understood by the early church is the revelation of the beginning and end of all things, and of human beings especially, *taking flesh, becoming embodied.*

In our time, however, the sacramental sinews that bind the members of Christ's ecclesial body together have largely been supplanted by the institutions and practices regulating the transactions of a state-centered, market-driven society. Comfortable in the well-worn ruts of conspicuous consumption, comparatively few Christians see their faith as anything other than a private, inward matter that makes their lives more fulfilling. They have been trained to regard the church as another vendor of goods and services, providing for their spiritual consumption and enjoyment, and thus are incapable of mounting a serious challenge to the sway of the global market's cult of productivity and consumption. For the most part the church has acquiesced in this matter, relegating "spiritual" questions to a realm beyond the everyday world where goods are bought and sold, rewards and punishments are meted out, and the young are raised and the elderly cared for, and in the process it has supplied religious justification for the global republic of production and consumption. Ecclesial practices have been reformatted to underwrite the individual in the role of consumer, encouraging each to choose from a vast inventory of religious symbols and doctrines, to select those that best express his or her private tastes and sentiments. Some like white bread, while others prefer whole wheat; some like the majesty of the Orthodox liturgy, while others are partial to the informality of Baptist services; some are drawn to the orderliness of the Reformed tradition, others the ecstasy of Pentecostal revivals; some prefer the wide range of spiritual goods and services offered by the suburban megachurch, yet others the eclectic mixture of ancient and postmodern in the so-called emerging church.

49. Wilken, *Christians as the Romans Saw Them*, 119.

Changes in sacramental practice and theory in the late medieval and modern contexts helped to prepare the way for the consumptive habits of modern piety. In the early church the notion of liturgy was not limited to cultic activity separate from the so-called profane areas of life. In Greek *leitourgia* designated a "public work"—that is, "an action by which a group of people become something corporately which they had not been as a mere collection of individuals—a whole greater than the sum of its parts." Starting with the Carolingian Renaissance in the ninth and tenth centuries, however, standard treatments of the concept of sacrament isolated it from its liturgical context, attempting to define as precisely as possible its *essence*—that is, "that which distinguishes it from the 'non-sacrament.'" Such debates posited for the first time a basic discontinuity between "symbol" and "reality," between what is "sacred" and what is "profane."[50]

Medieval debates concerning real presence in the Eucharist thus exhibit a gradual inversion of meaning that culminated in the late twelfth century. As I noted above, patristic and early medieval texts, in their threefold articulation of Paul's image of Christ's body, link together the sacramental body and the ecclesial body and posit a temporal gap between them and the historical body of Jesus, thereby constituting the contemporary performance of Christ's historical body making its journey toward the kingdom of God. In the later medieval period, however, it is the historical and sacramental bodies that were conjoined, and a synchronic gap opened between them and the ecclesial body. The consecrated bread and wine became the true body of Christ, and the liturgical emphasis shifted from historical incorporation into Christ's body and mission to awed contemplation of a sacred object venerated in the midst of grand spectacle. The visibility of the church as the performative locus of Christ's continued presence in the world was exchanged for the visibility of what took place on the altar.[51]

The intimate connection made by the patristic and early medieval church between the sacramental body (*corpus mysticum*) and the ecclesial body (*corpus verum*) was thus obscured by the dramatic reversal that took place between the meaning of sacrament and of sacrifice. Formerly the liturgical emphasis was on the active participation of the church—the true body of Christ performing his will—in the apocalyptic action of his sacrificial offering. Beginning in the late twelfth century, however, the meaning of sacrifice was made dependent on the sacerdotal consecration of the bread and wine, with the actions performed by the cleric becoming the dominant (and sometimes

50. Schmemann, *For the Life of the World*, 25, 137.
51. Cavanaugh, *Torture and Eucharist*, 213.

the sole) role in the proceedings. Since the words of consecration in some sense turn the bread and wine into the body and blood of Christ, what the church did in the Eucharist must be what Christ did with his body and blood—namely, offer them in sacrifice.[52]

As a result of these changes, the Eucharist came to be described not as liturgical action linking the church visibly to the sacrifice of Christ, but as object, with a concentration on the miracle produced in the symbols of bread and wine rather than on the transformation of the church by the presence of Christ in the liturgy. At the same time the redesignation of the church as *corpus mysticum* rendered its essence invisible: "The visibility of the church in the communal performance of the sacrament is replaced by the visibility of the Eucharistic object. Signified and signifier have exchanged places, such that the sacramental body is the visible signifier of the hidden signified, which is the social body of Christ."[53] Whereas in the patristic formula the historical body was manifested in its effects in the liturgical combination of a visible community or people and a secret (mystical) action, in later conceptualizations the visibility of the eucharistic symbols replaced the communal celebration and served as the visible indicator of the proliferation of the secret effects of grace and salvation that made up the real life of the church, which was now hidden.[54]

Severing the connection between the Eucharist and the church's offering of itself as the true body of Christ resulted in "a greatly diminished sense of the essentially social implications of the Christ's eucharistic presence."[55] With the eclipse of the corporate and social implications, combined with the introduction of new practices such as the elevation of the host, the celebration of the Eucharist was redirected toward the subjective devotional life of the individual in the isolation of his own thoughts and affections.[56] "The emphasis," writes Sarah Beckwith, "was increasingly on watching Christ's body rather than being incorporated in it."[57] According to Dom Gregory Dix, it did not stop with mere watching: "The part of the individual layman . . . had long ago been reduced from 'doing' to 'seeing' and 'hearing.' Now it is retreating within himself to 'thinking' and 'feeling.' He is even beginning to think that over-much 'seeing' (ceremonial) and 'hearing' (music) are detrimental to proper 'thinking' and 'feeling.'"[58] Nothing "inessential" could be allowed to

---

52. Dix, *Shape of the Liturgy*, 245–46.
53. Cavanaugh, *Torture and Eucharist*, 213.
54. Certeau, *Mystic Fable*, 83–84.
55. David L. Schindler, introduction to *Mystery of the Supernatural*, by de Lubac, xiii.
56. Morris, *Discovery of the Individual, 1050–1200*, 12.
57. Beckwith, *Christ's Body*, 36.
58. Dix, *Shape of the Liturgy*, 599.

intrude upon an individual's private encounter with the divine, a proscription that could conceivably extend to the sacramental elements themselves.

Churches that do not emphasize eucharistic observance are not immune to the privatization of Christian life by means of a reinterpretation of the sacraments. In the Baptist tradition, for example, the old habits of establishmentarianism—the advocacy of a state-established church (which would have been inconceivable prior to the Reformation)—have proven to be far more difficult to break than anyone ever imagined. The first generation of Baptists regarded the rulers of earthly regimes with a wary eye, because those rulers invariably laid claim to an authority over the church that belonged to Christ alone. In particular, these early Baptists claimed that the king had exceeded temporal powers granted to him by God when he claimed authority over the church in England. King Charles I, for example, declared in 1628, "Being by God's ordinance . . . Defender of the Faith and Supreme Governor of the Church within these our dominions, we hold it most agreeable to this our kingly office and our own religious zeal, to conserve and maintain the Church committed to our charge in unity of true religion and the bond of peace; and not to suffer unnecessary disputations, altercations or questions to be raised which may nourish factionalism both in the Church and commonwealth."[59]

Baptists rejected such claims as idolatrous, insisting that the church alone was the visible sign of the rule of Christ over all power in heaven and on earth, and thus earthly powers had no authority over Christ's body, nor were the king's decrees numbered among the divine ordinances. As the London Confession of 1644 puts it, Christ had established here in this age "a spirituall Kingdome, which is the Church, which he hath purchased and redeemed unto himselfe, as a peculiar inheritance: which Church, as it is visible to us, is a company of visible Saints, called & separated from the world, by the word and Spirit of God, to the visible profession of the faith of the Gospel, being baptized into that faith, and joyned to the Lord, and each other, by mutuall agreement, in the practical injoyment of the Ordinances, commanded by Christ their head and King."[60] Because Baptists believed that the rule of Christ claimed the whole of their lives, the church was, as Philip Thompson has put it, "the earthly arena in which the reign of Christ was embodied, and as such was an interruption and delegitimization of the false politics of the state."[61] The existence of Christ's "mystical body" (by this time the

59. Charles I, "King's Declaration," 481.

60. Lumpkin, *Baptist Confessions of Faith*, 165. The notion of "spirituall" here does not mean "nonworldly," as it would later be defined.

61. Thompson, "Sacraments and Religious Liberty," 46.

standard term designating the church as Christ's body), made visible to all by believer's baptism, intruded upon and called into question the authority of every other principality.

Early Baptists regarded their participation in the body of Christ as a visible sign of God's presence and activity before the rulers and authorities of the present age, gathered together by what they called Christ's ordinances (prayer, preaching, the devotional reading of Scripture, works of mercy, and the pastoral office) but especially by those ordinances explicitly called sacraments—namely, baptism and Eucharist. Baptists' understanding of these practices, and in particular their critique of and resistance to the Church of England, was rooted in their conviction that God's work of salvation could not be constrained by any human institution such as a temporal state. Idolatry, not liberty of conscience, was the principal sin of the crown's attempt to usurp divine authority over the church. The attention the Baptists gave to what constitutes the faithful practice of baptism reflects this concern. Baptism was for them the sacrament that conferred the proper significance on all bodies—communal as well as individual—and thus it relativized all other political expressions by locating true politics within the church. They were therefore concerned when the Church of England used infant baptism, in the words of Thomas Grantham, to bring persons "by the lump into the Name of Christian Churches."[62]

Once baptism had incorporated these early Baptists into the church's body politic, their day-to-day lives were not merely surveyed, categorized, inventoried, and supplemented by some sort of "spiritual" (i.e., therapeutic) benefit but were radically transfigured in a way that touched on every aspect of their existence, body as well as soul. They would have agreed with Dietrich Bonhoeffer's contention that repentance and faith are "not in the first place thinking about one's own needs, problems, sins, and fears, but allowing oneself to be pulled into the path that Jesus walks, into the messianic event."[63] And as they learned from firsthand experience, their participation in the apocalyptic event of Christ's life and passion brought them into conflict with those who actively sought to usurp the place and power of God.

There was a close link between the Baptist tradition of social and political dissent and Baptists' understanding of the sacraments.[64] They were persuaded

---

62. Cited in Thompson, "Sacraments and Religious Liberty," 46–47.

63. Bonhoeffer, *Letters and Papers from Prison*, 480.

64. Dissent is not an expression of unconstrained individuals but is intelligible only as an anomalous form of participation in an ongoing communal endeavor. The point of argument within a tradition is not ultimately to "win," which would locate the argument instead in the context of a competitive *agon* and not that of a *polis* seeking to bear witness to the triune

that Word and Spirit did not address the human heart directly but required ecclesial mediation. According to the *Orthodox Creed* of 1679:

> There is one holy catholick church . . . gathered, in one body under Christ, the only head thereof; which church is gathered by special grace, and the powerful and internal work of the spirit; and are effectually united unto Christ their head. . . .
> We believe the visible church of Christ on earth, is made up of several distinct congregations, which make up that one catholick church, or mystical body of Christ. And the marks by which she is known to be the true spouse of Christ, are these, viz., where the word of God is rightly preached, and the sacraments truly administered, according to Christ's institution, and the practice of the primitive church . . . ; to which church and not elsewhere, all persons that seek for eternal life, should gladly join themselves.[65]

According to these early Baptists, then, the church that challenges the authority of the king does not assemble at the initiative of its members but instead is gathered together by the working of God, which requires, among other things, a more theologically refined sense of remembrance. When Christians gather around the table, it is not we who recall Jesus to mind, but we call upon God to send the Holy Spirit to "remember" the new covenant enacted by his sacrifice. This is how we are joined to Christ and to one another as members of his body.

Early Baptists thus sought to recover for the circumstances of their time and place something of the social context and sensibilities that characterized the early church, for which the gospel was not at bottom a worldview but a people assembled together, not by their own will or decision but by the power of the Spirit, to be for the world the earthly-historical form of the crucified and risen Christ. "Christianity enters history not only as a message but also as a communal life, a society or city," writes Wilken, constituted by "inner discipline and practices, rituals and creeds, and institutions and traditions."[66] The initial trajectory plotted by the seventeenth-century Baptists was not, however, generally sustained by later generations. As their external circumstances improved—toleration in England, the institutionalization of religious liberty in the New World, and advances in social standing—the heirs of John Bunyan and Muriel Lester, Anne Hutchinson and Roger Williams made their peace with the earthly city. Like other ecclesial communities, Baptist churches

---

God. An argument's aim must always be to persuade and to be persuaded as the community seeks to come to one mind with respect to the truth.

65. Lumpkin, *Baptist Confessions of Faith*, 318–19.
66. Wilken, *Spirit of Early Christian Thought*, xv.

increasingly settled for the care of "souls," ceding virtually all claims on the bodies of their members to the civil authorities.[67] And as salvation was refigured as a private transaction between solitary individuals and God, even this limited jurisdiction was stripped from their purview. Baptism no longer accomplished anything concrete but only expressed what had occurred in the "experiences"—that is, the conscious mental goings-on—of individuals.[68] Abdication from the public realm effectively made the church incidental to salvation, reducing it to a *collegium pietatis*, a social club for the cultivation of a privatized spirituality.[69]

As a result of these and other changes, many Baptists, particularly in North America, embraced the division of spheres implemented under the auspices of the modern idea of religion, a division that they regarded as the liberation of faith from all political entanglements. One of the most prominent names in this retrenchment in the eighteenth and nineteenth centuries was that of John Leland of Virginia (1754–1841). Leland adopted Lockean and Madisonian theories about natural rights and voluntary associations to reconfigure historic Baptist convictions regarding liberty of conscience and the disestablishment of the church from the state. Liberty of conscience became "the inalienable right that each individual has, of worshipping his God according to the dictates of his conscience, without being prohibited, directed, or controlled therein by human law, either in time, place, or manner."[70]

Unfortunately, no world is free of regulatory modes of one sort or another. The modern Western mind has long been obsessed with the idea of freedom as self-making, self-possessing. From René Descartes to Karl Marx and William James, the vision of the detached, self-constituting individual has sent countless philosophers and novelists, critical theorists and artists on an errand for an existence completely unencumbered by anything not chosen by us.[71] Jean-Paul Sartre's portrayal is perhaps both the most precise and stark: "For human reality, to be is to *choose oneself*; nothing comes to it either from the outside or from within which it can *receive or accept*. Without any help whatsoever, it is entirely abandoned to the intolerable necessity of making itself be—down to the slightest detail."[72] Sartre could not be clearer: individuals have no choice but to choose to *make themselves be*.

67. M. Bell, *Apocalypse How?*, 129–30.
68. Swinburne, *Existence of God*, 244.
69. Bonhoeffer, *"Life Together" and "Prayerbook of the Bible,"* 45.
70. Leland, "Blow at the Root," 239.
71. Lash, *Beginning and the End of "Religion,"* 237–39.
72. Sartre, *Being and Nothingness*, 440–41 (emphasis original).

This picture of human freedom is a key component of the modern imaginary, and though it is a fiction, it accurately captures the archetypal moral yearning of a truly modern person: the autonomy characteristic of adolescence. This period in a person's life has its time, place, and form of freedom, but if this yearning persists, outliving its time and tasks, it enslaves "with iron bands." The time and task of adulthood is the acknowledgement of finite existence with others who also must acknowledge that existence, that human life is inextricably social and communal. A mature adult recognizes that we can and do receive and accept all kinds of things from beyond our individual selves, "language and identity, shelter and suffering, pain and delight, gratitude and disease."[73] Apart from these and an almost infinite number of other offerings, the human person does not even exist. In the most basic sense, we receive ourselves at the hands of others: who we are, how we learn how to perceive ourselves and the world around us, the meaning and purpose of our human being. We do not make ourselves be; *others let us be*. Conversely we let others be as well.[74]

To be a truly autonomous moral agent, then, is to be aware that choices are real precisely because they are constrained, first, by the "sheer thereness of others," and second, by all that I have done and undergone that made me the agent I am: "Adult autonomy—contrary to what is lazily assumed by much of our culture—is never the liberty to decide in abstraction from what others are, what others say. It is not, after all, the exclusive opposite of dependence." To choose is take up a stance in recognition of the impenetrable reality of others, to commit oneself to the risky business of being with or for them in that radical otherness.[75]

The position of Leland and his supporters unwittingly reestablished the church socially and politically, in a new form to be sure, but one that nonetheless fit perfectly into the world they thought they were challenging. The institutional disestablishment of "religion" they sought took place under the auspices of a social arrangement that sanctioned a moral identity of the church with the state and its commercial republic.[76] Cast now in the role of "autonomous individuals," women and men are required to render to "Caesar" (the political consortium of managerial government and the global market) their unconditional loyalty. This new emperor in his sovereign benevolence then permitted, or rather *guaranteed*, these newly minted individuals the right to "religious beliefs," which are perfectly free as long as they are perfectly private.

73. Lash, *Beginning and the End of "Religion,"* 240–41.
74. McCabe, *God Still Matters*, 10–11.
75. Williams, *Edge of Words*, 87.
76. See N. Hatch, *Democratization of American Christianity*.

The Return of Gnosticism

These shifts in sacramental practice were instrumental to the development of a kind of spirituality that is commensurate with a solitary career of self-determination, which is the highest good in liberal social orders. Such an aspiration presupposes the existence of a realm of nonhistorical freedom, where "autonomous" selves are not bound by the corporeal presence of other selves or the created world. In the process an ancient adversary of the church's distinctive social grammar has found opportunity once again to make a determined claim for the members of Christ's body. With the canonization of the myth of the unencumbered self by liberal social orders, religious piety and polity invariably tend toward Gnosticism, an age-old practice that teaches that faith and salvation are essentially private matters, with no real connection to history or social existence. Indeed, says Philip Lee, such tendencies represent "an attempt to escape from everything except the self."[77]

Harold Bloom, elaborating on Lee's insights, contends that the modern form of Gnosticism is so pervasive that even self-professed secularists and atheists tacitly embrace its view of the human self. Believer and nonbeliever join together to form "a religiously mad culture, furiously searching for the spirit," because "each of us is subject and object of the one quest, which must be for the original self, a spark of breath in us that we are convinced goes back to before the Creation." This gnosticized form of the Christian confession has for the most part kept the figure of Jesus, but it is "a very solitary and personal American Jesus, who is also the resurrected Jesus rather than the crucified Jesus or the Jesus who ascended again to the Father."[78] Indeed, writes Rodney Clapp, Christians in North America might not really want a Jesus rooted in history, for "that would be a particular Jesus who might reveal a particular God with a character and purpose different from our own."[79]

Bloom oversimplifies the convoluted genealogy of modern religiosity, overlooking, for example, its Stoic elements.[80] He nevertheless makes explicit the role that Gnostic notions have played in shaping the myth of a self that haunts a ghostly realm of ahistorical freedom, unencumbered by the bodily presence of other selves and by everything that inhabits the physical world. Consider the popular interpretation of the Protestant doctrine of justification by grace through faith that has become axiomatic in many churches. In

77. Lee, *Against the Protestant Gnostics*, 9–10.

78. Bloom, *American Religion*, 22, 32.

79. Clapp, *Peculiar People*, 35.

80. See Hardy and Ford, *Praising and Knowing God*, 144; cf. 94–99; MacIntyre, *After Virtue*, 168–70, 234–37; and Percy, *Sign-Posts in a Strange Land*, 83–88.

the Bible divine forgiveness and reconciliation constitute a visible sign of the new creation, an eschatological reality proleptically realized within this age and made known to its rulers and authorities by the body politic of Christ. Within the modern regime, however, forgiveness and reconciliation become a private transaction between God and the individual, abstracted from its apocalyptic context and unmindful of any consequences for the internal life of the church or its relationships with other forms of social life.

The privatizing of salvation in terms of the individual's standing *coram Deo*, before God alone, unwittingly contributed to the dubious conclusion that the essence of the gospel "is a knowing, by and of an uncreated self, or self-within-the-self, and the knowledge leads to freedom . . . from nature, community, other selves." This freedom exacts a high price from those who embrace it, "because of what it is obliged to leave out: society, temporality, the other. What remains, for it, is solitude and the abyss."[81] By contrast the sacraments, as they were originally performed, are public actions, incorporating women and men into the visible body of Christ, involving them in a communal and public disciplining of bodies that of necessity is political in nature, confronting the authorities and rulers of this world with a radically different constitution of human life within the apocalyptic action of the triune God.

Given the state of the world we now inhabit, the allure of Gnosticism is in some ways understandable. We see at virtually every turn the triumph of consumerism, the withering away of local associations that once bound people together in patterns of mutual obligation and enjoyment, the proliferation of individual rights without due regard for the goods that constitute the common welfare, and the expansion of technological networks devoted almost exclusively to means rather than ends. The natural and social world has become "nothing but a meeting place for individual wills, each with its own set of attitudes and preferences and who understand that world solely as an arena for the achievement of their own satisfaction, who interpret reality as a series of opportunities for their enjoyment and for whom the last enemy is boredom."[82] Finally, seemingly intractable racial and ethnic divisions and senseless violence place additional strain on the ability of liberal democracy and its commercial republic to manage the task of achieving and sustaining a truly human form of life.

In the final analysis, however, Gnosticism has no redeeming power for this world. When men and women seek to be free from other selves and from the created world, they only exacerbate their fragmented situation. In the words of

81. Bloom, *American Religion*, 37, 49.
82. MacIntyre, *After Virtue*, 25.

Martin Buber, "caprice and doom, the spook of the soul and the nightmare of the world," are bound inextricably together. They "get along with each other, living next door and avoiding each other, without connection and friction, at home in meaninglessness—until in one instant eye meets eye, madly, and the confession erupts from both that they are unredeemed."[83] Wendell Berry contends that the disintegration of communities and the disintegration of persons are the two epidemic illnesses of our time. They are related, he adds, as loneliness is necessarily bound up with the kind of public confusion that plagues us. These illnesses are not well understood, he adds, not because they have not been studied and discussed. The unrecognized source of the pathologies, he states, is the relation between the disintegrations of communities and persons and the disintegration of language: "My impression is that we have seen, for perhaps a hundred and fifty years, a gradual increase in language that is either meaningless or destructive of meaning. And I believe that this increasing unreliability of language parallels the increasing disintegration, over the same period, of persons and communities."[84] It was precisely into this fragmented and isolated world that God sent the Son, not to condemn it, but that it might be saved through him. It is into this same world that God now sends the church in the power of the Spirit to be salt and light, to continue Christ's mission of reconciliation and redemption, a public work that takes shape around sacramental action.

Telling the Little Narratives: Sacramental Performance in a Postmodern World

Many in recent years have argued that in the postmodern world the grand narrative of human development in the style of Hegel and Marx has reached an end and that from now on only little narratives that try to make sense only of local and contingent events can be told.[85] During this same time global capitalism has effectively established its presence and power as the most "rapacious grand narrative in the history of the West."[86] The regulatory schemes enforced by the combined efforts of the nation-state and the global market have radically reconfigured what it means to be human beings. The everyday activities and relationships of virtually every man, woman, and child on this planet are no longer attuned to the rhythms of nature, the changing of the

---

83. Buber, *I and Thou*, 108.
84. Berry, *Standing by Words*, 14.
85. See, for example, Lyotard, *Postmodern Condition*, 37–41, 60.
86. Coakley, *Powers and Submissions*, xiv.

seasons, the patterns of other life-forms, the peculiarities of particular places and times, or the institutions, crafts, and habits that once mediated human interaction with the rest of creation. These realities no longer serve as signs of the beginning and end of all things, and of reasoning creatures especially. Once every human being one encountered was sister, brother, cousin, parent, grandchild, a member of this household, that village, this tribe. Now we are groomed from birth to be an "individual" whose identity is determined not by being particular persons inhabiting particular times and places but by the undifferentiated role of producer and consumer in a global system of governance, accumulation, and exchange. These regulatory mechanisms have uprooted social relationships and personal identities that were once embedded in local associations and have redistributed them via technological networks that extend across vast distances in time and space.

If the body of Christ is to help its members resist complete assimilation to the ways of this regime of coercion and commerce while at the same time fully engaging it at both the institutional and the practical levels, writes Nicholas Boyle, the church will "need to draw its moral strength not from its international presence but from its claim to represent people as they are locally and distinct from the worldwide ramifications of their existence as participants in the global market." In its efforts to embody the social grammar of God's apocalyptic regime, then, the Christian community must learn how to tell "the little narratives of the victims of the grand process, the stories of what the big new world is squeezing out or ignoring . . . full of details which the new world will dismiss as superficial and inessential."[87]

These little narratives find their interpretive context in the journey of the church to God's kingdom, orchestrated in this age through the sacraments. When men and women pass through the waters of baptism and partake of the bread of life and the cup of salvation at the Lord's table, they submit themselves to the all-encompassing claim of Jesus on their lives disclosed in the service of the Word. Jesus's dramatic encounters with his contemporaries recorded in Scripture—often set in the context of table fellowship—become figures for our own encounters with Christ through reading the Bible in community. When this occurs, the solid line that modern methods of interpretation typically draw between the "world of the Bible" and the "real world out there," between what the Bible "meant" and what it "means,"[88] begins to dissipate. The canonical texts provide the performative images in terms of which the members of Christ's body may discern their present circumstances

87. Boyle, *Who Are We Now?*, 91–92.
88. See Stendahl, "Biblical Theology, Contemporary," 418–32.

and decide among alternative courses of action in ways that will allow them in the future to remain faithful to the *anamnēsis* of Jesus.

"From the standpoint of the Church," writes Williams, "the events around Jesus make possible those new modes of human being spoken of, symbolized and enacted in the Church, and the appropriation and transformation of Jewish paradigms in a radically different context. To explore the continuities of Christian patterns of holiness is to explore the *effect* of Jesus, living, dying and rising."[89] As we follow Jesus in baptism and then take our seats at the last meal that he shared with his closest friends, we discover patterns of actions and encounters that make up the timely process of creation's convergence and divergence in relation to its messianic center. Meeting Jesus once again around the table of disciples plunges us back into the world precisely as it teeters on the threshold between two ages. As we partake of his board of fare, each of us is given new roles to play, unfamiliar points on which to stand and speak, and perhaps most importantly, a new company of actors with which to perform, gathered "from every tribe and language and people and nation" (Rev. 5:9). The aim of baptism and Eucharist in our circumstances, then, is to take isolated worker-consumers and produce martyrs—that is, witnesses to the apocalyptic activity of God in Christ.

This road company of the messianic kingdom thus does not merely mark the passage of time. Her members are instead "drawn into a share in the vulnerability of God, into a new kind of life and a new identity. They do not receive an additional item called faith; their ordinary existence is not reorganized, found wanting in specific respects and supplemented: it is transfigured as a whole."[90] By inscribing in our bodies the social grammar by which human beings are drawn into the vulnerability of God, the Eucharist transposes our circumstances into a confrontation between the present world and the age to come inaugurated by Jesus's life and ministry. The social practices and institutions that bound the members of the early church together in a new style of public life continue to serve as a definitive sign to the world that this new creation has dawned. Through our confession of Christ's lordship—sealed by baptism, celebrated in the eucharistic feast, and lived out daily in a holy life of service and fellowship—we announce to the world in both word and deed that the end toward which history is moving is not determined by those whom this age calls powerful, but by the one who gathers together all things in heaven and on earth in the crucified Messiah of Israel.

89. Williams, "Unity of Christian Truth," 92 (emphasis original).
90. Williams, *On Christian Theology*, 41.

The irruption of the messianic reign of God in the midst of a fallen creation establishes the goal toward which all things tend, and it also sets the limits for the exercise of power by all worldly authorities. In and through the commonwealth of the church, everything in the created order, all life, is "now, at once, immediately confronted with a claim that is non-negotiable in the sense that in the end God will irrefutably be—God."[91] To be re-membered by God in Christ is to be caught up in Christ's mission to and for the world, the end of which is to glorify God and to gather up the whole of creation in the great activity of delighting in the beauty of God manifested in every aspect of the cosmos.[92] Because the whole of our existence as human beings is claimed and transfigured by the drawing-near of the reign of God to this fallen world, Christ's followers must attend in particular to the cares and concerns that make up the business of everyday life: building houses, tending gardens, buying and selling, marrying and giving in marriage, and raising children. As we Christians engage in these public activities, our goal is not simply to survive in what can at times be a hostile environment. The primary task is rather to glorify God in the world (John 17:20–24), which takes place in the generative interaction between the liturgy of the Eucharist and the "liturgy"—that is, the public work—of mission.

The connection between the two forms of the liturgy is exemplified in the relationship between the Eucharist and the practice of hospitality.[93] The sharing of bread around the Lord's table invokes the common life and purse of the first disciples, whom Jesus formed into a new household that relativized the claims of their biological or ethnic families on their material resources (cf. Mark 3:31–35; 10:29–31). Before the bread is blessed at Christ's table, it is a sign of a fallen creation, a world in rebellion, dominated by fear, greed, and division. But when it is blessed, it becomes a sign of God's new creation, a realm where perfect love casts out fear, generosity reaches out to the stranger in the gate, and reconciliation heals the world's divisions. John Chrysostom thus exhorts Christians to practice hospitality on the basis of the eucharistic feast:

> Do you wish to honor the Body of Christ? Do not despise him when he is naked. Do not honor him here in the church building with silks, only to neglect him outside, when he is suffering from cold and from nakedness. For he who said, "This is my Body," is the same who said, "You saw me, a hungry man, and you did not give me to eat." Of what use is it to load the table of Christ? Feed the hungry and then come and decorate the table. You are making a golden chalice

91. McClendon, Doctrine, 66.
92. Schindler, "Christology and the Imago Dei," 176–77.
93. See E. Newman, Untamed Hospitality.

and you do not give a cup of cold water? The Temple of your afflicted brother's body is more precious than this Temple. The Body of Christ becomes for you an altar. It is more holy than the altar of stone on which you celebrate the holy sacrifice. You are able to contemplate this altar everywhere, in the street and in the open squares.[94]

This shared meal prefigures the hope of the messianic age, when the rich will give up their capital and the poor will be well fed.

As these actions suggest, encounters with Jesus at his table never leave us as we are but "force to light hidden directions and dispositions that would otherwise never come to view, and thus make the conflicts of goals and interests between people a *public* affair." Those who engage the risen Christ in this manner thus discover that they become a perpetual question to themselves. All that they had formerly assumed was true, everything that had once appeared good and right and proper in their world, whatever they said or did, is constantly exposed to a new and unexpected light. There are, of course, no guarantees about these engagements. With some, as with the figure of the rich ruler (Luke 18:18–25), the inability to grasp their status as a cherished creature of God "becomes visible and utterable in the form of complicity in rejecting Jesus." With others, as with Zacchaeus (19:1–10), the "readiness to come to judgment and to recognize the possibility of truth and meaning becomes visible and utterable in the form of discipleship, abiding in the community created by God's love."[95]

As I noted in the previous chapter, the love that creates the disciple community should not be confused with cheap sentiment. The sacramental remembering of Christ's body in its social and personal aspects takes place according to well-established patterns attested to in the New Testament. Our baptism is an immersion into the death of Christ (Rom. 6:3–4; cf. Mark 8:34), and the celebration of the Lord's table "always and necessarily operates between the two poles of Maundy Thursday and Easter Sunday, between Gethsemane and Emmaus, between the Upper Room before the crucifixion and the Upper Room to which the risen Jesus comes." Our participation in the life of God in the world occurs in the apocalyptic interval made actual by the eucharistic feast. This gathering continually signifies the restoration of a fellowship broken time and again by human infidelity. The communal practice of discernment, forgiveness, and reconciliation is thus presupposed by this meal. In this meal "the wounded body and the shed blood are inescapably present."[96]

94. John Chrysostom, *Homilies on the Gospel of St. Matthew* 50.4–5.
95. Williams, *On Christian Theology*, 32 (emphasis original).
96. Williams, *Resurrection*, 40.

It is the obligation of each member of Christ's body to make her or his own the intrusion of the wounded body of Jesus into a world that is ordered around a different set of practices and dispositions. As vital as baptism and Eucharist are, they do not by themselves cultivate the habits of life and language that reveal to the world God's messianic regime. The practices of spiritual formation—prayer, confession, the giving and receiving of counsel, forgiveness and reconciliation, fasting, hospitality, and the works of mercy—are a necessary complement to the work of these other constitutive activities of the church, enabling Jesus's followers to embody in their daily lives signs of the ultimate meaning and destiny of creation. It is to these practices of spiritual formation, and especially their interaction with the modes of regulating human conduct promoted by the state and market, that we now turn.

6

HOLY VULNERABLE

Spiritual Formation for a Pilgrim People

You should love God unspiritually, that is, your soul should be unspiritual and stripped of all spirituality.

Meister Eckhart, *Sermon 83*

In an address to the ecumenical conference held in Fanø, Denmark, in August 1934, Dietrich Bonhoeffer posed a key question to the conferees: How does peace come about? Is it the result of international peace treaties, economic investment in developing countries, or universal peaceful rearmament? According to Bonhoeffer, it is through none of these, for they confuse peace with safety: "There is no way to peace along the way of safety. For peace must be dared. It is the great venture. It can never be safe. Peace is the opposite of security." In the end, "Peace means to give oneself altogether to the law of God, wanting no security, but in faith and obedience laying the destiny of the nations in the hand of Almighty God, not trying to direct it for selfish purposes. Battles are won, not with weapons, but with God. They are won where the way leads to the cross."[1]

1. Bonhoeffer, "Church and the Peoples of the World," 307–8.

The great venture of peace is part and parcel of the church's interpretive surmise about human existence as lived in relation to God. As members of Christ's body, Christians are re-membered by the Spirit to serve as a sign to all that in the end peace, rather than conflict, will have the final say and that vulnerability, not security, forms the path leading to that which alone truly deserves the name of peace: "a perfectly ordered and perfectly harmonious fellowship in the enjoyment of God, and of one another in God."[2] Practices that cultivate women and men capable of leading such extraordinary lives while "living fully in the midst of life's tasks, questions, successes and failures, experiences, and perplexities"[3] are among the constitutive activities that establish the Christian community as a distinctive body politic that promotes "its own laws and its own patterns of behavior."[4]

In the first few centuries of the church, those who wished to transfer their allegiance to this new body politic were required to submit to a lengthy and rigorous process lasting three years or more.[5] The extent of their participation in the life of community was carefully circumscribed to protect the mystery of the community from profanation. Those who were not yet baptized were allowed to attend the first part of the liturgy, consisting of readings from Scripture, singing, prayer, and proclamation, but were often dismissed before the Eucharist was celebrated. As the catechumens made progress in practices of reading the Bible, learning the creeds, prayer, hospitality, forgiveness, and reconciliation, which they learned through imitation from those more experienced in the life of virtue, their level of involvement gradually increased. The whole process was taken very seriously, such that men and women could, if their apprenticeship in the catechetical process was deemed insufficient, be denied membership.[6]

Contrast the profundity, rigor, and seriousness of the early church's modes of spiritual formation with what regularly passes for spirituality in our time and place. One popular trend is a custom-designed deity for discriminating modern consumers, most often one that is "a gentle twin of the one they grew up with. He is wise but soft-spoken, cheers them up when they're sad, laughs at their quirks. He is, most essentially, validating, like the greatest of friends. . . . The God they choose is more like a best friend who has endless time for their needs, no matter how trivial."[7] At bookstores and discount

---

2. Augustine, *City of God* 19.17.
3. Bonhoeffer, *Letters and Papers from Prison*, 486.
4. Wilken, *Christians as the Romans Saw Them*, 118–19.
5. Hippolytus, *Treatise on the Apostolic Tradition* 17.28.
6. Navone, *Seeking God in Story*, 14; Budde, *(Magic) Kingdom of God*, 67–68.
7. Rosin, "Beyond 2000," A1.

malls across North America, one can find countless self-help books that claim to help individuals discover their own, true spiritual identity. What these discriminating shoppers of spiritual goods and services finally want to know is, How will following this spiritual path improve my quality of life? Bottom line, what does this deity (or whatever constitutes the object of spiritual attention) do for me?

Both types of spiritual formation are inextricably linked with different habits, appetites, affections, and relationships that specify and enact divergent interpretations of what human life is all about. Each presupposes a distinctive interpretive stance that must be examined in connection with the respective regimes of power that constitute and regulate the social bodies within which each is set. Any discussion of the nature of spiritual formation that fails to consider the institutions and practices that constitute these competing regimes will invariably provide an incomplete and misleading picture.

It lies beyond the scope of the present work to discuss in detail the rich variety of practices of Christian spiritual formation—prayer, confession, fasting, hospitality, the giving and receiving of counsel, rites of forgiveness and reconciliation, and the works of mercy. I concentrate instead on some of the ways these activities, working in concert with the other constitutive practices of the church, help Jesus's followers make the social grammar of the messianic regime of God their own. Within this mode of life our everyday existence begins with the acknowledgment of our vulnerability as creatures, or as the Bible refers to it, the fear of God. This vulnerability is sanctified, made holy, in the incarnation, where the exchange of love between the first two persons of the Trinity opens itself, through the activity of the Spirit, to all creation. As we are caught up in this exchange, we learn to embrace our contingent existence as given to us by the Creator of all, whom we also learn to love as the one who first loved us. The love of God for creation manifested through the incarnation of the Word and the sending-forth of the Spirit, in turn, defines the aim of spirituality as *holy vulnerability*, the concurrence of "'non-grasping' humanity and authentic divine power itself 'made perfect in weakness.'" In the politics of the Spirit, then, vulnerability is scripted not as a stereotypically female weakness but as "a (special sort of) 'human' strength." Perhaps, writes Sarah Coakley, "Jesus may be the male messenger to empty 'patriarchal' values."[8]

The type of vulnerability that I am talking about here is not a self-abnegation but a vulnerability held together, in paradoxical fashion, within "the 'space' in which non-coercive divine power manifests itself."[9] Apart from

8. Coakley, *Powers and Submissions*, 25.
9. Coakley, *Powers and Submissions*, 5.

this "space" within which God is revealed in the suffering and resurrection of Christ, there is nothing holy about the kind of vulnerability that gives rise to the unnecessary and unjust suffering experienced by so many. Moreover, as those caught up in Christ's kenotic vulnerability as pilgrims in this age, we are summoned to solidarity with those persons and groups who are vulnerable to the lust for power and control.

That said (and it must be said repeatedly), if Christian formation is divorced from the social grammar of God's apocalyptic action in Christ, it is stripped of its integrity and purpose and converts into a virulent and idolatrous form of impiety according to which we become both "subject and object of our own quest."[10] Picturing ourselves as the subject and object of our own individual spiritual quests does not mean, however, that our lives have become our own. Who we are and what we do, in public *and* in private, are instead caught up in an economy of desire that is no longer related to any shared set of goods. The social grammar of the earthly city determines not particular acts but the range of possible acts available to us as individuals—that is, as workers and consumers. The control this malformation of the self exercises over us is therefore anonymous and indirect, more akin to seduction than coercion, but precisely for this reason all the more sweeping.

Consumption, Production, and Spiritual Formation

The church of late antiquity knew that if the distinctiveness of its spiritual disciplines from the formative influences of pagan society were compromised, the social space that the body of Christ needed to reproduce itself as a distinctive body politic would at some point collapse in on itself. Just such a contraction gradually occurred in the decades and centuries following the church's accommodation with Rome. Rigorous spiritual formation, which once was expected of everyone, was increasingly restricted to those entering religious orders, with the catechumenate for lay men and women truncated and eventually abandoned. A dual ethic emerged, with the more demanding "evangelical counsels" reserved for members of religious orders and the less demanding "precepts" for everybody else,[11] the latter often little more than "respectable unbelief."[12]

The dual ethic not only fostered the conception that religious orders formed an ascetic elite that achieved perfection through self-denial but paradoxically

10. Bloom, *American Religion*, 217.
11. See, for example, Aquinas, *Summa theologica* I-II.108.4.
12. Yoder, *Royal Priesthood*, 57.

made a way of life consistent with the status and mission of the church as the body of Christ more remote when monasticism was called into question during the age of Reformation. Bonhoeffer argues in this regard that Martin Luther, though an unrelenting critic of this dual standard, unwittingly confirmed Constantine's covenant with the church. He acknowledges that this was of course not what Luther wanted, that with his doctrine of grace he sought a complete ethic for everyone, not just for the religious orders. But when Luther proclaimed the costly grace of the gospel, he had two decades behind him in which he sought to live under the law: "Luther could cry 'grace alone' because he knew Christ as the one who calls to discipleship. What is true as a final consequence is false as a presupposition, and what is obedience as a final consequence is disobedience as a presupposition." As a result, writes Bonhoeffer, a "minimal ethic was victorious," with the existence of the Christian becoming indistinguishable from that of the secular citizen: "Hence now the essence of church invisible. This fundamentally misunderstands the New Testament message. Innerworldliness [is] now no longer possibility but rather has become principle."[13]

A similar situation exists in our time and place, with the existence of the Christian virtually indistinguishable from that of the conspicuous consumer. The formation of members of Christ's body, always a fluid, dynamic, and precarious process centered in the life and worship of the church, has largely been eviscerated by determined competition from powerful institutions and processes that are also interested in shaping human affections, dispositions, and appetites around habits of consumption and the gratification of desire that directly challenge the formation of Christian practices. The aim of these habits is to make people fit for unfettered consumption, and the extent to which they succeed will at the same time make them unfit for discipleship. One need only consider how marketing and advertising transvalue, say, the purchase of an automobile, into a statement about one's perceived identity, be it hip, sophisticated, or macho. The two regimes of moral and intellectual formation, because they seek to form persons to act in accordance with certain social ends, are fundamentally incompatible.[14]

Many in the affluent areas of the world would no doubt find it difficult even to imagine a way of life that does not have as its primary purpose making consumer choices that will guarantee their personal welfare and satisfy their private interests in every sphere allotted to them by the commercial institutions of the earthly city. To be sure, women and men are finite, mortal

13. Bonhoeffer, "Contemporizing New Testament Texts," 432.
14. Budde and Brimlow, *Christianity Incorporated*, 61.

beings, and we must eat, drink, clothe ourselves, secure shelter, till the land, and fashion instruments of all sorts, just to mention a few things. We must, in other words, consume in order to live (and thus we must produce). Far too many of us, however, live instead to consume. The current regime carefully orchestrates day-to-day existence around habits of consumption that no longer serve any higher purpose but have become ends in themselves, to be desired for their own sake. Not only are these habits out of proportion to what human beings need to flourish as creatures made in the image of God; they have largely transformed the nature of our most intimate relationships with other people.

The unchecked ability of capitalism to prescribe what is valuable, innovative, normal, pleasing, and repulsive erects imposing barriers to the formation of habits and convictions that are intrinsic to the body of Christ. In times past certain modes of public demeanor were considered either desirable or not because they were related to accepted standards regulating the common good and therefore there were "proper" and "improper" objects of desire. Communities large and small promoted (if not always achieving) a harmonious polyphony of desire, orchestrated around an accepted hierarchy of goods. In a neoliberal social order, on the other hand, a new economy of desire has been introduced. Unconstrained appetite is emphasized, together with the manipulation and control of this process, forming women and men to see themselves almost exclusively as consumers.[15] A new spiritual order has thus been promoted, or rather the lack of rational order—a cacophony of appetite. In this mode of regulating day-to-day life, to be a person is to be a consumer; virtually everything else is optional to this identity. These options (including making friends, getting married, and having children) are configured as products to be consumed, and the value of every product is determined by its market share—that is, its ability to please the consumer.

We should not be surprised in such circumstances to see spirituality marketed as yet one more commodity, or the selling of commodities as a form of spirituality. It has become a private and inward matter, a type of therapy designed to make one's life more fulfilling, a diet plan for one's soul, as it were, complete with "before" and "after" testimonies.[16] It is now altogether natural to talk about a relationship with God as another good or service for one's personal enjoyment, an effective way to be in harmony with the universe, cope with the stress and confusion of twenty-first-century life, overcome substance abuse, fashion more stable families, enhance one's self-esteem, and in general live more satisfying

---

15. Milbank, *Theology and Social Theory*, 33.
16. A good example of the marketing of spirituality is Moore's *Care of the Soul*.

lives. It is a product, furthermore, that does not require any sort of communal mediation (indeed, that is often explicitly rejected as antithetical to true spirituality) but may be enjoyed in the privacy of one's own home, head, and heart.

Spirituality is not only a commodity or service in a global economy, nor are human beings merely consumers. The capitalist formation of identity and desire also serves an important role in shaping human beings into compliant and efficient workers. The demands of capitalist regimes have always caused a considerable amount of havoc in the lives of women and men, and globalization, with the dispersal of production, finance, and commerce beyond local and national borders, has only intensified these tendencies. Most if not all of the social relations that traditionally defined who people were and what they should do and that mediated their relationship to governing authorities and their neighbors are quickly dissolving. Men and women have been reduced to the status of "individuals," performing a series of functions in accordance with the expectations of the market and under the watchful eye of the sovereign state. Maintaining these units of production is expensive, and thus their time must be kept at an optimum flexibility. Any group or community that might have an impact on their availability—family, neighborhood, ethnic group, church, synagogue, or mosque—represents a potentially disruptive practice, and all ties to them must be loosened or, if possible, severed altogether.

A flexible workforce fit for a global regime, however, exacts a high price in human terms. The employees that remain after repeated downsizings and outsourcings are often overworked, alienated from management, and cynical about their prospects for the future. Corporate firms are thus interested in the potential of spirituality to implant a shared vision and sense of excitement and purpose in the office, behind the counter, and on the shop floor. At the same time, however, they are suspicious of anything as particular and as potentially disruptive as the church. They are willing to work with established religious institutions, provided that those institutions' rituals and beliefs support the firm's goals and work to deepen the loyalty and productivity of the employees. And though many in the corporate spirituality movement claim that their ideas are independent of historic Christian faith, they are nevertheless quite willing to engage in the widespread exploitation of "a variety of Christian concepts, values, and symbols that have been detached and separated from the contexts of believing communities. Notions of transcendence, vocation, and covenant—which for most people in the United States and many Western capitalist countries make little sense apart from the Christian experience—now exist as free-standing but empty categories, to be filled according to the profit and efficiency strategies of corporate managers."[17]

17. Budde and Brimlow, *Christianity Incorporated*, 47–48.

The reconfiguration of spirituality to help make consumers/workers fit for a global market represents a natural extension of civil religion, the purpose of which, as I noted in chapter 4, is contingency management—that is, sacralizing the present social order as divinely sanctioned. For centuries in Europe, Australia, and the Americas, the church provided beliefs, values, ceremonies, and symbols that gave sacred meaning to the body politic of the earthly city, providing a thin Christian veneer that conferred an abiding sense of unity and purpose and transcended all internal conflicts and differences while relating the earthly city's practices and institutions to the realm of ultimate reality.[18] The church's civic responsibility was twofold: to serve as moral conscience and to ameliorate the suffering incurred by those who slipped between the cracks. "The church, in this understanding," says Anthony Robinson, "is a center of civic life, one that provides an avenue by which the most fortunate and powerful can be of help to the less fortunate and least powerful."[19] Concentrating the practice of charity in the hands of the fortunate and powerful is not an accidental feature of modern civil religion, for it grants to the wealthy and influential few the privilege of defining and providing for the common good.[20]

The acute social and economic dislocation associated with global capitalism has only intensified this quandary and acts as a catalyst for political fragmentation. These circumstances have diminished the capacity of states to secure social order, giving rise to ethnic, nationalist, and religious groups that undermine the prerogatives and primacy of the state. Though we typically associate these trends with certain "hot spots" in the world (Africa, the Middle East, Central and South America), they produce a considerable amount of anxiety among the oligarchs in Europe, Australia, and North America. "With capitalism rendering whole segments of American society economically unnecessary," write Michael Budde and Robert Brimlow, citing African American men as a prime example, "politicians and opinion leaders worry about the 'dis-uniting of America,' the collapse of 'public spiritedness,' and the decline of civic virtue as manifested in voting and support for elected officials."[21]

According to Budde and Brimlow, the traditional form of civil religion in the United States, with its recognizable Puritan republican heritage and biblical imagery (city set on a hill, the new Jerusalem, God's chosen people), no longer provides the sort of religious legitimation needed in a globalized setting that is "sufficient, in the words of Voltaire, to keep the servants from stealing the silver, but not the type likely to encourage religious practices and norms at odds with

18. See Linder, "Universal Pastor," 734.
19. Copenhaver, Robinson, and Willimon, *Good News in Exile*, 16.
20. See Long, *Goodness of God*, 249–50.
21. Budde and Brimlow, *Christianity Incorporated*, 14–15.

capitalism, patriotism, or the essentials of the system as presently constituted." The standard reason given is that this sort of religion can no longer account for the experiences of society's excluded—women, minorities, dissenting voices.[22] In other words, a "thick" account of what constitutes a good life, one that is embedded in particular forms of life and contingent social practices, is supposedly too wedded to these particularities to encompass the vast diversity of convictions and values that human beings embrace in today's global village. What is needed is a spirituality that is divorced from social practices that might disrupt attention and take allegiance away from one's loyalty and obligation to the state and market. A personalized piety that is internalized in beliefs, attitudes, and feelings, and not one that is tied to outward observance, will help the powers that be accumulate the social capital, "the stock of social relations and shared values,"[23] that underwrites the unconstrained exercise of self-interest.

Piety, Power, and the Earthly City

The modern sense of the word *spirituality*, emphasizing the inner goings-on of the individual divorced from material issues of the production and reproduction of life, represents a radical shift in meaning from the word's standard usage in the church prior to the twelfth century. Beginning with the Pauline correspondence in the New Testament, the Greek adjective *pneumatikos*, often translated "spiritual," was associated with *pneuma*, the Spirit whom the early Christians proclaimed was in Jesus and who was also the gift of the risen Christ to his followers. A spiritual person was someone whose whole way of acting in and relating to the world was under the influence of the Holy Spirit, and thus one who manifested the presence of the Spirit in the world. He or she was therefore not somebody who shunned the material world of time and space, but one in whom the Spirit dwelt, one who was engendered and empowered by God. *Spirituality*, accordingly, did not refer to a property that one possessed or a discrete facet of one's private inner life, but to a pattern of personal growth and maturation that took place within the community of those who had been gathered together by the risen Lord "to be a kingdom and priests serving our God" (Rev. 5:10). It was associated with the active presence of Christ through the work of the Spirit as the source and power of the Christian life, and not with the cultivation of extraordinary inner experiences, though of course it involved a range of affections, desires, and loves.[24]

22. Budde and Brimlow, *Christianity Incorporated*, 16.
23. Budde and Brimlow, *Christianity Incorporated*, 19.
24. Sheldrake, *Spirituality and History*, 42–43.

Spiritual formation in the early church thus found its occasion and significance in the radical restructuring of bodily life and language brought about by the intrusion of God's messianic regime into a fallen world. The task set before each believer by this intrusion, writes Rowan Williams, is to make "his or her own that engagement with the questioning at the heart of faith which is so evident in the classical documents of Christian belief." This process of interrogation has little in common with fashionable notions about the relative nature of all human endeavors, nor does it encourage romantic sentiments about persons who, while half-believing, withhold assent from all commitments in order to preserve their moral and intellectual autonomy. "The question involved here," Williams insists, "is not our interrogation of the data, but its interrogation of us. It is the *strangeness* of the ground of belief that must constantly be allowed to challenge the fixed assumptions of religiosity; it is a *given*, whose question to each succeeding age is fundamentally one and the same. And the greatness of the great Christian saints lies in their readiness to be questioned, judged, stripped naked and left speechless by that which lies at the center of their faith."[25]

The goal of this lifelong process of spiritual allocution and interpellation, of "being unmade to be remade,"[26] is to be fully incorporated into the mystery of God's will, hidden from the foundation of the world but now revealed in Christ (Eph. 1:9–10), gathering together all things and inaugurating in the midst of the conflict and violence of the present age an alternative history for all creation that is reestablished through redemptive suffering.[27] When considered from this standpoint, Jesus's faithfulness brings about the inbreaking of the long-awaited reign of God, and with it the initial rhythms and harmonies of a new creation and new humanity manifested in the church's polyphony of life. In and through the ecclesial practices of prayer, fasting, confession, and the like, the Spirit draws women and men from every tribe, nation, language, and people into Christ's body, a process that culminates with their participation in his dying and, in the age to come, in his rising.

In this ecclesial context, prayer and contemplation are not divorced from theological reflection. In the words of Evagrius of Pontus, "If you are a theologian, you will pray truly; and if you pray truly, you will be a theologian."[28] Research, study, argument, and reflection on God and his ways with the world thus "find their source and their completion only in prayer."[29] Rigorous theo-

---

25. Williams, *Wound of Knowledge*, 1 (emphasis original).
26. Williams, *Wound of Knowledge*, 8, 13.
27. See Milbank, "Second Difference," 227.
28. *Evagrius of Pontus*, 199.
29. Torrell, *Saint Thomas Aquinas*, 1:157.

logical inquiry, rightly conceived, comprises "an aspect of the mystical journey by means of which God is leading creatures back into unity with the divine life. Theology is the attempt to notice how this is happening, to articulate the stages of the community's journey, to point ahead to the One who alone could mystically arouse the uplifting ecstasy that always leads beyond." *Spirituality*, if we wish to retain this term at all, pertains properly to the impression made by the encounter with God that takes place within the new network of communal relationship and perception that is provided by the church as the fellowship of the Spirit.[30]

The erosion of this sense of what it means to be spiritual may be traced to the convergence of a number of factors that emerged over a period of several hundred years and began to coalesce during the high Middle Ages. According to Colin Morris's classic account, eucharistic practice shifted during the eleventh and twelfth centuries from a communal emphasis to a mode of devotion focused on the inner experience of the individual. Confessional practices began to emphasize the importance of self-examination, with a growing distinction between public penance and the inner sorrow that marked true repentance, the latter being that which God most valued. A new interest in and study of the inner workings of the soul emerged during this time, with an awareness of the degree to which a variety of motivations, affections, and appetites were involved in an individual's spiritual progress. Pronounced shifts in the doctrines of salvation and eschatology also exerted an influence, as patristic descriptions of Christ's cosmic triumph over death, the devil, and sin were supplanted by a preoccupation with the pains of Christ in his passion. Finally, the hope of the Christian shifted from the gathering-together of all things in Christ to a concern with the fate of the individual after death.[31]

It is not surprising, then, that beginning around the twelfth century the idea of *spiritualitas* began to have new connotations. Leading the way was a new philosophical trend among medieval scholastic theologians, who began to use this term to refer to what pertains to the soul as contrasted with the body, which was part of a sharper distinction between "spirit" and "matter" or "body." The adjective *spiritualis* was increasingly applied to intelligent creatures (that is, human beings) as opposed to nonrational beings, with the effect of vacating its Pauline moral sense and taking on a meaning "more radically opposed to corporeality."[32] Though for a time this new sense stood

30. McIntosh, *Mystical Theology*, 6–7, 56.

31. Morris, *Discovery of the Individual, 1050–1200*, 12, 47, 70–79, 139–52; see also McIntosh, *Mystical Theology*, 64–65; McGinn, "Love, Knowledge, and Mystical Union in Western Christianity," 7–24.

32. Sheldrake, *Spirituality and History*, 43.

side by side with its former meaning, says Bernard McGinn, there is little doubt that scholasticism helped to give birth to "conceptions of spirituality which willy-nilly used it as the reason for giving the physical world and especially the human body a largely negative role in what they conceived of as authentic Christian life."[33] Thus began a privatizing tendency in the history of spirituality in the church, with increasing emphasis placed on the interior state of the soul and especially on how one achieved ever-more-refined stages of inner purity and exaltation.[34]

As *spiritualitas* became restricted to a person's private, interior life, it also was divorced from the intellectual concerns of theology, such that fewer and fewer were competent to integrate spirituality and theological inquiry in their own lives.[35] "How few of them are saints," complains Denys the Carthusian in the fifteenth century, "Thomas [Aquinas] and but few others."[36] This stands in marked contrast to the church fathers, writes Hans Urs von Balthasar, who had at their disposal "all the rational methods of distinguishing and defining for the clarification of concepts; they were used in the fierce controversies with heretics, both by individual theologians and by councils. But . . . these methods were not the determining factor in the construction of their theology. Even polemical works such as Irenaeus's *Adversus Haereses*, Athanasius's *Contra Arianos*, Hilary's *De Trinitate*, Gregory of Nyssa's *Contra Eunomium* were embedded in a spiritual, sapiential setting which became more and more pronounced as the decisive element."[37] A drastic revision of the concept of intellect was thus taking place, one that would drive a deep wedge between the rational and affective aspects of the soul. As Denys Turner says of this development, it was widely thought that "if we are to enter into the true 'mystical' darkness of the divine, then the intellectual knowledge of the philosopher has to be set aside in order to leave room for the God of faith, known, it is said, not by intellect, but by love. For *amor ipse notitia est*, love is itself a kind of knowing, of which intellect can know nothing."[38]

The erosion of the ecclesial context that had secured the continuity of theology and spiritual formation did not, however, occur in a social vacuum. It was connected with institutional changes, including a significant shift in the setting for learning, from the monastery to the cathedral school and university.

33. McGinn, "Letter and the Spirit," 3.
34. McIntosh, *Mystical Theology*, 7.
35. McIntosh, *Mystical Theology*, 63.
36. Denys the Carthusian, *Difficultatum Praecipuarum Absolutiones* a5, cited in Turner, *Faith, Reason and the Existence of God*, 77.
37. Balthasar, *Word Made Flesh*, 214.
38. Turner, *Faith, Reason and the Existence of God*, 77–78; see also Turner, *Darkness of God*, 186–273; Coakley, *Powers and Submissions*, 78–82.

In the monasteries the course of theological study had been concerned with the preparation of students for discerning the hidden depth of the Bible. According to Jean Leclercq, the purpose of reading the classical texts of Greek and Roman antiquity was "to educate young Christians, future monks, to 'introduce' them to Sacred Scripture and guide them toward heaven by way of *grammatica*. To put them in contact with the best models would, at one and the same time, develop their taste for the beautiful, their literary subtlety, as well as their moral sense."[39]

In the cathedral schools and universities, by contrast, there was a revival of interest in the liberal arts in the ninth and eleventh centuries, and these arts were applied directly to the interpretation of sacred Scripture.[40] The relationship between the study of Scripture and the liberal arts was gradually reversed, initiating a movement that, when combined with the rise to prominence of dialectical inquiry and scholastic disputation, diverted attention away from the monastic maintenance of spiritual life in the company of friends and toward more technical inquiries and secular applications involving the "literature" and "history" of the past.[41] Though not yet a situation in which rational inquiry was completely severed from a concern for the spiritual life, a gradual dissociation took place as new "masters of the divine books" and "doctors of the sacred page" began to exercise a magisterial authority over the reading of Scripture that became more and more desacralized.

According to Henri de Lubac, these learned scholars became "professors of Sacred Scripture" and "university men" before their time. Students crowded around their mentors not as monks did after their work to hear the *collatio* of their abbot, a practice set within the framework of the daily office, but as those eager to see who would triumph in whatever *disputatio* was taking place. And though they did manage to accumulate more scientific knowledge, they were also prone to a greater spirit of disquiet: "How many of them seek to be taught only with a view to making a career and have already begun their drive to achieve honors! . . . It is the rising tide of 'science' in the almost modern sense of the word that pushes aside humble spiritual commentary as belonging to inferior stages of growth."[42] The seeds that would later blossom into the divorce of theological inquiry from the work of spiritual formation began to be sown in these new educational institutions as early as the ninth century.

39. Leclercq, *Love of Learning and the Desire for God*, 149.
40. See Evans, *Old Arts and New Theology*.
41. De Lubac, *Medieval Exegesis*, 55; Sheldrake, *Spirituality and History*, 39–40; cf. Sheehan, *Enlightenment Bible*.
42. De Lubac, *Medieval Exegesis*, 49.

The shift from "humble spiritual commentary" to "scientific" approaches to Scripture exemplifies the altered relationship between spirituality and theology in the late medieval setting. It played a significant role in the general demise of the kind of theological hermeneutics practiced by the church fathers, who sought to catch a glimpse of the beauty of truth itself in a world spoken by God. As this tradition of reading Scripture and the world was replaced by more "modern" forms of interpretation in medieval academies, the close relationship between the *signa* of the world and the *signa* of Scripture also began to unravel, imperceptibly at first, and then more quickly as the world moved into the sixteenth century. Together with the rise of late medieval nominalism, which combined "a highly sophistical analysis of given theological propositions with a deep skepticism about the human mind's capacity to abstract beyond the immediate data of sense experience,"[43] the separation of scholastic and mystical theology was all but secured.

Gender may have also played a role in the redirection of spirituality to the interior lives of individuals. Grace Jantzen notes that when the preeminent representatives of theology were predominantly male and frequently occupied important ecclesiastical offices (Augustine, Gregory the Great, and Bernard of Clairvaux), spiritual formation was embraced as central to the public life and essential to the practice of the church. As more and more women became prominent in the field, it came to be thought of as a strictly private matter, something that was susceptible to "hysteria" and thus to be kept separate from the public life of the church, particularly in its role within the political structures of Christendom. "It was only with the development of the secular state," Jantzen writes, "when religious experience was no longer perceived as a source of knowledge and power, that it became safe to allow women to be mystics." With spirituality safely sequestered in the realm of the private and personal, having little or nothing to do with the public realm in general and politics in particular, it was possible to see such matters as "compatible with a woman's role."[44]

In any event, by the time of Teresa of Ávila (1515–82), the movements that made up the interior drama of the soul were elevated to institute a momentous hermeneutical shift within the late medieval church. Michel de Certeau rightly notes that prior to the sixteenth century the world was "perceived as *spoken by God.*" A tacit sacramentality to the world thus supplied the interpretive key for understanding it in the context of God's apocalyptic activity. But by the sixteenth century that perception had largely dissipated, and the material

---

43. Williams, *Wound of Knowledge*, 140.

44. Jantzen, *Power, Gender and Christian Mysticism*, 326; cf. McIntosh, *Mystical Theology*, 63–64; Coakley, *Powers and Submissions*, 50.

world had "become opacified, objectified, and detached from its supposed speaker." The refined feelings and ecstatic experiences of the inner self became the site for glimpsing the beauty of truth in place of the more public speech of God in the created order. "This *I* who speaks in the place of (and instead of) the Other," says Certeau, "also requires a *space* of expression corresponding to what the world was in relation to the speech of God."[45]

In effect the focus of the doctrine of transubstantiation had shifted from the bread and wine on the altar to the individual's thoughts and feelings. Teresa's "interior castle," says McIntosh, "becomes the imaginal realm in which the divine speech can still be heard, but now the language of that speech is constituted by the inner movements of the soul. The soul itself is 'but the inarticulate echo of an unknown Subject,' thus it needs a dramatic imaginary inner stage upon which to act out and narrate the mysterious and inexpressible touch of 'Unknownness.'"[46] The inner movements of the soul, its mind, and especially its memory were no longer viewed as *vestigia trinitatis*,[47] footprints of the Trinity, but were seen as the last refuge for the divine in a world no longer grounded in mystery. In the process the "contemplative" became a solitary figure, a "professional," as it were, in spiritual matters. He or she "recedes, introverts, 'abstracts,' from normal practical reasoning for his [or her] own particular purposes in relation to God."[48]

This new conception of spirituality presupposes the invention of detached personal identity, important elements of which Nicholas Boyle traces to a highly formalized technology of the self developed by the fourteenth-century erotic mysticism known as the *devotio moderna*. The economic relations that were being instituted at that time eventually led to the creation of the bourgeois class in the city-states of Italy, Germany, and the Hanseatic League. Underwriting the development of this new regime of accumulation was the creation of a system of monetary exchange, banking, and bookkeeping practices that distinguished for the first time between capital and income. "Money is the great leveler," Boyle notes, since "cash from a prince is no better than cash from a pastry cook."[49] The rise of a system of monetary exchange fueled tension between the ideas of the new, politically unemancipated bourgeoisie and the feudal rulers who saw themselves in terms of the great structure of medieval theology and anthropology.

45. Certeau, *Mystic Fable*, 188 (emphasis original).
46. McIntosh, *Mystical Theology*, 69; the embedded quotations are from Certeau, *Mystic Fable*, 188–89.
47. Augustine, *Trinity* 6.10, 213.
48. Coakley, *Powers and Submissions*, 82.
49. Boyle, *Who Are We Now?*, 156; cf. Sheldrake, *Spirituality and History*, 51–52.

According to Boyle, the creation of a money economy was a necessary step toward forgetting that human beings are of creaturely necessity producers occupying a specific place within a mode of production, and not detached egos but participants in a larger story. The mystics of the *devotio moderna*, with their systematic methods of prayer and meditation, prompted this self-induced amnesia by conceiving of a detached self-identity as a universal possibility and by imagining a state of consumption without production that was in principle accessible to all and thus not tied to a particular class in the feudal order: "The mystic has glimpsed a fulfillment of humanity which is outside time, that is, outside the productive nexus, and best imagined as boundless, but personal enjoyment." Under the influence of this picture, women and men learned to imagine themselves no longer as apprentices who must learn and grow as they make their way through life but as selves born complete and mature into the world, magically endowed with both economic and intellectual capital, ready to make consumer choices about material and spiritual goods without first having produced something or concerning themselves about those who do produce products or provide services to be consumed.[50]

An ironic twist in the plot of this story occurred in the late seventeenth century with the condemnation of the allegedly quietist teachings of French spiritual writer Madame Guyon. Her exhortation to radical resignation and disconnection from the external world not only reinforced the drift of spirituality toward a preoccupation with interior states of consciousness but also gave rise to the suspicion within the Catholic church that the whole topic of spirituality was "too refined, rarified and separated from ordinary Christian life,"[51] most especially the sacraments and the teaching authority of the church. Partly in reaction to Guyon and others, a new theoretical discourse developed that sought to order the individual's struggle for inner perfection in properly orthodox ways. To aid this theorization, inspired in part by the neo-scholastic obsession with good order and detailed classification, a new terminology emerged. The term *mystical theology* was commandeered from Pseudo-Dionysius and pressed into service to describe the novel sense of spirituality. According to Mark McIntosh,

> Whereas for [Pseudo-Dionysius] the term referred to the "knowledge" disclosed to Christians as they themselves are known and transformed by the unknowable God, now it comes to be used as a technical term for theoretical teaching about the soul's process of sanctification. Here was a double irony, for just as Madame Guyon's language about the utter *resignation* of the self was in fact

50. Boyle, *Who Are We Now?*, 154, 156–57; cf. Coakley, *Powers and Submissions*, 86.
51. Sheldrake, *Spirituality and History*, 43.

an elaborate *rhetoric* of the self, so what might have seemed a turn away from this perspective (to the supposedly more scientific "mystical theology") turns out to be a new and ever more baroque *technology of the self.*[52]

We should not, however, lay blame for the privatization of spirituality solely at the feet of Rome. The Protestant Reformation contributed its fair share to this radical reorientation of spirituality, beginning with Luther's division of every human being into an inner and outer person, the former standing solely before God (*coram Deo*) in conscience and the latter in the historical sequence of particular acts, as one stands before one's fellow human beings (*coram hominibus*). He writes in his famous essay on the freedom of the Christian that human beings have a twofold nature, one spiritual and the other bodily. The spiritual nature is no longer that which has to do with the Spirit, but that which is juxtaposed over against the body—that is, the "spiritual, inner, or new man." The bodily nature is the "carnal, outward, or old man." And though it is true that "in the sight of men a man is made good or evil by his work," we must take care not to think that in doing these works we are "justified before God by them, for faith, which alone is righteousness before God, cannot endure that erroneous opinion."[53]

With his division of the human being into two natures, Luther consolidates the late medieval interiorization and individualization of faith. A hard-and-fast dichotomy between faith and works became the norm in Protestant spirituality, such that "law" (in virtually any sense of the term) and "works" are by definition outside of grace. Nevertheless, keeping the law and doing good works are necessary to the maintenance of the earthly city if not to true faith. Separate spheres of life are therefore isolated, one for each of the two natures. The temporal world, where goods and services are bought and sold, rewards and punishments are meted out, wars are fought and enemies subjected, and women and men are forced to seek their own individual interests, can now be understood *etsi deus non daretur*, even if God does not exist. The present age does not depend on the irruption of God in Jesus Christ into the world for its meaning, nor does the latter add anything of substance to it; the spiritual world of hidden faith has little or nothing to add to the course of the temporal world, save, of course, for the general sentiment that the temporal world, too, is ultimately subject to the sovereignty of God.

The seeds of Luther's division of the human being into two discrete selves germinated in the Puritan piety of the seventeenth and eighteenth centuries.

---

52. McIntosh, *Mystical Theology*, 8 (emphasis original).

53. Luther, *Freedom of a Christian*, 278, 295, 298. Boyle contends that so-called Cartesian dualism is more properly attributed to Luther. Boyle, *Who Are We Now?*, 158.

According to Charles Taylor, the English Puritans thoroughly rejected the medieval conception of contemplation, in which matters of the "spirit" are reserved for those in religious communities and thus divorced from everyday life, "i.e., those aspects of human life concerned with production and reproduction."[54] Their rejection of contemplation in favor of everyday life entails a commitment to social leveling and to the belief that the good life is something that everyone can achieve. The virtues of commerce and the knowledges that serve the new regime of capitalist accumulation displace those that attended the medieval hierarchical ordering of society. A new conception of vocation develops that is no longer connected to the priesthood or monastery but that sanctifies any kind of employment deemed useful and imputed to use by God. All such callings are thus equal, and one's participation in them is to be judged not by the activity itself, because the temporal sphere is relatively autonomous, but by "the *spirit* in which one lives what everyone lives, even the most mundane existence." We both trivialize and corrupt the theological concept of vocation—which in Scripture pertains to Jesus's call to follow him, a calling that never steps out from under the shadow of the cross—when we use it in association with neoliberalism's conception of the common good: security, wealth, and the opportunity to generate more of both.

Taylor also contends that the Puritans set aside virtually all practices of mediation for the spiritual life, rejecting the traditional view that the power of God is more intensely present in certain holy places, times, and persons. Now each person "stands alone in relation to God: his or her fate—salvation or damnation—is separately decided." Redemption thus reconceived is the exclusive provenance of God, and the traditional role of the church as the mediator of God's salvific work in the world is effectively vacated. Personal commitment becomes the sole determining factor: "Salvation by faith thus not only reflected a theological proposition about the inanity of human works but also reflected the new sense of the crucial importance of personal commitment. One no longer belonged to the saved, to the people of God, by one's connection to a wider order sustaining a sacramental life, but by one's wholehearted personal adhesion."[55]

The isolation of one's true, interior life of faith from the life and activity of the body (both individual and ecclesial), perpetuating the fiction of the detached personal identity, produces a sense of the self unfettered by social and geographical ties. The illusion that we can substantially cut ourselves loose from the familial and communal relations of accountability into which

54. Taylor, *Sources of the Self*, 211.
55. Taylor, *Sources of the Self*, 216–17.

we were born and which nurtured us over the years and fashion our lives according to self-selected scripts is one of the most tragic aspects of our present predicament. As poet Micheal O'Siadhail laments,

> Freedom. We sang of freedom
> (travel lightly, anything goes)
> and somehow we became strangers
> to each other, like gabblers
> at cross purposes, builders of Babel.[56]

What the modern world initially promoted as a quest toward freedom turned out instead to have been "an adventure that held the seeds of its own destruction within itself, within its attenuated definition of human nature and its inadequate vision of human destiny. What we got was not self-freedom but self-centeredness, loneliness, superficiality, and harried consumerism."[57] The result of our impiety has not been the freedom from others and from nature that we were promised, but confusion, frustration, cynicism, despair, and alienation. The sweet savor of liberty for which we longed has left the bitter taste of falsehood in our mouths. The more vigorously we sought our freedom, the more thoroughly we enslaved ourselves, our neighbors, and the whole of creation within the techniques, instruments, and structures that we devised to facilitate our emancipation.

The Politics of the Spirit and the Art of Vulnerability

In contrast to the self-centeredness, loneliness, superficiality, and harried consumerism endemic to the modern quest for freedom, the significance of Jesus's activity and passion can be grasped only in the generative context that the Holy Spirit shapes and directs within the body of Christ. The gift of the Spirit, though it cannot be contained by any created thing, constitutes and animates the ecclesial community of faith, creating and sustaining a people who offer to the world a different kind of existence in which relations misshapen by death and sin are transfigured into patterns of life and wholeness. It is in the Spirit that women and men learn that God's address to the world in Christ is ultimately a word of redemption, that life and not death is the goal of creation. Spiritual formation, therefore, is inseparable from the politics of the Spirit.

56. O'Siadhail, "Freedom," 117.
57. Hauerwas and Willimon, *Resident Aliens*, 50.

Though the reference to the Holy Spirit is consistent with the subject of spirituality, linking it with politics might come as a surprise to many of us, accustomed as we are to the notion that spirituality is strictly a private matter, having principally to do with our interior lives. When one looks closely at the consistent witness of the Scriptures, however, this reaction itself seems curiously out of place, for the generative images that typically describe the activity of God and the response of human beings in both the Old and New Testaments are almost exclusively political images. The fact that many find the predominance of political images in the Bible strange is itself revealing, disclosing more about who we are and how we deal with the world than perhaps any other aspect of modern life.

The principal locus of the Spirit's activity in the New Testament is not the individual believer but the gathered community of disciples. Salvation does not consist of Christ rescuing isolated souls from life's traumas by recruiting them for an otherworldly existence, but of the Holy Spirit adding to the *koinōnia* (a standard term in the political vocabulary of Paul's day) of Christ's body, the church. As a fruit of the Spirit's labors in creation, it is the church (and not heaven as such) that stands in tension with the world. In short, the church—the community of peace and reconciliation, the city of redemption from the powers and rulers of the present age—is the goal of God's saving work in creation. Who Christians are as individuals, therefore, both derives from and contributes to our involvement in this communion, this commonwealth, which is the body politic of Christ.

The term *politics in the Spirit*, says William Stringfellow, "refers comprehensively to the total configuration of relationships among humans and institutions and other principalities and the rest of created life in this world." It names both the arena of God's mysterious activity in this world, the infinite self-giving that is the triune Godhead enacted in time and space in Christ's passion and triumph, and the impact of the divine presence and power "upon the fallen existence of this world, including the fallen life of human beings and that of the powers that be. Politics points to the militance of the Word of God incarnate, which pioneers the politics of the Kingdom which is to come." Spiritual formation in this context has to do with "*a reiteration of the act of creation in the Word of God* . . . renewing human life (and all of created life) in the midst of the era of the fall, or during the present darkness, in which the power of death apparently reigns."[58]

Spiritual formation for the members of Christ's earthly-historical body is therefore set firmly in the political context of God's apocalyptic regime.

58. Stringfellow, *Politics of Spirituality*, 25–26, 30 (emphasis added).

There is of course an intensely personal dimension to this discipline, but it is neither at the outset nor in the end a private matter. Spiritual formation is an ecclesial affair, intersecting with every aspect and every concern of life. No field of human endeavor and inquiry stands outside its purview, because our quest for God is not one quest alongside all the others—personal relations; social policies; relations of production, accumulation, and consumption; scientific research; literature; music; and art—which human beings undertake.[59] Spiritual formation impinges on all these areas, not to dictate to them how to go about their business but to help us follow the concrete ways these activities link together the events that make up the rhythms and harmonies of our day-to-day existence and that direct us toward God.

The politics of the Spirit begins with the fear of God, which takes hold of us, says Martin Buber, when the whole of our existence between birth and death becomes incomprehensible and uncanny.[60] Only when we have accepted deep down (in our bones, so to speak) that we do not hold the deed to our own lives, nor to anything or anyone else in the world, can the habits and relations of life that echo the rhythms of God's own internal self-giving relations begin to take shape in our lives. The fear of God entails accepting our existence as *gift*, and to accept this is to come face-to-face with our contingency, our vulnerability as creatures. And from this fact, says Nicholas Lash, "nothing follows. Here we are. This is how things are. That's it. No safety belts, no metacosmic maps or guidebooks, no mental cradles for our 'ultimate' security."[61]

At the outset of our apprenticeship in the Spirit's discipline, then, we discover that our existence resides in incomprehensible, ineffable mystery. This is not, writes Buber, "the relative mystery of that which is inaccessible only to the present state of human knowledge and is hence in principle discoverable. It is the essential mystery, the inscrutableness of which belongs to its very nature; it is the unknowable."[62] The mystery eludes all categories of our understanding and shatters every form of security that we devise to protect ourselves from the vulnerability implied in the world's giftedness. Consequently, there are no experts in the knowledge of matters divine, for the God who, according to Scripture, knows us in Jesus Christ is unknowable as such, "the You that in accordance with its nature cannot become an It."[63] There is, however, a spiritual art to living with the mystery, and the aim of this art is holy vulnerability.

59. Lash, *Theology on the Way to Emmaus*, 8–12.
60. Buber, *Eclipse of God*, 36.
61. Lash, *Believing Three Ways in One God*, 39.
62. Buber, *Eclipse of God*, 36.
63. Buber, *I and Thou*, 123.

The spiritual art of vulnerability presents a fundamental challenge to the prevailing ethos of state and market, which requires the identification of a discrete and secure "subject" as the proper locus of choice and action, a subject whose intellectual appetite is governed by the desire to own, use, and then dispose of what is known.[64] This subject (which can be a person or an institution such as a corporation, an army, or a nation-state) designates "a *place* that can be delimited as its *own* and serve as the base from which relations with an *exteriority* composed of targets or threats . . . can be managed. As in management, every 'strategic' rationalization seeks first of all to distinguish its 'own' place, that is, the place of its own power and will, from an 'environment.'"[65] Scholars give the name of instrumental rationality to this sort of strategic calculation of power. Though it involves complex forms of reasoning, instrumental rationality is, very simply, a way of coping with the world that continually strives to subject all things, even life itself, to its control. In striving for control, instrumental reasoning recognizes no boundaries, acknowledges no limitations, encounters no mystery, and allows no exemptions from its all-embracing quest for mastery. No *thing* lies outside the scope of its calculating gaze, including the divine.

On the long trek through time toward the world to come, by contrast, we must learn that the nature of the mystery that accounts not only for our existence as human beings but for the world as a whole is shrouded in impenetrable darkness. God is not an object, a thing or person that we can encounter, identify, categorize, compare, and contrast along with all the other things and persons that make up the world. *What* God is will forever remain unknown to us. In the words of Dante,

> For, trusting to man's reason, mad is he
> who hopes to plumb the endless ways of those
> three Persons in substantial unity.

> Be satisfied with "*so it is,*" O Man,
> for if you could have known the whole design,
> Mary would not have had to bear a son.[66]

Our most adequate analogy for conceiving of our relation to the unknown God is provided by intimate human relationships, which exhibit a mysterious nature in their own right. When we meet people for the first time, we normally begin the process of getting to know them by gathering information about

64. Griffiths, *Intellectual Appetite*, 140–43.
65. Certeau, *Practice of Everyday Life*, xix, 35–37 (emphasis added).
66. Dante, *Purgatory* 3.34–39.

them: where they work, whether they are married, how many children they have, from what part of the world they come, where they went to school, and so on. In other words, we relate to them, for the most part, as one more object or thing in the world. But as we get to know them better, as we begin to acquire a shared history with each other, as the stories that narrate the plot of our lives become increasingly intertwined, such information, while still a factor in the relationship, moves into the background. As this common history develops, friends and family can no longer be identified by simply referring to the aforementioned list of facts; they become more complex, harder to describe, possessing a depth not seen at first. The closer we are to people, writes Lash, "and the better we understand them, the more they evade our cognitive 'grasp' and the greater the difficulty that we experience in giving adequate expression to our understanding. Other people become, in their measure, 'mysterious,' not insofar as we *fail* to understand them, but rather insofar as, in lovingly relating to them, we succeed in doing so."[67]

The fear of God is therefore not a permanent dwelling place of postmodern despair to which we are condemned, but as Buber expresses it, a "dark gate" through which we move into the everyday, which is where we address the dilemmas and delights of our existence before God. Once a person crosses this threshold, it is the embodied reality of day-to-day life, not the private recesses of the individual heart, that is "henceforth hallowed as the place in which he has to live with the mystery. . . . That the believing man who goes through the gate of dread is directed to the concrete contextual situations of his existence means just this: that he endures in the face of God the reality of lived life, dreadful and incomprehensible though it be. He loves it in the love of God, whom he has learned to love."[68] We human beings must, in other words, begin in the concreteness and vulnerability of our own existence, with all its uncertainty and uncanniness. Only then are we in a position to grasp the divine act of creation and redemption as the overflow of intertrinitarian love and, as a consequence of being taken up into the divine exchange of love through our communal praise and adoration, are we able to love.

In a fallen and rebellious creation, foreboding evils deepen the darkness that attends the mystery: disease, war, hunger, cruelty, and abuse, the mere threat of which affects our daily lives in innumerable ways. And then for all things comes death, the single most determinative aspect of our creaturely existence. In the words of Pope John Paul II, the "daily experience of suffering—in one's own life and in the lives of others—and the array of facts which seem

---

67. Lash, *Easter in Ordinary*, 236.
68. Buber, *Eclipse of God*, 36–37.

inexplicable to reason are enough to ensure that a question as dramatic as the question of meaning cannot be evaded. Moreover, the first absolutely certain truth of our life, beyond the fact that we exist, is the inevitability of our death. Given this unsettling fact, the search for a full answer is inescapable."[69] It is not surprising, then, that so many Christians are tempted to bypass this first step and move straight to the comfort afforded by an affirmation of God's love. "The essence of the American," writes Harold Bloom, "is the belief that God loves her or him, a conviction shared by nearly nine out of ten of us, according to a Gallup poll."[70]

As with most forms of temptation, however, this is one we should avoid, for as Buber observes, the one "who begins with the love of God without having previously experienced the fear of God, loves an idol which he himself has made, a god whom it is easy enough to love."[71] Thus we must return often to the Bible's scripting of spiritual maturity as a holy vulnerability and to the divine love that Scripture describes as fierce and all-consuming, which would have us sacrifice our lives and even those of our children, a love that presupposes rather than replaces the fear of God as the point of departure for the polyphony of life in Christ. But without this gut-level grasp of just how fragile and besieged, how insecure and out of control human life really is, the wisdom and wholeness that characterize spiritual maturity will lie forever beyond our reach.

This is not to say that the fear of God is somehow in opposition to love for God. The point is rather that it makes sense to speak of loving God only when the relationship between God and ourselves is already well established, when we love God for who God is and not as we might want him to be. "What is needed above all else," says Augustine, "is to be converted by the fear of God to wishing to know his will, what he bids us seek and shun. Now this fear of necessity shakes us with thoughts of our mortality and of our death to come, and so to say nails our flesh and fixes all the stirrings of pride to the wood of the cross." Together with the meekness that comes with piety, he writes, the fear of God teaches us to heed the commandment in Scripture that "God is to be loved on God's account, and one's neighbor on God's account."[72]

The fear of God is also a protest against a spirituality without suffering, which assumes that God calls men and women into being and into communion apart from the pain and distress of the world. Spirituality without suffering and conflict has to do with the gods of this world, not the God of Jesus Christ.

69. John Paul II, *Fides et Ratio*, 40.
70. Bloom, *American Religion*, 17.
71. Buber, *Eclipse of God*, 36.
72. Augustine, *Teaching Christianity* 2.7.

As I noted in chapter 3, the cross comes about because of the kind of world we have made for ourselves, a world bent not toward God but toward violence and death. Crucifixion is what happens to human beings when they are faithful to God rather than to the rulers of the present age. Forms of piety that leave us feeling safe, sated, and secure do not share in the messianic suffering of God but are rooted in the deceptions of the present age.

Holy vulnerability, however, should never be confused with a fatalistic acceptance of the status quo. As Buber notes, the fact that in the fear of God "one accepts the concrete situation as given to him does not, in any way, mean that he must be ready to accept that which meets him as 'God-given' in its pure factuality. He may, rather, declare the extremest enmity toward this happening and treat its 'givenness' as only intended to draw forth his own opposing force. But he will not remove himself from the concrete situation as it actually is; he will, instead, enter into it, even if in the form of fighting against it."[73] Bonhoeffer expresses something similar in a meditation on the petition "thy Kingdom come" in the Lord's prayer:

> Praying for the kingdom cannot be done by the one who tears himself away from his own misery and that of others, who lives unattached and solely in the pious hours of his "own salvation." . . . The hour in which the church prays for the kingdom today forces the church, for better or worse, to identify completely with the fellowship of the children of the Earth and world. It binds the church by oaths of fealty to the Earth, to misery, to hunger, to death. It renders the church completely in solidarity with that which is evil and with the guilt of their brothers. The hour in which we pray today for God's kingdom is the hour of the most profound solidarity with the world, an hour of clenched teeth and trembling fists.[74]

The hope that is ours in Christ, in other words, does not deny the darkness that casts its shroud over the present order of things, but neither does it succumb to that despair that is finally the worship of necessity.

We must therefore never confuse Christ's acceptance of suffering, nor his insistence that his disciples must follow him down this same path, with passivity in the face of it. Abuse and suffering are endured in hope of the new creation, relying on whatever God may will, "and this," says Williams, "is preeminently the gift of the Spirit." Our suffering is conformed to the pattern of Christ "by the presence of the same Spirit of protest, trust and hope." The follower of Christ "meets pain in acceptance and *hope*; he or she confronts

73. Buber, *Eclipse of God*, 37–38; see also Lash, *Believing Three Ways in One God*, 108.
74. Bonhoeffer, "Thy Kingdom Come!," 289.

it, identifies with those experiencing it, and then struggles through it to grow into new humanness, more capable both of pain and of love. . . . The Spirit is the 'pledge,' the Spirit is that which more and more conforms to Christ; and so the Spirit is that which impels us forward, which creates hope out of our cries of protest in the present. We protest because we have tasted the reality of new life."[75]

The spirituality promoted by state and market, by contrast, seeks constantly to capitalize on our fear of death so that they might manipulate our creaturely vulnerability and anxiety to consolidate their hold upon our loyalty. Popular piety similarly corrupts the insatiable human longing for wholeness and integrity with the lure of security, safety, stability, and predictability through the eradication of suffering. The quest for security and its corruption of God's creation manifests itself in a variety of ways. In some the *libido dominandi*, the lust for mastery, runs roughshod over our created solidarity with one another and with all the world, as we are alternatively encouraged, enticed, and threatened to seek safety and stability by taking ownership of the people and things around us. We strive to transform God's gift of communion with other people and things into private property, commodities to be possessed and disposed of as it suits our needs. Others who are "numbed by terror and acknowledged impotence retreat into varieties of personal and moral individualism, places of private feeling and individual 'experience.'"[76] In these persons the quest for security serves to drive them further and further away from the pain and disappointment of day-to-day contact with others, in a vain attempt to carve out an inner world of safety and tranquility within themselves. They flee to the inner garden of the soul to be alone with Jesus.

The fear of God, on the other hand, does not mark the end of our understanding of the divine mystery, but only its point of departure. The art of knowing God as ineffable has been interpreted by Christians down through the centuries in terms of sharing in the paschal mystery of Christ. In the words of Paul, "If we have been united with him in a death like his, we will certainly be united with him in a resurrection like his" (Rom. 6:5).[77] The idea of mystery, in other words, does not denote simply God's infinite incomprehensibility, though it does presuppose it. When early Christian authors adopt the Greek terminology of what is secret or hidden (*mystikos*) from the Hellenistic mystery cults,[78] they use it principally in relation to what they regard as the hidden depth of meaning in the Bible. For figures such as Clement and

75. Williams, *Wound of Knowledge*, 12 (emphasis added).
76. Lash, *Easter in Ordinary*, 85.
77. Cf. McIntosh, *Mystical Theology*, 41.
78. Stroumsa, *Hidden Wisdom*, 31–45.

Origen, the story of God's people narrated in Scripture has its secret meaning revealed and articulated by Christ, the incarnate Logos of God: "Christ is the hermeneutical key who opens a vast treasury of meaning, giving access to God's eternal will for creation; the exegetical process of arriving at this new knowledge is referred to as mystical, and the knowledge itself comes also (for Origen) to be designated as such."[79]

The Christian invocation of the concept of mystery, with the attendant notions of knowing and loving God, has therefore had a christological and pneumatological focus from the beginning. It does not designate some sort of esoteric inner experience but the hidden meaning and transformative understanding disclosed in Christ about God's presence and activity in the world. In the movement of self-giving love, the triune God creates the world and, in the missions of the Word and the Spirit, chooses not to be God apart from a fallen and lost world. In the end, writes McIntosh, "the mystical is not simply the ineffable incomprehensibility of God (no matter whether that incomprehensibility is thought of in ancient Neoplatonic terms or modern post-Kantian ones); rather what is most *mysterious* is not the divine being per se but precisely the infinite self-giving of God which is the fundamental characteristic of the divine Trinity and is enacted in history in the life, death and resurrection of Jesus."[80]

Only as we come to know the unknown God, then, can we truthfully know ourselves. Augustine was among the first to observe how the knowledge of God and self-knowledge, while distinct, are finally inseparable: "Let me, then, confess what I know about myself, and confess to what I do not know, because what I know of myself I know only because you shed your light on me, and what I do not know I shall remain ignorant about until my darkness becomes like bright noon before your face."[81] The art of vulnerability is, at bottom, a process of self-discovery, made possible by the work of the Spirit within the common venture of discipleship that belongs to the community of Jesus. And this means that at the heart of this shared journey into the mystery of God revealed in Christ is the discipline of unselfing.

Contemplation and the Discipline of Unselfing

Once we have crossed the threshold of the dark gate into the everyday, we are ready to undertake the discipline of unselfing, of being unmade so that we

79. McIntosh, *Mystical Theology*, 42.
80. McIntosh, *Mystical Theology*, 44 (emphasis added).
81. Augustine, *Confessions* 10.5.

can be remade. This notion will no doubt make some uncomfortable, as it sounds all too similar to the destructive habits of self-abnegation that some in our world have either been persuaded or forced to accept. Unfortunately, many have good reason to be suspicious of such ideas. The biblical notions of repentance, servanthood, and self-sacrifice have routinely been detached from the social practices that made the early church a subversive organization to the Romans and have been reinscribed within the habits and relations of the prevailing culture and society, where they are normally reserved for certain people, especially women and the marginalized.[82]

We should, however, take care not to allow distortions to determine our response to God and the world. Sarah Coakley argues that there is a long-term danger in the repression of all forms of vulnerability and in the failure to regard all questions of fragility, suffering, and self-emptying save in terms of victimization. Such responses tend to presume the very questions they beg about power, gender, and identity—namely, "the alignment of 'males' with achieved, worldly power, and women with the lack of it. The presumption is that women *need* 'power'—but of what sort?"[83] Acting on these impulses would not result in freedom but would continue our captivity within the structures and aims of the modern world in the form of an antithetical bondage.[84] Both forms of the quest for security—retreating within oneself and striving for mastery of self and others—constitute pathologies that have contributed to the dismembering of Christ's body and the vitiating of our witness.

The exhortation to enter into the vulnerability of Christ's ecclesial body, aptly expressed in the hymn of Philippians 2, "Let the same mind be in you that was in Christ Jesus," is "not an invitation to be battered; nor is its silence a silenc*ing*." If anything, writes Coakley, it nurtures in us the virtue of courage, that we might speak with a prophetic voice. Through the practice of contemplation we enter into "the subtle but enabling presence of a God who neither shouts nor forces, let alone 'obliterates.'" If we refuse to engage in this practice, we turn away from the grace of God that invites us to enter into this presence. "Thus the 'vulnerability' that is its [i.e., contemplation's] human condition is not about asking for unnecessary and unjust suffering (though increased self-knowledge can indeed be painful); nor is it . . . a 'self-abnegation.' On the contrary, this special 'self-emptying' is not a negation of the self, but the place of the self's transformation and expansion into God."[85]

82. See Jantzen, *Power, Gender and Christian Mysticism*; Hampson, *Theology and Feminism*.
83. Coakley, *Powers and Submissions*, 32–33 (emphasis original).
84. Lash, *Theology on the Way to Emmaus*, 55–56.
85. Coakley, *Powers and Submissions*, 35–36.

The spiritual discipline of unselfing interrupts the processes of forming our identity as disembodied consumers and faceless producers in order to cultivate a new self within the community of Jesus, one that is not confined by its Adamic past but liberated for its future in the messianic kingdom. Who we are as persons is not something that already lies potentially within each of us, needing only to be set free from the shackles of other people's expectations. Who each of us is, the name by which each of us will be called (Rev. 2:17), is rather a task to be perfected in grace within the body of Christ, the details of which take a lifetime to complete.[86] Only over time can we achieve our identity in Christ, signs of which may arise from time to time but the definitive understanding of which will be revealed only when God will be all in all.[87]

In keeping with its trinitarian context, the process of unselfing takes the form of a story. Not just any story, however, and not a story that each of us gets to write for ourselves according to our own individual tastes. It is instead the account of a journey with a fellow group of travelers that reconstructs the sense and direction of our lives. If spiritual formation is truly an engagement with the questioning at the heart of faith that permeates the classical documents of the early church, then the form it takes is the rewriting of our autobiographies that occurs as we are caught up in the communion, the *community*, of Christ. The politics of the Spirit has basically to do with each member of Christ's body becoming a coauthor of the story of Jesus—a story with a multitude of characters, countless twists in the plot, and numerous confrontations with the present order of things. As we move through the often-traumatic process from self-possession to self-giving and from unrestrained desire and acquisitiveness to maturity and wholeness, our individual stories find their meaning and purpose in the history of the Spirit with God's people.

Spiritual formation, working in concert with the other practices of the church, has no purpose apart from this story. Baptism begins our involvement in the politics of the Spirit as the sign and seal of our induction into a new society, marking the passage from life to death to life eternal and the transfer of our citizenship from the realm of darkness to the kingdom of light. Immersion in the baptismal waters relativizes all previous definitions of identity based on class, ethnic or national origin, and gender, so that these matters no longer determine who we are as persons. Together with the Spirit's endowment of every member of the community with her or his own distinctive role (the spiritual *charisma*), baptism establishes a new mode of social relations within the community, a way of relating that, unlike the brand of equality

---

86. Williams, *Wound of Knowledge*, 21; Coakley, *Powers and Submissions*, 139.

87. Williams, *On Christian Theology*, 287–89; Ward, *Cultural Transformation and Religious Practice*, 78.

prescribed by neoliberalism, does not treat us as faceless, interchangeable integers of production and consumption.

The discipline of unselfing divests us of the illusion that "I" exist apart from creation, apart from history, apart from a community and a tradition, apart from the habits and relations that make up my dealings with others. It is a discipline of demythologizing the working assumptions of contemporary existence, foremost among which is the idea that each of us is free to make up our own story, which presupposes that our lives belong to us rather than being a gift. A leading motif in the modern myth is the claim that each of us already possesses in the privacy of our inner selves a "fixed point of certainty and unshakable reassurance in our most unstable and insecure world."[88] In short, we have been enchanted by a picture of ourselves as gods, unconstrained by the material forces and historical relations of the created order, "spectators of a distanced spectacle."[89] In the end the effective denial of our creatureliness is the desire to be rid of God so that we might determine our own identity and destiny.

The consequences of this founding illusion of modernity have been devastating not only for human beings but for all of God's creatures. The origins of modern science can be traced in no small measure to the desire to subject nature to our ownership and control, so that we might safeguard ourselves from her many menaces and manage her resources for our benefit. When we thus picture ourselves in timeless caprice as lords and masters of the physical world, rather than recognizing our place within it, God's creation "becomes something manipulable for the sake of the values we have chosen. It becomes the stock of resources on hand for the fulfillment we value."[90] As the earth staggers under the weight of pollution, waste, squandered resources, and now climate change on an unprecedented scale, we cannot ignore the fact that the knowledges we so proudly developed to secure our freedom from nature's menace now enslave us along with the physical world. In effect, we traded away our spiritual birthright for the promise of security and self-determination, and we received instead a new and more pervasive form of bondage.

As Luther knew so well, the discipline of unselfing embraces God's judgment: "He who judges himself and confesses his sin justifies God and affirms his truthfulness, because he is saying about himself what God is saying about him."[91] But as with the fear of God, divine judgment is not finally a cause for despair or hopelessness. The Spirit judges us in Christ not by uttering words of condemnation but through complex processes of interaction that "force to

88. Lash, *Easter in Ordinary*, 18.
89. Poteat, *Polanyian Meditations*, 267.
90. Rouse, *Knowledge and Power*, 66.
91. Luther, *First Lectures on the Psalms II*, 93.

the light hidden directions and dispositions that would otherwise never come to view, and thus make the conflicts of goals and interests between people a *public* affair." The Spirit takes Jesus's interactions with the people he encountered during his lifetime, dramatically narrated in Scripture as "a series of ritual, quasi-legal disputations," and transforms every new social setting and every historical circumstance into "an event of judgment in that it gives the persons involved definitions, roles to adopt, points on which to stand and speak. They are invited to 'create' themselves in finding a place within this drama—an improvisation in the theater workshop, but one that purports to be about a comprehensive truth affecting one's identity and future."[92]

Judgment is therefore a necessary precondition for conversion, when a person shifts her or his allegiance from one set of powers to another and from one measure of reality to another—namely, "the reality of God which has become manifest in Christ in the reality of the world."[93] The work of the Spirit in and through the church as it "plays away from home" is "to make explicit what is at stake in particular human decisions or policies, individual and collective, and in this sense bring in the event of judgment, the revaluation of identities."[94] In contrast, the false piety fostered by neoliberalism reconfirms the prevailing habits and relations of the world and thus comprises a de facto legitimation of the status quo. Such politics is in the end nonjudgmental, in both the popular and biblical senses of that term, and is therefore incapable of displaying God's love for the world incarnated in the crucified one.

For those who stand before God within the body of Christ, judgment brings not condemnation but the possibility of genuine freedom joined with a new capacity to participate in the divine exchange of love. As we shed the vanity that is the quest for security, the world's grip upon us also starts to relax. The freedom of a holy vulnerability

> takes the form of dispossession, letting go, surrendering the title-deeds we forged. . . . Emancipation, letting things and people go from our grasp . . . is how life in the Spirit is to be lived; which is to say: it is how we are to die. What occurs in death is, in the last resort, the same for all of us: we are deprived of all possessions, "even of ourselves." To learn to die (which is, of course, the way that finite creatures learn to live) is, therefore, to learn to relate to each and every person, thing, disease, event, delight, that we encounter, neither as enemy nor as possession but as gift, as friend.[95]

92. Williams, *On Christian Theology*, 32 (emphasis original).
93. Bonhoeffer, *Ethics*, 197.
94. Williams, *On Christian Theology*, 33.
95. Lash, *Believing Three Ways in One God*, 103.

The art of vulnerability in the *koinōnia* of the Spirit thus conveys a distinct freedom, one that is different from modern simulacra. Most people, if asked to define freedom, will usually do so as freedom *from* something or someone. Freedom is, essentially, the opportunity (and the right) to be a tyrant over one's own affairs. This conception of freedom is still mired in the picture of the self as an individual who in the essence of his being is unfettered by relations with his fellow creatures, and those relations into which such an individual does enter are, and always will be, his choice.

In the church, by contrast, we learn to live—quite literally—out of control, emancipated from the promise of self-mastery with which the earthly city lures us yet which it will never allow us to achieve. Contemplation, which is the end of the practice of spiritual formation, is not an esoteric preoccupation but, as Williams says, "a deeper appropriation of the vulnerability of the self in the midst of the language and transactions of the world."[96] We learn through a contemplative way of life to give back our habits, our relations, our attempts at knowledge, our very lives. As we do so we cultivate the virtue of patience, divesting ourselves of our feeble and vain attempts at security, "sometimes in darkness not unlike Gethsemane."[97] The freedom that is the gift of the Spirit (2 Cor. 3:17) is therefore signified by the freedom *of* and *for*. It is the freedom *of* our adoption as the daughters and sons of God, the freedom of servanthood within the household of Christ, to be there *for* the other. Within this household, freedom is a gift that can never be possessed and a power that can never become ours, and yet it is a gift and power in which we share in the Spirit through our participation in the *koinōnia* of the people of God.

The freedom of the Spirit, therefore, does not have anything to do with that specter that modernity calls the human ego, a Gnostic apparition that only haunts its body but really does not belong to it. Human beings only begin to learn what freedom is when we learn what it means to be some*body*—that is, when we know *viscerally* that human life is vested in and is nothing apart from our bodies and that our bodies are inextricably woven into the social and material fabric of God's creation. Freedom is thus tied up upon our interactions and exchanges with others—parents, relatives, neighbors, the institutions of state and market—and with all created things. The freedom of Christ involves even our enemies, for only as the followers of Jesus are liberated to love those who seek to do them harm do they have assurance that they are making progress on their journey toward that liberty, that *liberality*, which *is* the reign of God. The life of freedom thus requires intense and

96. Williams, "Theological Integrity," 148.
97. Lash, *Believing Three Ways in One God*, 81.

rigorous schooling within the context of the messianic community and its distinctive skills and institutions.

The freedom that comes through the politics of the Spirit is itself formed by the other practices of the church. Through our participation in these activities we come to understand that emancipation is the gift and effect of getting caught up in a true story that transfigures our fate as finite, fallen beings into our destiny as redeemed and cherished creatures. But the realization of this destiny does not take place apart from confrontation and conflict. The sacraments always situate us in the context of Jesus's death and resurrection, and thus in the context of the faithfulness of Christ being met time after time by the infidelity of friend and foe alike. These practices nurture what Johann Baptist Metz calls the memory of suffering, in the light of which "it is clear that social power and political domination are not simply to be taken for granted but that they continually have to justify themselves in view of actual suffering." The art of vulnerability, in which the victims of suffering and oppression provide contrapuntal dissonance, challenges the world to justify itself in light of the human cost it exacts, but at the same time it also extends the divine offer of new life in the messianic community, the historical sign of God's peaceable kingdom.[98]

To be buried and raised with Christ in baptism, therefore, not only begins the process of accepting our vulnerability before God but also makes explicit the role of the disciple in the biblical drama. The Bible, together with the church fathers, teaches that the true and perfect disciple of Christ is the martyr, the one who is ready to go with Jesus to the cross.[99] The sharing of bread and cup within the family of God is likewise never simply a fellowship meal but concretely embodies the divine summons to share in "God's sufferings at the hands of a godless world."[100] As I noted in chapter 5, the origins of this meal are invariably set in the context of Jesus's betrayal by his disciples on the night before his death. The story of the Eucharist, then *and* now, thus does not ignore the suffering associated with everyday life, nor does it cover over our complicity in it; rather, it incorporates these within its costly solidarity with the world. As with baptism, the Eucharist also affirms and proclaims God's vindication of suffering, both Christ's and ours, in the community of the crucified.

Finally, though the practice of spiritual formation rejects the quest for security that holds the world in its grip, Christ's followers are not left adrift in chaotic waters without a sense of direction or assistance. In that community

98. Metz, *Faith in History and Society*, 115.
99. Zizioulas, "Early Christian Community," 39.
100. Bonhoeffer, *Letters and Papers from Prison*, 480.

where men and women live by "the conviction of things not seen" (Heb. 11:1), relying on the grace of the one who subjects the world to God's will through his weakness and suffering, we learn to discriminate between the fraudulent offer of certainty and security, which is forever beyond our reach, and the kind of certitude that develops through our continuing faithfulness to Christ, who on the cross accepted our vulnerability as his own. By contrast, the calculating cynicism that is cultivated by many in our culture, as they seek to preserve their autonomy by describing all commitments as self-interested pursuits, is but "the irresponsible dilettantism which we call 'bad faith.'"[101] But for "those who are the called, both Jews and Greeks," the discipline of following Christ with one's brothers and sisters is "the power of God and the wisdom of God" (1 Cor. 1:24).

The goal of the politics of the Spirit is the ability to live and work as artisans of the age to come while dwelling in the midst of the present age. To do this we must understand the social grammar of neoliberal capitalism, its ways of organizing human life and action. In particular, we must attend to its fundamental impulse, the lust for mastery, which drives the quest for security and certainty that lies at the root of what is often mistaken for true spirituality. We must cooperate with our earthly neighbors in the pursuit of the material goods necessary to mortal life, but without surrendering to the worship of necessity, which insists that we have no alternative but to act in accordance with the limitations this age would impose on us. This will require habits of discernment that allow us to discriminate between uses of these goods that are open to God's activity in Christ and may therefore be rightly directed toward the peace of the heavenly city and uses that are closed to that activity and are incompatible with the church's art of vulnerability.

101. Lash, *Believing Three Ways in One God*, 19.

7

DWELLING AGAIN IN TENTS

Living in Tension with the Earthly City

"O people who can rest
    assured to see the light of Heaven someday,
    your desire's only care and only quest.

May grace soon melt the film of sin away,
    that from a conscience finally made clear
    may fall the river of your memory;

Graciously tell me—and I'll hold it dear—
    if any of you hails from Italy.
    My knowing it may bring some good to you."

"My brother, each man is a citizen
    of one true city. What you mean to say
    is, 'who once lived a pilgrim in that land.'"

Dante Alighieri, *Purgatory*

According to the ancient Egyptians, the social world that developed around the fecundity of the Nile River was the place around which all life, including that of the gods, was ordered in perpetuity. Imperial Rome declared itself to be the eternal city, to whose legions the celestial powers set no limits, world or time, but bequeathed the gift of empire without end. In more recent times the nation-state has staked its claim to Rome's political mantle as "*the City*, a permanent and 'eternal' City, *Urbs aeterna* . . . an ultimate solution of the human problem."[1] And now the global marketplace proclaims itself to be the privileged site where all reality must henceforth always be strategically conceived and coordinated. The common thread here is the notion that some particular place or institution within this world provides the standpoint from which all things are rightly named, assessed, and pursued.

As citizens of the *civitas peregrina*, the one true city on pilgrimage through this world toward the age to come, Christians believe that these places and the institutions that support them are destined to pass away. Because our true homeland and commonwealth still lies before us, we do not narrate the unfolding of history in relation to any particular place in this world but privilege instead the apocalyptic activity of God in Jesus Christ. We see ourselves as a company of nomads, living, as it were, in "tents" in the various places to which God has sent us to serve as sign, instrument, and foretaste of his intentions for the world.

Because the two cities are mixed together and entangled in this time before the consummation of all things, Christians must learn to make wise use of the same goods and to endure with patience the same evils as the citizens of the *civitas temporalis* do, all the while bearing witness to the one "who has made peace with God and peace among human beings."[2] Like everyone else, then, we must eat, drink, find clothing, secure shelter, till the land and fashion instruments of all sorts, marry and give in marriage, raise and protect children, bury parents, and cope with natural disasters, debilitating disease, and social upheavals. We are called to do so according to a different faith, a different hope, and a different love that enable us to engage the world as a missional people, and to do so without succumbing to forms of acting and speaking that domesticate, marginalize, and exploit the church's life, language, and witness.[3]

Knowing how to live and work as citizens and envoys of the heavenly city that is to come while dwelling in the midst of the present world and engaging with all whose yearnings are open to God's intrusion into the world is a primary aim of the spiritual art of holy vulnerability. An important dimension of our calling as members of Christ's body, then, is to develop the skills and habits that will enable us to work and play as artisans of the age to come in the middle of a world that labors under the reign of sin and death. In particular,

1. Florovsky, "Empire and Desert," 135.
2. Bonhoeffer, *"Life Together" and "Prayerbook of the Bible,"* 33.
3. Augustine, *City of God* 1.35; 18.54.

we need to acquire those virtues of discernment that allow us to discriminate between uses of goods that are compatible with the irruption of God into the world in Christ and those that foreclose on that possibility. In addition, we must learn to recognize idolatrous practices and institutions that would have us confess an alien faith, pursue a false hope, and embody a lesser love, a temptation to which too many of us have succumbed too often.

In this last chapter, I discuss some of the recurring tendencies in the social grammar of the earthly city that set the context in which Christians are called on to practice the art of pilgrimage. In one way or another the tendencies we need to oppose are linked to what Augustine calls the *libido dominandi*, the lust for mastery, which is predicated in manifold ways on the possession, threat, and use of coercive power, and finally on death and the fear of death. This desire to take charge of our lives, to carve out zones of security for ourselves, permeates every aspect of a fallen world, including those involved in the reproduction of life in all its facets. Of all the manifestations of this desire to dominate the world about us, however, none is more persistent and destructive than war.

War and the *Libido Dominandi*

Though by its existence the church challenges claims to our allegiance on the part of the state and the market, it does not compete with these temporal authorities for control over geographical space, nor does it seek to determine what are the best means to achieve such control. It is tasked to seek the welfare of the earthly city, which requires that we cooperate with our earthly neighbors in the pursuit of the material goods necessary to life in this age. Indeed, in virtually every case we cannot avoid some sort of cooperation, because the two cities are mingled together at present. At the same time we need to oppose "the vagaries of neoliberal capitalism without committing to the conceit that we can evade it."[4] We must therefore discover how to make use of the same goods and endure the same evils as the citizens of the earthly city do, but direct those goods and sufferings to a different and more salutary end.[5]

Our pursuit of these goods, therefore, must not hinder our worship of the one supreme and true God or injure true faith and godliness, for it is worship that finally allows us to name these vagaries truthfully. In our desire to cooperate with the earthly city, to play on its home turf, as it were, we must be on guard against the lure of the *libido dominandi*, its false promise that

4. Hargaden, *Theological Ethics in a Neoliberal Age*, xxi.
5. Augustine, *City of God* 19.17.

we can make this world new by dint of our own efforts. It is this fundamental desire to control our surroundings that holds the world in its grip, and it is what led the rulers and authorities to rebel against God's intrusion in the world by condemning Christ to death, and when they did so, this same desire condemned them to be the form of the world that is passing away. By contrast, Christians are called upon to cultivate the kind of holy vulnerability that allows us to use earthly goods without resort to the moral authority of death, so that we might direct their use toward that alone which can truly be called peace, "a perfectly ordered and perfectly harmonious fellowship in the enjoyment of God, and of one another in God."[6]

The lust for mastery is perhaps the most virulent form of idolatry, the setting of our mind and heart, loyalty and confidence, hopes and fears on something other than the grace and mercy of God. It gives rise to the worship of necessity, which is the affirmation of the present order as the enduring nature of things. Things just *are* as we now find them, and we must therefore work with these givens. The worship of necessity proclaims that we have no alternative but to act in accordance with the limitations necessity would impose on us. This worship renders absolute our impotence, leaving us completely enthralled to authorities at whose thrones we believe we have no choice but to kneel.[7]

The idolatrous worship of necessity informs much of what counts as modern social analysis (including much of what is labeled "Christian social ethics") and also sets the stage for literature. Reinhold Niebuhr, for example, gives tacit consent to the givenness of the present order of things when he accepts without protest or qualification the "fact" that "society is in a perpetual state of war."[8] Not only does such an assumption presuppose an understanding of the world markedly at odds with Scripture, in that it presupposes an ontology of original violence (a view advocated by early Gnostics); it also confers upon the managerial politics of the nation-state and the ever-expanding sphere of global capitalism the status of a theodicy.[9] These mechanisms are mythically ordained to manage individual and "tribal" self-interests so as to maintain an optimum balance of relative goods, but in the process they also perpetuate the ancient heroic *agōn* celebrated (in somewhat different ways) by both Machiavelli and Nietzsche.

In a fascinating essay on the peculiar use of grotesque ideas and images in Southern fiction, Flannery O'Connor labels the picture of reality underwriting

6. Augustine, *City of God* 1.pref.; 19.17.
7. Lash, *Believing Three Ways in One God*, 108.
8. Niebuhr, *Moral Man and Immoral Society*, 19.
9. Milbank, *Theology and Social Theory*, 27–48.

the worship of necessity as a "realism of fact." Under the influence of the social sciences, this brand of realism establishes for the novel a kind of literary orthodoxy that associates the movement of social forces, the typical fidelity to the way things look and happen in what passes for normal life, as the only legitimate material for long fiction. Readers and critics alike look to "literature as a mirror and guide for society" and seek writers who will serve as the handmaids of their time. After all, the reader wants to be lifted up, to be reassured that what has fallen is at least offered the chance to be restored. He wants a work that will either torment his senses or raise his spirits, transporting him instantly "either to a mock damnation or a mock innocence." The reader is not wrong to look for this motion, writes O'Connor, "but what he has forgotten is the cost of it. His sense of evil is diluted or lacking altogether and so he has forgotten the price of restoration."[10]

The worship of necessity wears many guises, but we encounter it most poignantly in the assertion that war is a regrettable but necessary part of human life and that we must therefore be prepared as good citizens to sacrifice for our homeland, the nation-state. Though this might seem like a straightforward, reasonable, and disinterested assertion, the invocation of the concept of sacrifice, drawn from the realm of cultic ritual and observance, links it to the practice of idolatry. From time to time, so the argument goes, blood must be offered to the gods, to the powers and principalities that determine the warp and woof of the universe. Granted, most nations and peoples would prefer to offer the lives of the enemy, of "them," and not those of their own youth, but sacrifice in some form must nevertheless be made.

Though some may be scandalized by a cultic description of war, our own speech betrays us, for while the making of offerings to bloodthirsty deities is not generally in the working vocabulary of most nations, the language of martyrdom and sacrifice, expropriated from the language of the church, most certainly is. Time and again those in the military who have died for their country are extolled as having made "the supreme sacrifice."[11] The question immediately arises: To whom do we offer this sacrifice, if not to the gods? If we respond, to the God of Abraham and Sarah, then it would seem that we are tacitly admitting that Christ's sacrifice was not sufficient for the sins of the world, that he did not "once for all" enter in the eternal Holy of Holies to obtain our redemption (Heb. 9). If we say instead that we offer it to the nation-state of which we are a part, we are granting to a part of the

10. O'Connor, "Some Aspects of the Grotesque in Southern Fiction," 814, 818–20.
11. Hedge, *War Is a Force That Gives Us Meaning*; Marvin and Ingle, *Blood Sacrifice and the Nation*; Gamble, *War for Righteousness*.

created order an honor that belongs solely to God. And if the answer is, we offer this sacrifice to ourselves, or to our posterity, then we explicitly embrace the sin of Adam, seeking not only to be like the gods but to be such on our own terms (Gen. 3).[12]

Ted Smith, for example, chronicles the way that the bloodshed and carnage of the American Civil War has been narrated by the likes of John Brown, abolitionist Henry C. Wright, Harriet Beecher Stowe, and liberal theologian Horace Bushnell as an atoning sacrifice of blood that would renew the nation and give it a sense of its role in divine providence.[13] In *Upon the Altar of the Nation: A Moral History of the American Civil War*, historian Harry Stout gives conditional assent to the thesis that the sacrifice of so many had a redemptive element to it. As the casualties escalated to unimaginable levels, Stout writes, people began to attribute a mystical element to the conflict, "a sort of massive sacrifice on the national altar. The Civil War taught Americans that they really were a Union, and it absolutely required a baptism of blood to unveil the transcendent dimensions of that union."[14]

Perhaps some will dismiss the notion of sacrifice as "just a metaphor," though I doubt that many of those whose world and sense of self were decisively shaped by war through the ages would accept such a summary dismissal. But even if we are successful in this regard, then other problems arise that are associated with the desire to deny the idea and the practice of sacrifice.[15] We twenty-first-century heirs of the Enlightenment have been trained to believe that it is our sacred task to create a world that makes sacrifice a thing of the past. We were told that we could achieve this goal by fashioning a world of unencumbered freedom where all our limits are freely chosen and where our god or gods (should we choose to worship them) are little more than highly personable cosmic therapists who help to realize our true selves when we need them but at other times will politely not interfere with our self-directed lives.[16]

From the standpoint of the gospel, however, the story that men and women can by their own wits live without sacrifice, at least from now on, is a form of cheap grace founded on a lie. It is cheap grace because it seeks to evade

12. Augustine notes that "Adam and Eve would have been better fitted to resemble gods if they had clung in obedience to the highest and true ground of their being, and not, in their pride, made themselves their own ground. For created gods are gods not in their own true nature, but by participation in the true God." Augustine, *City of God* 14.13.

13. T. Smith, *Weird John Brown*, 165–68.

14. Stout, *Upon the Altar of the Nation*, xxi. Stout adds that in spite of the use of sacral ideas about the war, it was ultimately a failure in that it did not include the women and men of African descent for whom it was fought. Stout, *Upon the Altar of the Nation*, xxii.

15. I am indebted to Stanley Hauerwas for what follows. See *In Good Company*, 165–68.

16. See C. Smith, *Soul Searching*, 162–63.

the continuing effects of the sacrifices extracted in the past. Willie Jennings says in this regard that it is premature to speak of racial reconciliation before articulating the profound deformities of our age.[17] It is a lie because it creates false memories that instigate more sacrifices that are even more damnable, because these stories prevent us from acknowledging the suffering and death of the past as sacrifice. No doubt most Americans feel terrible about the suffering that has taken place in the past, particularly by excluded peoples—African Americans, other people of color, Native Americans, women, Jews, the poor, and so forth. We hope that our recognition of past prejudice, slavery, segregation, and genocide is a sign of our goodwill and essential righteousness. And so we deceive ourselves by saying that now that we have acknowledged our guilt about the sweat and blood of past generations offered up to idols against their wills, we just need to try to be and to do better. Though such measures are implemented from sincere motives, what is often overlooked by the inclusion of these stories within the metanarrative of neoliberal capitalism is that these excluded peoples become victims all over again, involuntarily inscribed into a history narrated by those who profited either directly or indirectly by their suffering.

The truth be told, sacrifice never comes to an end in the earthly city; "History," as Hegel reminds us, is a slaughter-bench.[18] From the standpoint of life lived "according to the flesh"—that is, apart from cross and resurrection—time unfolds in response to the offering of blood to the gods of war, who constantly renew their demand for the lives of human beings, and we have no choice but to obey meekly, hoping against all rational expectation that this will be the last time that we shall have to bloody our hands. All the while we seek new scapegoats to explain our past aggressions and take comfort in the illusion that since we have diagnosed the cause and thereby remedied it, we shall soon have no reason to offer sacrifice. The particular scapegoat that the Enlightenment identified as the catalyst for war was "religion," and so it narrated history as the past violence of warring religious parties to justify the sovereignty of nation-states over the affairs of humankind. Mark Lilla puts this prejudice in its starkest form: "The reason human beings in war commit acts no animal would is, paradoxically, because they believe in God."[19] What Lilla does not grasp, says Ted Smith, is the way he not only fails to capture accurately the truth of the matter but also misses completely the ways the state foments its own violence and promotes its use by nonstate actors and agencies.[20]

17. Jennings, *Christian Imagination*, 10.
18. Hegel, *Philosophy of History*, 21.
19. Lilla, *Stillborn God*, 84.
20. T. Smith, *Weird John Brown*, 41–51.

The attacks of September 11, 2001, on New York and Washington, DC, gave new life to the practice of scapegoating religion, now in the demonized form of "fundamentalist" or "radical" religion, which is then linked with terrorism. This way of describing the current state of affairs is part of a larger narrative, according to which (1) there is a dichotomy between the religious and the secular, (2) the religious is irrational and dangerous, and therefore (3) the religious must be constantly reined in by "reason," instantiated in secular state power. Delimiting the human condition in this manner establishes an other who is essentially irrational, fanatical, and violent, which in turn authorizes coercive measures against this other. In our time and place, writes William Cavanaugh, "the Muslim world especially plays the role of religious Other. *They* have not yet learned to remove the dangerous influence of religion from political life. *Their* violence is therefore irrational and fanatical. *Our* violence, by contrast, is rational and peacemaking, and sometimes regrettably necessary to contain *their* violence."[21] The not-so-subtle message is that the only good religion is one in which everyone acts like good American Protestants, holding their religion lightly.

The good news of God's intrusion into the world in Christ and his church is that we are freed from the presumption that war is our fate. In the offering of our Passover lamb, sacrifice comes to its proper end, its proper purpose; for in this, the offering of God to God, God refuses to let the never-ending slaughter-bench determine the course of human history. And through our liturgically configured participation in this, the end of sacrifice, we are saved from our illusions concerning what will save us from the bloodshed that has dominated the story line of history, and thus from the worship of necessity. The God of Jesus Christ is a bloody and bloodied God, and our salvation is equally so, because we are called upon not to offer the other up to death for our security but to offer ourselves, to be martyrs, to offer testimony to the end of sacrifice in the sacrifice of the Passover lamb. Baptism can therefore never be "just a symbol," for it is the washing that readies our bodies for burial, preparing us to share in the true history of the world as citizens of the one true city and just regime, bearing witness to that time when death will be no more.

The apocalyptic perspective of the gospel that informs our participation in Christ's sacrifice embodies what O'Connor calls a realism of distances. Realists of this sort believe that life is essentially mysterious, that women and men exist in a created order and respond freely to its laws, which for O'Connor are found in "the virgin birth, the Incarnation, the resurrection."[22] What we see

21. Cavanaugh, "Sins of Omission," 35 (emphasis original).
22. O'Connor, "Letter to A," 953.

close at hand is of interest insofar as it allows us to traverse the (nonspatial) distance to an experience of mystery itself. The realist of distances is interested in what we do not understand rather than in what we do, in possibility rather than in probability. He is interested in characters "who are forced out to meet evil and grace and who act on a trust beyond themselves—whether they know very clearly what it is they act upon or not." For the artisan whose understanding of the world is not impoverished by a realism of fact, every thing is also a sign, thus combining in itself two points, one in the concrete and the other in "a point not visible to the naked eye, but believed in by him firmly, just as real to him, really, as the one that everybody sees."[23]

Natural and Unnatural Life

When we are caught up, body as well as soul, in God's sacrifice for the welfare of the world, we become citizens of the commonwealth of the new creation, characters in a drama that does not take its cues from what is near at hand. Instead, the miraculous sign of the resurrection, God's declaration that life and not death will have the final word in the end, plots our words and deeds. The refusal to engage in the worship of necessity through the offering of sacrifice in war is thus one of the marks of the church's life and witness to a world in thrall to the lust for mastery. At the same time, however, war is the exceptional case. In most circumstances Christians cannot evade the vagaries of nation-state and market but must cooperate in some manner and to some extent with the world and its ways of regulating the necessities of everyday life. How do we determine which uses of material goods cultivate true faith and godliness, allowing the peace of the heavenly city to be manifested in the midst of the earthly city?

To this end Dietrich Bonhoeffer retrieves the idea of the natural as a helpful way of relating the eschatological trajectory of the church to the use we are to make of earthly goods.[24] He develops it as a mediating concept between the created as such, in order to take into account the fallenness of humankind, and the sinful, in order to include the created. By entering into natural life, Christ transforms it into the time that precedes the age to come and directs it toward the justification of all things in the messianic reign of God. The concept of the natural denotes a moment of independence and self-development for the created as such, with a relative freedom appropriate to it. Within this freedom,

23. O'Connor, "Some Aspects of the Grotesque in Southern Fiction," 816.
24. Bonhoeffer is influenced here by Josef Pieper's *Reality and the Good*; see Pieper, *Living the Truth*.

however, "there is a difference between its right use and its misuse, and this is the difference between the natural and the unnatural; there is therefore a relative openness and a relative closedness for Christ." The natural is, therefore, that within creation that is directed toward the coming of Christ, while the unnatural is that which has closed itself off against Christ's coming.[25]

The formal determination of the natural is provided by God's intention to preserve the world and direct it toward Christ, and thus what is natural can be discerned only in relation to Christ. Materially, it is the form of preserved life itself, embracing the whole of creation. Reason belongs to this material dimension as the source of knowledge of itself. It is not a divine principle that can elevate human beings above the natural to the supernatural but is itself a part of creation that has been graciously preserved by God, participating wholly in the natural. Its function is to "take in" (in Bonhoeffer's German, *vernehmen*) as a unity that which is whole and universal in reality. The natural and reason are thus correlated with each other, the former as the form of being of the preserved life, the latter as the form of its awareness. Reason thus shares fully in the effects of the fall, perceiving "only what is given in the fallen world, and, indeed, exclusively according to its content."[26]

The categories of natural and unnatural function typologically as anticipations and refusals, respectively, of the messianic regime of God in Jesus Christ. The natural can therefore not be defined or understood apart from the event of grace. On its own it cannot compel the coming of Christ (hence, the grace of God's apocalyptic action is truly unmerited), nor can that which is unnatural make it impossible: "In both cases the real coming is an act of grace."[27] As Aquinas expresses it, human beings are created with a natural desire to see and participate in God, but that desire can be realized only by God's gracious initiative.[28] The church's constitutive practices provide the means by which Christians recognize as either natural or unnatural the activities and habits that foster our pursuit of the necessities of life within the earthly city.

The incarnation can never serve as God's affirmation of the natural in abstraction from the cross and resurrection. The humanity of Jesus does not ratify the established world and human life as it exists in a fallen world, nor does it give credence to the worship of necessity. There can be no greater error, says Bonhoeffer, than to separate the three elements of the event of grace: "In becoming human we recognize God's love toward God's creation; in the crucifixion God's judgment on all flesh; and in the resurrection God's

25. Bonhoeffer, *Ethics*, 173–74.
26. Bonhoeffer, *Ethics*, 174–75.
27. Bonhoeffer, *Ethics*, 173–74.
28. Aquinas, *Summa contra gentiles* 3.51–53.

purpose for a new world."[29] True creatureliness is only followable in terms of the relationship between the present age and the age to come, or between nature and grace, made visible in this age by the actions and speech of the risen Christ's earthly-historical body. We can affirm with Aquinas that grace does indeed perfect nature, but this does not mean that that nature will be recognizable to those in thrall to the worship of necessity when Christ is done with it, or "at least not until Christ transforms them as well."[30]

With this conception of the natural we are able to acknowledge what God has created and to relate it to the unveiling of God in the person and community of Christ. There remains that within the created that has not been completely effaced by the fall and thus retains its sacramentality, its character as *signum*, the product of God's speech. It is perfectible in the sense of being capable of being reimagined and recontextualized by the workings of grace as markers of God's eternal commonwealth and is therefore conducive to the cultivation of virtue and the worship of the one true God. Seen in this light, the natural is "that form of life preserved by God for the fallen world that is directed towards justification, salvation and renewal through Christ."[31]

Bonhoeffer's discussion of the natural provides a point of departure for developing our sense of what is involved in being artisans of the age to come in the midst of the present age, but we must proceed with caution. Because the incarnation does not simply ratify the world as it is presently ordered, there is no reason to assume, for example, that we owe unquestioned allegiance to the nation-state or that we are obligated to participate in the ever-increasing (and ultimately unsustainable) levels of consumption required to continually prime the pump of a global economy. Our involvement in the natural realm is a matter of discernment, which requires the use of reason directed toward the peace of God's regime. As artisans of the age to come, we must become "connoisseurs of reason"[32] in receptiveness to the irruption of the reign of Christ in the present age.

Economy and Gift

Because our lives are entangled within "the hegemony of the binary model of market-plus-state,"[33] we Christians cannot avoid the nation-state and its absolute monopoly on the "legitimate" use of force nor exempt ourselves from

29. Bonhoeffer, *Ethics*, 157.
30. Budde, *Borders of Baptism*, 126.
31. Bonhoeffer, *Ethics*, 174.
32. Lentricchia, *Ariel and the Police*, 133.
33. Benedict XVI, *Caritas in Veritate*.

the patterns of production, exchange, and consumption in a global market that oversees the distribution of goods all people need. The question for the artisans of the age to come is therefore not whether we shall live in and by the state's sphere of authority or the necessary exchanges of markets, but which uses of the goods overseen by them are natural and which are not. As a nomadic people intermingled with the citizens of this world, we have no choice but to participate in the workings of this regime. We must therefore "do business" with the institutions of the state and the global market, and "the first duty of the critic is to understand our position and not succumb to delusions."[34] To acknowledge this is not to capitulate to the demands of either institution but to identify the starting point for developing a faithful Christian response to it.

What we do have a choice about is the *manner* of our interaction. It belongs to Christian connoisseurs of reason to discern between natural and unnatural uses of the public goods that are necessary to life in the body and that are overseen by the institutions of the earthly regime. These goods are not limited to consumer products and services such as water, sewer, power, and fire protection, but include schools, judicial systems, communication networks, and the professions, trades, trade unions, and occupations that allow us to provide needed goods for ourselves, our families, and neighbors. Christians may therefore participate in political forums that range from local school boards to national assemblies, from long-established institutions to spontaneous demonstrations, to appeal for the wise use of these goods—for example, when the civil rights movement promoted voter registration as part of its campaign to end Jim Crow segregation.

Since the incarnation does not ratify the world as it is, Christians are not obligated to fill all the slots, provide all the services of the earthly regime, or make sure that history comes out right. Such tendencies are much more typical of Stoicism, a moral and spiritual tradition that is, as Daniel Hardy and David Ford observe, "timid and orderly, leaving the passions free for economics, war and collective sport."[35] In the body of Christ, the Spirit sets us free to engage as a deliberative body in the vital and yet difficult activity of discerning what constitutes a natural mode of consumption or which among the many trades, occupations, and professions within the earthly city are open to the peace of the inbreaking reign of God and which are not.

Augustine thus determined (in keeping with church teaching at the time) that with his baptism he would need to resign his position as a teacher of

---

34. Boyle, *Who Are We Now?*, 81.
35. Hardy and Ford, *Praising and Knowing God*, 144.

rhetoric, which in classical Roman society put one on the path to success. The tools of rhetoric were not devoted to God's law but used as weapons for "lying follies and legal battles." Indeed, he acknowledged that some might judge that he had sinned in this matter "by allowing [himself] to remain even for an hour in a professional chair of lying once [his] heart was fully intent on [God's] service."[36] In other circumstances, good uses may be found for professions not typically associated with the works of corporeal and spiritual mercy. Bankers, for example, could use their skills and position to help low-income families rise above subsistence levels, which in turn would allow them to contribute to the common good.

In addition to the wise use of goods regulated by the current regime of the earthly city, the church is called on to offer alternatives to that regime's patterns of accumulation and forms of managing behavior, thereby providing tangible signs of the reality of God in Christ, not in the church's proper "religious" place at the margins of life but in the midst of the world of production and use. These alternatives will not be part of a social order that humans enact for themselves through contracts between autonomous individuals (a form of exchange that both presupposes and perpetuates forms of reasoning governed by the *libido dominandi*). As I observed previously, it is the incarnation that is the basis for this alternative ordering of material goods. All things on earth and in heaven, including the use of the things necessary for this bodily life, have been caught up in this ultimate exchange between God and humankind. This *oikonomia* can only be received as divine gift, beginning with baptism and then received ever anew at the feast at the Lord's table, where we learn that "because there is one bread, we who are many are one body, for we all partake of the one bread" (1 Cor. 10:17). The alternative initially takes form around Christ's table, undercutting the monopoly that the type of exchange ordered by the lust for mastery holds in the present age.

In the prevailing regime of market-plus-state, by contrast, men and women are severed from the overlapping relationships that once existed within families, churches, guilds, and other local social groupings, their authority usurped by the state. Thus extracted from organic communities, stripped of their identities as daughter, son, Christian, Muslim, and so on, they are transformed into "individuals"—that is, interchangeable units of production and consumption. Thus "freed," they are compelled to enter into contractual relationships, the formal nature of which stipulates that human beings are essentially unencumbered agents who engage others solely on the basis of self-interest. "Rather than 'cohere' directly to one another," writes Cavanaugh,

36. Augustine, *Confessions* 9.2.

"we relate to each other through the state by the formal mechanism of contract." Property, including the product of their labor, becomes commodified and thus alienable.[37]

In the community fashioned in the Spirit around the Eucharist, a different mode of exchange is inaugurated, one that binds us to the risen Christ and to one another by drawing our relationships, including those having to do with earthly goods, into the infinite plenitude of God's triune life. The gift of Christ's body sets aside the primacy of contractual exchange and the marginalization of the gift relationship to the private sphere, where the recipient is rendered passive and the giver experiences giving as an alienation of property. In God's gift of the Son to the world, the Father is not alienated from the gift but goes with the gift, is in the gift.[38] In return an exchange of sorts is expected of the recipient, though not one that presumes to return to God something that might be lacking in the divine life, "since there is nothing extra to God that could return to him."[39]

Within the economy of divine plenitude, the expected return of the gift on the part of the recipient is not one that can be preestablished by contract, for it too must bear the character of the countergiver. In the alternative economy of Christ's ecclesial body, writes Cavanaugh, "this type of giving is perfected as the dualism of giver and recipient are collapsed; Christ is the perfect return of God to God. In the Eucharist, we receive the gift of Christ not as mere passive recipients, but by being incorporated into the gift itself, the Body of Christ. As members of the Body, we then become nourishment for others—including those not part of the visible Body—in the unending trinitarian economy of gratuitous giving and joyful reception."[40]

As recipients of God's prevenient gift, artisans of the age to come look for opportunities to cultivate types of associations that in the material realm lend themselves to this mode of gift exchange. Through these relationships we come to share more deeply in the life and goodness of God, and along the way we develop rich conceptions of the common good for those outside the body of Christ to contemplate, while at the same time helping to foster the ability of all to contribute to it. These associations do exist, but often on a scale that seems inconsequential in a global economy: Catholic Worker houses of hospitality, community- or church-supported agriculture programs (CSAs),[41]

---

37. Cavanaugh, "City," 192–93, 195.
38. Cavanaugh, "City," 195.
39. Milbank, "Can a Gift Be Given?," 133.
40. Cavanaugh, "City," 195–96.
41. For more information on community- or church-supported agriculture, see the Alternative Farming Systems Information Center website at www.nal.usda.gov/afsic/csa.

Habitat for Humanity building projects, cooperative stores, community development associations,[42] and community gardens and fair-trade exchanges.[43] In addition to these forms of exchange there are the corporeal works of mercy: feeding the hungry, clothing the naked, welcoming the stranger, assisting the poor, visiting those who are sick or in prison, and burying the dead.[44] But then again, should scale be a determining factor for an endeavor that began with a handful of fishermen and widows cowering in fear before the most powerful empire the world had to that time ever known?

These gratuitous and joyful relationships of giving and receiving do not treat others as either superfluous or instrumental to one's own appetites but as occasions for us to love gratuitously, just as God has loved us. These relations are sustained by what Alasdair MacIntyre calls the virtue of just generosity, which issues in actions that in a real sense are uncalculating, in that there is no strict proportionality of giving and receiving. That is to say, "those from whom I hope to and perhaps do receive are very often, even if not always, not the same people as those to whom I gave. And what I am called upon to give has no predetermined limits and may greatly exceed what I have received. I may not calculate what I owe on the basis of what others have given me."[45]

According to MacIntyre, there is a form of rationality that accompanies just generosity, a prudent calculation that is required if one is to have something to give: industriousness in acquiring property, thrift in saving, and discrimination in giving so that the truly needy may receive.[46] However, though this linking of just generosity with a modified form of prudential calculus is more natural than a system tethered solely to surplus desire and unconstrained self-interest, it still presupposes the normative standing of an economy of scarcity in which the principle of marginal utility reigns supreme. In the divine gift economy, by contrast, the plenitude of divine charity eternally shared within the Godhead becomes available to all. The unnatural competition for scarce resources is overcome, as finitude is seen as an opportunity to learn the true significance of creaturely freedom and the other is seen as the one we are called to love. Desire is thereby redirected as a generosity that is gratuitous

42. Perkins, *Restoring At-Risk Communities*.

43. For more information on fair-trade opportunities, see the website of the Fair Trade Federation at www.fairtradefederation.com.

44. The danger in emphasizing these sorts of ventures is that they seem to focus on the symptoms of capitalism's pathologies without addressing the systemic causes, but as Daniel Bell points out, one of the spiritual works of mercy is admonishing sinners. Bell, "Sacrifice and Suffering," 358n68.

45. MacIntyre, *Dependent Rational Animals*, 126.

46. MacIntyre, *Dependent Rational Animals*, 126.

and for that reason as just, flowing from the reciprocity of gifts within the body of Christ.

The body of Christ, then, is not without its own source of power for dealing with the earthly regime, particularly as the rulers and authorities of this age seek under the influence of the *libido dominandi* to confine all things within their own panoptic brand of universality, their own ersatz "catholicity," as it were. The church challenges their idolatrous pretensions to express and exhaust the human world to the extent that it attends to the lives of people as they are locally, distinct from the implications of their fragmentary existence as interchangeable producers and consumers in the global market. The church needs to replot on a human scale the stories of those who are but ciphers within the hegemonic strategies of the state and the global market—to relocate their stories within the face-to-face exchanges that can take place only at the level of local forms of ecclesial association—congregation or parish, diocese, and the like.[47] To those deprived of houses, lands, siblings, and parents, the church is called to offer "houses, brothers and sisters, mothers and children, and fields, with persecutions—and in the age to come eternal life" (Mark 10:30).

Where, Then, Does the Church Stand Now?

It is fitting that I conclude by returning to the question with which I began: Where, then, do we stand? As members of the ecclesial body of Christ, we stand where we have always stood since Pentecost (though far too often we have lost our sense of direction): on pilgrimage toward the city whose architect and builder is God, serving the places in which we now find ourselves as both sign of the age to come and vehicle of passage for this world through time. As we have seen, this form of life requires new habits of life and language, new ways of assessing the world in which we live, new practices binding us to the body of Christ that is our salvation. If in this particular place we are to be weaned from the myth that the nation-state is our true homeland and unconstrained consumption our highest good, we will need to be formed according to a different faith, a different hope, and a different love.

We dare not confuse these theological virtues with value judgments that have principally to do with abstract ideas that individuals choose in isolation from their material relations with their neighbors and with the world about them. These virtues are instead dispositions of character that transpose simple seeing into discernment and mere existing into holy habitation, and they are

47. Boyle, *Who Are We Now?*, 92.

formed only in the company of friends through participation in a shared network of constitutive practices. These sorts of friendships are cultivated as women and men from every tribe, language, people, and nation pass through the baptismal waters that admit them to the eucharistic feast, where around the table of the risen Lord we are caught up by the power of the Spirit into the way of Jesus Christ and the vulnerability of God's pilgrim city.

We should not, however, place too much stock in our virtues, as important as they are for the journey. In her short story "Revelation," O'Connor describes a vision that came just after sundown one day to Ruby Turpin as she was washing down her hogs. Mrs. Turpin was someone who had always prided herself on being a respectable person, working hard every day, doing for the church, having a little of everything and "the God-given wit to use it right," including hogs that were "cleaner than some children." In her vision she saw "a vast horde of souls" making their way to their true homeland. As she looked at the company of saints rumbling toward heaven on a bridge of light extending upward from the earth "through a field of living fire," Mrs. Turpin was astonished to see that people like her were not leading the procession. Instead there were "white trash, clean for the first time in their lives," black folks in white robes, "and battalions of freaks and lunatics shouting and clapping and leaping like frogs." Her kind was bringing up the rear, "marching behind the others with great dignity, accountable as they had always been for good order and common sense and respectable behavior. They alone were on key. Yet she could see by their shocked and altered faces that even their virtues were being burned away." For a time Mrs. Turpin did not move but kept her eyes fixed "on what lay ahead." She eventually turned to make her way up the darkening path to the house. "In the woods around her the invisible cricket choruses had struck up, but what she heard were the voices of the souls climbing upward into the starry field and shouting hallelujahs."[48] May we have eyes to see and ears to hear what the Spirit is saying to us as we tend to our business.

---

48. O'Connor, "Revelation," 654.

BIBLIOGRAPHY

Anderson, Benedict. *Imagined Communities: Reflections on the Origin and Spread of Nationalism*. Rev. ed. New York: Verso, 1991.

Anselm. *Proslogion, with the Replies of Gaunilo and Anselm*. Translated by Thomas Williams. Indianapolis: Hackett, 1995.

Aquinas, Thomas. *Summa contra gentiles*. Translated by Anton C. Pegis, FRSC. Notre Dame, IN: University of Notre Dame Press, 1975.

———. *Summa theologica*. Rev. ed. Translated by Fathers of the English Dominican Province. New York: Benziger, 1948.

Aristotle. *The Politics*. Translated by Carnes Lord. Chicago: University of Chicago Press, 1984.

Asad, Talal. *Genealogies of Religion: Discipline and Reasons of Power in Christianity and Islam*. Baltimore: Johns Hopkins University Press, 1993.

Athanasius the Great of Alexandria. *On the Incarnation: Greek Original and English Translation*. Translated by John Behr. Yonkers, NY: St. Vladimir's Seminary Press, 2011.

Augustine. *The City of God against the Pagans*. Edited by R. W. Dyson. New York: Cambridge University Press, 1998.

———. *The Confessions*. Translated by Maria Boulding. New York: New City, 1997.

———. "First Homily on First John." In *Augustine: Later Works*, edited by John Burnaby, 260–69. Philadelphia: Fortress, 1955.

———. *Teaching Christianity: "De Doctrina Christiana."* Translated by Edmund Hill, OP. New York: New City, 1996.

———. *The Trinity*. Translated by Edmund Hill, OP. New York: New City, 1991.

Balthasar, Hans Urs von. *A Theology of History*. San Francisco: Ignatius, 1994.

———. *The Word Made Flesh*. Vol. 1 of *Explorations in Theology*. San Francisco: Ignatius, 1989.

Barnett, Victoria J. *Bystanders: Conscience and Complicity during the Holocaust.* Westport, CT: Praeger, 1999.

Bauerschmidt, Frederick Christian. "Walking in the Pilgrim City." *New Blackfriars* 77 (November 1996): 504–18.

Bauman, Zygmunt. *Postmodern Ethics.* Oxford: Blackwell, 1993.

Baxter, Michael. "'Overall, the First Amendment Has Been Very Good for Christianity'— NOT! A Response to Dyson's Rebuke." *DePaul Law Review* 43 (Winter 1994): 423–46.

Beckwith, Sarah. *Christ's Body: Identity, Culture, and Society in Late Medieval Writings.* New York: Routledge, 1993.

Begbie, Jeremy. *Theology, Music and Time.* Cambridge: Cambridge University Press, 2000.

Beiner, Ronald. *What's the Matter with Liberalism?* Berkeley: University of California Press, 1992.

Bell, Daniel M., Jr. "Sacrifice and Suffering: Beyond Justice, Human Rights, and Capitalism." *Modern Theology* 18 (July 2002): 333–59.

Bell, Mark R. *Apocalypse How? Baptist Movements during the English Revolution.* Macon, GA: Mercer University Press, 2000.

Benedict XVI. *Caritas in Veritate.* Encyclical. Vatican City: Holy See, 2009. http://w2 .vatican.va/content/benedict-xvi/en/encyclicals/documents/hf_ben-xvi_enc_2009 0629_caritas-in-veritate.html.

Benjamin, Walter. *Illuminations.* Translated by Harry Zohn. New York: Schocken, 1969.

Berger, Peter L. *The Sacred Canopy: Elements of a Sociological Theory of Religion.* Garden City, NY: Doubleday, 1967.

Berry, Wendell. *Standing by Words.* San Francisco: North Point, 1983.

———. *What Are People For?* New York: North Point, 1990.

Bloom, Harold. *The American Religion: The Emergence of the Post-Christian Nation.* New York: Simon & Schuster, 1992.

Blowers, Paul M. "The *Regula Fidei* and the Narrative Character of Early Christian Faith." *Pro Ecclesia* 6 (Spring 1997): 199–228.

Bonhoeffer, Dietrich. "The Church and the Peoples of the World." In *London: 1933–1935,* edited by Keith Clements, translated by Isabel Best, vol. 13 of *Dietrich Bonhoeffer Works,* 307–10. Minneapolis: Fortress, 2007.

———. "Contemporizing New Testament Texts." In *Theological Education at Finkenwalde: 1935–1937,* edited by H. Gaylon Barker and Mark S. Brocker, translated by Douglas W. Stott, vol. 14 of *Dietrich Bonhoeffer Works,* 413–33. Minneapolis: Fortress, 2013.

———. *Creation and Fall: A Theological Exposition of Genesis 1–3.* Edited by John W. de Gruchy. Translated by Douglas Stephen Bax. Vol. 3 of *Dietrich Bonhoeffer Works.* Minneapolis: Fortress, 1997.

———. *Discipleship*. Edited by Geffrey B. Kelly and John D. Godsey. Translated by Barbara Green and Reinhard Krauss. Vol. 4 of *Dietrich Bonhoeffer Works*. Minneapolis: Fortress, 2001.

———. *Ethics*. Edited by Clifford J. Green. Translated by Reinhard Krauss et al. Vol. 6 of *Dietrich Bonhoeffer Works*. Minneapolis: Fortress, 2005.

———. *Letters and Papers from Prison*. Edited by John W. de Gruchy. Translated by Lisa E. Dahill et al. Vol. 8 of *Dietrich Bonhoeffer Works*. Minneapolis: Fortress, 2010.

———. *"Life Together" and "Prayerbook of the Bible."* Edited by Geffrey B. Kelley and Albrecht Shonherr. Translated by Daniel W. Blosch and James H. Burtness. Vol. 5 of *Dietrich Bonhoeffer Works*. Minneapolis: Fortress, 1996.

———. "The Nature of the Church." In *Ecumenical, Academic, and Pastoral Work: 1931–1932*, edited by Victoria J. Barnett et al., translated by Anne Schmidt-Lange et al., vol. 11 of *Dietrich Bonhoeffer Works*, 269–332. Minneapolis: Fortress, 2012.

———. Sanctorum Communio: *A Theological Study of the Sociology of the Church*. Edited by Clifford J. Green. Translated by Reinhard Krauss and Nancy Lukens. Vol. 1 of *Dietrich Bonhoeffer Works*. Minneapolis: Fortress, 1998.

———. "Thy Kingdom Come!" In *Berlin: 1932–1933*, edited by Larry L. Rasmussen, translated by Isabel Best et al., vol. 12 of *Dietrich Bonhoeffer Works*, 285–97. Minneapolis: Fortress, 2009.

Bottum, Joseph. "Christians and Postmoderns." *First Things* 40 (February 1994): 28–32.

Boyarin, Daniel. *A Radical Jew: Paul and the Politics of Identity*. Berkeley: University of California Press, 1994.

Boyle, Nicholas. *Who Are We Now? Christian Humanism and the Global Market from Hegel to Heaney*. Notre Dame, IN: University of Notre Dame Press, 1998.

Brueggemann, Walter. *The Land: Place as Gift, Promise, and Challenge in Biblical Faith*. 2nd ed. Minneapolis: Fortress, 2002.

Buber, Martin. *Between Man and Man*. Translated by Ronald Gregor-Smith. New York: Routledge, 2002.

———. *The Eclipse of God: Studies in the Relation between Religion and Philosophy*. Translated by Maurice S. Friedman, Eugene Kamenka, Norbert Guterman, and I. M. Lask. Atlantic Highlands, NJ: Humanities Press International, 1988.

———. *I and Thou*. Translated by Walter Kaufmann. New York: Scribner's, 1970.

———. *Kingship of God*. 3rd ed. Translated by Richard Scheimann. Atlantic Highlands, NJ: Humanities Press International, 1990.

Buckley, James J. "A Field of Living Fire: Karl Barth on the Spirit and the Church." *Modern Theology* 10 (January 1994): 81–102.

Budde, Michael. *The Borders of Baptism: Identities, Allegiances, and the Church*. Eugene, OR: Cascade, 2011.

———. *The (Magic) Kingdom of God: Christianity and Global Culture Industries*. Boulder, CO: Westview, 1997.

Budde, Michael, and Robert Brimlow. *Christianity Incorporated: How Big Business Is Buying the Church*. Grand Rapids: Brazos, 2002.

Bullard, Scott W. *Re-membering the Body: The Lord's Supper and Ecclesial Unity in the Free Church Traditions*. Eugene, OR: Cascade, 2013.

Burrell, David B., CSC. *Freedom and Creation in Three Traditions*. Notre Dame, IN: University of Notre Dame Press, 1993.

Burrell, David B., CSC, and Elena Malits, CSC. *Original Peace: Restoring God's Creation*. New York: Paulist Press, 1997.

Calvin, John. *Institutes of the Christian Religion*. Translated by Ford Lewis Battles. Philadelphia: Westminster, 1960.

Cameron, Averil. *Christianity and the Rhetoric of Empire: The Development of Christian Discourse*. Berkeley: University of California Press, 1991.

Campbell, Colin. *The Romantic Ethic and the Spirit of Modern Consumerism*. Oxford: Blackwell, 1987.

Capes, David B. "The Lord's Table: Divine or Human Remembrance?" *Perspectives in Religious Studies* 30 (Summer 2003): 199–209.

Catherine of Siena. *Dialogue*. Translated by Suzanne Noffke, OP. New York: Paulist Press, 1980.

Cavanaugh, William T. "The City: Beyond Secular Parodies." In *Radical Orthodoxy: A New Theology*, edited by John Milbank, Catherine Pickstock, and Graham Ward, 182–200. New York: Routledge, 1999.

———. "'A Fire Strong Enough to Consume the House': The Wars of Religion and the Rise of the State." *Modern Theology* 11 (October 1995): 397–420.

———. "Sins of Omission: What 'Religion and Violence' Arguments Ignore." *Hedgehog Review* 6 (Spring 2004): 34–50.

———. *Theopolitical Imagination: Discovering the Liturgy as a Political Act in an Age of Global Consumerism*. New York: T&T Clark, 2002.

———. *Torture and Eucharist: Theology, Politics, and the Body of Christ*. Oxford: Blackwell, 1998.

Certeau, Michel de. *The Mystic Fable*. Vol. 1. Translated by Michael B. Smith. Chicago: University of Chicago Press, 1992.

———. *The Practice of Everyday Life*. Translated by Steven Rendall. Berkeley: University of California Press, 1984.

Charles I. "The King's Declaration." In *Documents of the English Reformation*, edited by Gerald Bray, 481–82. Minneapolis: Fortress, 1994.

Chenderlin, Fritz, SJ. *"Do This as My Memorial": The Semantic and Conceptual Background and Value of* Anamnēsis *in 1 Corinthians 11:24–25*. Rome: Biblical Institute Press, 1982.

Cicero. *De re publica, De legibus*. Translated by Clinton Walker Keyes. Cambridge: Harvard University Press, 1951.

Clapp, Rodney. *Border Crossings: Christian Trespasses on Popular Culture and Public Affairs*. Grand Rapids: Brazos, 2000.

———. *A Peculiar People: The Church as Culture in a Post-Christian World*. Downers Grove, IL: InterVarsity, 1996.

Clement of Alexandria. *Protrepticus*. In vol. 2 of *The Ante-Nicene Fathers*. Edited by Alexander Roberts and James Donaldson. 1885. Repr., Peabody, MA: Hendrickson, 1994.

Coakley, Sarah. *Powers and Submissions: Spirituality, Philosophy and Gender*. Oxford: Blackwell, 2002.

Cochrane, Charles Norris. *Christianity and Classical Culture: A Study of Thought and Action from Augustus to Augustine*. London: Oxford University Press, 1940.

Copenhaver, Martin B., Anthony B. Robinson, and William H. Willimon. *Good News in Exile: Three Pastors Offer a Hopeful Vision for the Church*. Grand Rapids: Eerdmans, 1999.

Dahl, Nils. *Jesus in the Memory of the Early Church*. Minneapolis: Augsburg, 1976.

Dante Alighieri. *Paradise*. Translated by Anthony Esolen. New York: Modern Library, 2004.

———. *Purgatory*. Translated by Anthony Esolen. New York: Modern Library, 2004.

Dawson, John David. *Christian Figural Reading and the Fashioning of Identity*. Berkeley: University of California Press, 2002.

de Lubac, Henri, SJ. *Catholicism: Christ and the Common Destiny of Man*. Translated by Lancelot C. Sheppard and Elizabeth Englund, OCD. San Francisco: Ignatius, 1988.

———. *Medieval Exegesis: The Four Senses of Scripture*. Vol. 1. Translated by Mark Sebanc. Grand Rapids: Eerdmans, 1998.

———. *The Mystery of the Supernatural*. Translated by Rosemary Sheed. With an introduction by David L. Schindler. New York: Crossroad, 1998.

———. *Scripture in the Tradition*. Translated by Luke O'Neill. New York: Herder & Herder, 2000.

Dix, Dom Gregory. *The Shape of the Liturgy*. With additional notes by Paul V. Marshall. New York: Seabury, 1982.

Dostoevsky, Fyodor. "The Dream of a Ridiculous Man." In *The Best Short Stories of Dostoevsky*, translated by David Magarshack, 263–85. New York: Modern Library, 1955.

Eagleton, Terry. *The Illusions of Postmodernism*. Oxford: Blackwell, 1996.

Eusebius. *The History of the Church*. In vol. 1 of *The Nicene and Post-Nicene Fathers*, Series 2, edited by Philip Schaff, 73–387. 1890. Repr., Peabody, MA: Hendrickson, 1994.

———. *In Praise of the Emperor Constantine*. In vol. 1 of *The Nicene and Post-Nicene Fathers*, Series 2, edited by Philip Schaff, 581–610. 1890. Repr., Peabody, MA: Hendrickson, 1994.

———. *Life of Constantine*. In vol. 1 of *The Nicene and Post-Nicene Fathers*, Series 2, edited by Philip Schaff, 481–559. 1890. Repr., Peabody, MA: Hendrickson, 1994.

Evagrius of Pontus. *Evagrius of Pontus: The Greek Ascetic Corpus*. Translated and edited by Robert E. Sinkewicz. New York: Oxford University Press, 2003.

Evans, G. R. *Old Arts and New Theology: The Beginnings of Theology as an Academic Discipline*. Oxford: Clarendon, 1980.

Field, Lester L., Jr. *Liberty, Dominion, and the Two Swords: On the Origins of Western Political Theology (180–398)*. Notre Dame, IN: University of Notre Dame Press, 1998.

Figgis, John Neville. *Studies of Political Thought from Gerson to Grotius, 1414–1625*. Cambridge: Cambridge University Press, 1956.

Fish, Stanley. "Boutique Multiculturalism, or Why Liberals Are Incapable of Thinking about Hate Speech." *Critical Inquiry* 23 (Winter 1997): 378–95.

Florovsky, Georges. "Empire and Desert: Antinomies of Christian History." *Greek Orthodox Theological Review* 3 (Winter 1957): 133–59.

Fox, Richard Wightman. *Reinhold Niebuhr: A Biography*. San Francisco: Harper, 1987.

Francis. *Address of His Holiness Pope Francis to the Pilgrimage from El Salvador*. Vatican City: Holy See, 2015. http://w2.vatican.va/content/francesco/en/speeches /2015/october/documents/papa-francesco_20151030_el-salvador.html.

Freeman, Curtis W. *Contesting Catholicity: Theology for Other Baptists*. Waco: Baylor University Press, 2014.

Fukuyama, Francis. "The End of History?" *National Interest* 16 (Summer 1989): 3–18.

Gallie, W. B. *Philosophy and the Historical Understanding*. New York: Schocken, 1964.

Gamble, Richard M. *The War for Righteousness: Progressive Christianity, the Great War, and the Rise of the Messianic Nation*. Wilmington, DE: ISI, 2003.

Geertz, Clifford. *The Interpretation of Cultures*. New York: Basic Books, 1973.

Gelasius (pope). "Letter Twelve to Emperor Anastasius." In *Church and State in Early Christianity*, by Hugo Rahner, SJ, translated by Leo Donald Davis, SJ, 173–76. San Francisco: Ignatius, 1992.

Gewirth, Alan. *Reason and Morality*. Chicago: University of Chicago Press, 1978.

Grant, George. *Time as History*. Toronto: University of Toronto Press, 1995.

Greene, Graham. *The Power and the Glory*. New York: Penguin, 1991.

Griffiths, Paul J. *Intellectual Appetite: A Theological Grammar*. Washington, DC: Catholic University of America Press, 2009.

Guroian, Vigen. *Incarnate Love: Essays in Orthodox Ethics*. 2nd ed. Notre Dame, IN: University of Notre Dame Press, 2002.

Hampson, Daphne. *Theology and Feminism*. Oxford: Blackwell, 1990.

Hardy, Daniel W., and David F. Ford. *Praising and Knowing God*. Philadelphia: Westminster, 1985.

Hargaden, Kevin. *Theological Ethics in a Neoliberal Age: Confronting the Christian Problem with Wealth.* Eugene, OR: Cascade, 2018.

Harmon, Steven R. *Baptist Identity and the Ecumenical Future: Story, Tradition, and the Recovery of Tradition.* Waco: Baylor University Press, 2016.

Harrison, Peter. *"Religion" and the Religion in the English Enlightenment.* New York: Cambridge University Press, 1990.

Harvey, Barry. *Another City: An Ecclesiological Primer for a Post-Christian World.* Valley Forge, PA: Trinity Press International, 1999.

Hatch, Derek C. *Thinking with the Church: Toward a Renewal of Baptist Theology.* Eugene, OR: Cascade, 2018.

Hatch, Nathan O. *The Democratization of American Christianity.* New Haven: Yale University Press, 1989.

Hauerwas, Stanley. *In Good Company: The Church as Polis.* Notre Dame, IN: University of Notre Dame Press, 1995.

Hauerwas, Stanley, and William H. Willimon. *Resident Aliens: Life in the Christian Colony.* Nashville: Abingdon, 1989.

Havel, Václav. *Living in Truth.* Edited by Jan Vladislav. London: Faber and Faber, 1987.

Hedge, Chris. *War Is a Force That Gives Us Meaning.* New York: Anchor, 2003.

Hegel, Georg Wilhelm Friedrich. *The Philosophy of History.* Rev. ed. Translated by J. Sibree. New York: Wiley, 1944.

Herberg, Will. *Protestant, Catholic, Jew: An Essay in American Religious Sociology.* Garden City, NY: Anchor, 1960.

Heschel, Abraham. *Sabbath: Its Meaning for Modern Man.* New York: Farrar, Straus & Giroux, 1951.

Hippolytus. *The Treatise on the Apostolic Tradition.* Edited by Gregory Dix and Henry Chadwick. Ridgefield, CT: Morehouse, 1992.

Hobbes, Thomas. *Leviathan.* Edited by Edwin Curley. Indianapolis: Hackett, 1994.

Ignatius of Antioch. *Epistle to the Romans.* In vol. 1 of *The Ante-Nicene Fathers.* Edited by Alexander Roberts and James Donaldson. 1885. Repr., Peabody, MA: Hendrickson, 1994.

Jantzen, Grace M. *Power, Gender and Christian Mysticism.* Cambridge: Cambridge University Press, 1995.

Jefferson, Thomas. *Notes on the State of Virginia.* Query 17, "Religion." In *The Writings of Thomas Jefferson,* edited by William Peden, 157–61. Chapel Hill: University of North Carolina Press, 1954.

Jennings, Willie James. *The Christian Imagination: Theology and the Origins of Race.* New Haven: Yale University Press, 2010.

Jenson, Robert. "How the World Lost Its Story." *First Things* 36 (October 1993): 19–24.

———. *The Triune God.* Vol. 1 of *Systematic Theology.* New York: Oxford University Press, 1997.

Jeremias, Joachim. *The Eucharistic Words of Jesus*. Translated by Norman Perrin. Philadelphia: Fortress, 1966.

John Chrysostom. *Homilies on the Gospel of St. Matthew*. Translated by Tissa Balasuriya. Maryknoll, NY: Orbis, 1979.

John Paul II. *Fides et Ratio*. Encyclical. Boston: Pauline Books and Media, 1998. Also available at the Vatican website: http://w2.vatican.va/content/john-paul-ii /en/encyclicals/documents/hf_jp-ii_enc_14091998_fides-et-ratio.html.

Johnson, Kelly S. *Fear of Beggars: Stewardship and Poverty in Christian Ethics*. Grand Rapids: Eerdmans, 2007.

Kant, Immanuel. *Critique of Pure Reason*. Translated by Norman Kemp Smith. New York: St. Martin's, 1965.

———. *Religion within the Boundaries of Mere Reason, and Other Writings*. Translated by Allen Wood and George Di Giovanni. New York: Cambridge University Press, 1998.

Kantorowicz, Ernst H. *The King's Two Bodies: A Study in Mediaeval Political Theology*. Princeton: Princeton University Press, 1985.

Kasper, Walter Cardinal. "Current Problems in Ecumenical Theology." Vatican City: Holy See, 2003. http://www.vatican.va/roman_curia/pontifical_councils/chrstuni /card-kasper-docs/rc_pc_chrstuni_doc_20030227_ecumenical-theology_en.html.

Kent, John H. S. *The End of the Line? The Development of Christian Theology over the Last Two Centuries*. Philadelphia: Fortress, 1982.

Kermode, Frank. *The Genesis of Secrecy: On the Interpretation of Narrative*. Cambridge: Harvard University Press, 1979.

Ladner, Gerhart B. "Aspects of Medieval Thought on Church and State." *Review of Politics* 9 (1947): 403–9.

Lash, Nicholas. *The Beginning and the End of "Religion."* New York: Cambridge University Press, 1996.

———. *Believing Three Ways in One God: A Reading of the Apostles' Creed*. Notre Dame, IN: University of Notre Dame Press, 1993.

———. *Easter in Ordinary: Reflections on Human Experience and the Knowledge of God*. Charlottesville: University Press of Virginia, 1988.

———. *Theology on the Way to Emmaus*. London: SCM, 1986.

Leclercq, Jean, OSB. *The Love of Learning and the Desire for God*. 2nd ed. Translated by Catharine Misrahi. New York: Fordham University Press, 1974.

Lee, Philip J. *Against the Protestant Gnostics*. New York: Oxford University Press, 1987.

Lehmann, Paul L. *Ethics in a Christian Context*. New York: Harper & Row, 1963.

Leithart, Peter J. *The End of Protestantism: Pursuing Unity in a Fragmented Church*. Grand Rapids: Brazos, 2016.

Leland, John. "A Blow at the Root." In *The Writings of John Leland*, edited by L. F. Greene, 235–55. New York: Arno, 1969.

Lentricchia, Frank. *Ariel and the Police*. Madison: University of Wisconsin Press, 1988.

Lilla, Mark. *The Stillborn God: Religion, Politics, and the Modern West*. New York: Knopf, 2007.

Linder, Robert D. "Universal Pastor: President Bill Clinton's Civil Religion." *Journal of Church and State* 38 (Autumn 1996): 733–49.

Locke, John. *A Letter concerning Toleration*. Edited by James H. Tully. Indianapolis: Hackett, 1983.

Lohfink, Gerhard. *Does God Need the Church? Toward a Theology of the People of God*. Translated by Linda M. Maloney. Collegeville, MN: Liturgical Press, 1999.

Long, D. Stephen. *The Divine Economy: Theology and the Market*. New York: Routledge, 2000.

———. *The Goodness of God: Theology, the Church, and Social Order*. Grand Rapids: Brazos, 2001.

Lortz, Joseph. *The Reformation: A Problem for Today*. Translated by John C. Dwyer, SJ. Westminster, MD: Newman, 1964.

Loughlin, Gerard. *Telling God's Story: Bible, Church and Narrative Theology*. New York: Cambridge University Press, 1996.

Lowe, Walter. "Prospects for a Postmodern Christian Theology: Apocalyptic without Reserve." *Modern Theology* 15 (January 1999): 17–24.

Luhmann, Niklas. *Religious Dogmatics and the Evolution of Societies*. Translated by Peter Beyer. New York: Mellen, 1984.

Lumen Gentium: Dogmatic Constitution on the Church. Vatican City: Holy See, 1964. http://www.vatican.va/archive/hist_councils/ii_vatican_council/documents/vat-ii_const_19641121_lumen-gentium_en.html.

Lumpkin, William L. *Baptist Confessions of Faith*. Rev. ed. Valley Forge, PA: Judson, 1969.

Luther, Martin. *First Lectures on the Psalms II: Psalms 76–126*. Vol. 11 of *Luther's Works*. Edited by Hilton C. Oswald. St. Louis: Concordia, 1976.

———. *The Freedom of a Christian*. In *Three Treatises*, 261–316. Translated by W. A. Lambert. 2nd ed. Philadelphia: Fortress, 1970.

Lyotard, Jean-François. *The Postmodern Condition: A Report on Knowledge*. Translated by Geoff Bennington and Brian Massumi. Minneapolis: University of Minnesota Press, 1984.

MacIntyre, Alasdair. *After Virtue*. 2nd ed. Notre Dame, IN: University of Notre Dame Press, 1984.

———. *Dependent Rational Animals: Why Human Beings Need the Virtues*. Chicago: Open Court, 1999.

———. "Epistemological Crises, Dramatic Narrative, and the Philosophy of Science." In *Why Narrative?*, edited by Stanley Hauerwas and L. Gregory Jones, 138–57. Grand Rapids: Eerdmans, 1989.

———. *Whose Justice? Which Rationality?* Notre Dame, IN: University of Notre Dame Press, 1988.

Markus, R. A. *Saeculum: History and Society in the Theology of St Augustine.* Rev. ed. Cambridge: Cambridge University Press, 1988.

Marvin, Carolyn, and David W. Ingle. *Blood Sacrifice and the Nation: Totem Rituals and the American Flag.* New York: Cambridge University Press, 1999.

Mawson, Michael. *Christ Existing as Community: Bonhoeffer's Ecclesiology.* Oxford: Oxford University Press, 2018.

McCabe, Herbert, OP. "Comment." *New Blackfriars* 48 (February 1967): 226–29.

———. *God Matters.* London: Geoffrey Chapman, 1987.

———. *God Still Matters.* Edited by Brian Davies, OP. New York: Continuum, 2002.

McClendon, James Wm., Jr. *Doctrine.* Vol. 2 of *Systematic Theology.* Nashville: Abingdon, 1994.

———. *Ethics.* Rev. ed. Vol. 1 of *Systematic Theology.* Nashville: Abingdon, 1986.

———. *Witness.* Vol. 3 of *Systematic Theology.* Nashville: Abingdon, 2000.

McClendon, James Wm., Jr., and James M. Smith. *Convictions: Defusing Religious Relativism.* Rev. ed. Valley Forge, PA: Trinity Press International, 1994.

McGinn, Bernard. "The Letter and the Spirit: Spirituality as an Academic Discipline." *Christian Spirituality Bulletin* 1 (Fall 1993): 1–10.

———. "Love, Knowledge, and Mystical Union in Western Christianity: Twelfth to Sixteenth Centuries." *Church History* 56 (March 1987): 7–24.

McIntosh, Mark A. *Mystical Theology: The Integrity of Spirituality and Theology.* Oxford: Blackwell, 1998.

Mensch, Elizabeth, and Alan Freeman. *The Politics of Virtue: Is Abortion Debatable?* Durham, NC: Duke University Press, 1993.

Merton, Thomas. *The Wisdom of the Desert.* New York: New Directions, 1970.

Metz, Johann Baptist. *Faith in History and Society: Toward a Practical Fundamental Theology.* Translated by David Smith. New York: Seabury, 1980.

Meyer, Ben F. *The Early Christians: Their World Mission and Self-Discovery.* Wilmington, DE: Michael Glazier, 1986.

Milbank, John. *Being Reconciled: Ontology and Pardon.* New York: Routledge, 2003.

———. "Can a Gift Be Given? Prolegomena to a Future Trinitarian Metaphysic." *Modern Theology* 11 (1995): 119–61.

———. "'Postmodern Critical Augustinianism': A Short *Summa* in Forty-Two Responses to Unasked Questions." *Modern Theology* 7 (April 1991): 225–37.

———. "The Second Difference: For a Trinitarianism without Reserve." *Modern Theology* 2 (1986): 213–34.

———. *Theology and Social Theory: Beyond Secular Reason.* Oxford: Blackwell, 1990.

———. *The Word Made Strange: Theology, Language, Culture*. Oxford: Blackwell, 1997.

Moore, Thomas. *Care of the Soul: A Guide for Cultivating Depth and Sacredness in Everyday Life*. New York: HarperCollins, 1992.

Morris, Colin. *The Discovery of the Individual, 1050–1200*. New York: Harper & Row, 1972.

Mullins, E. Y. *The Axioms of Religion: A New Interpretation of the Baptist Faith*. Philadelphia: American Baptist Publication Society, 1908.

Murdoch, Iris. *The Sovereignty of Good*. New York: Routledge, 2001.

Murray, John Courtney, SJ. *We Hold These Truths: Catholic Reflections on the American Proposition*. Lanham, MD: Sheed and Ward, 2005.

Navone, John, SJ. *Seeking God in Story*. Collegeville, MN: Liturgical Press, 1990.

Neuhaus, Richard John. "Three Constellations of American Religion." *First Things* 111 (March 2001): 71–77.

Newman, Elizabeth. *Attending the Wounds on Christ's Body: Teresa's Scriptural Vision*. Eugene, OR: Cascade, 2012.

———. *Untamed Hospitality: Welcoming God and Other Strangers*. Grand Rapids: Brazos, 2007.

Newman, John Henry. *An Essay on the Development of Christian Doctrine*. Notre Dame, IN: University of Notre Dame Press, 1989.

———. "The Nature of Faith in Relation to Reason." In *Fifteen Sermons Preached before the University of Oxford between A.D. 1826 and 1843*, 202–21. Notre Dame, IN: University of Notre Dame Press, 1997.

Niebuhr, Reinhold. *Moral Man and Immoral Society: A Study in Ethics and Politics*. New York: Charles Scribner's Sons, 1960.

Nietzsche, Friedrich. *The Antichrist*. In *The Portable Nietzsche*, translated by Walter Kaufmann, 565–656. New York: Penguin, 1954.

Nisbet, Robert A. *The Quest for Community: A Study in the Ethics of Order and Freedom*. New York: Oxford University Press, 1953.

Novak, David. "Edith Stein, Apostate Saint." *First Things* 96 (October 1999): 15–17.

Nussbaum, Martha C. *Cultivating Humanity: A Classical Defense of Reform in Liberal Education*. Cambridge: Harvard University Press, 1997.

Oberman, Heiko Augustinus. *The Harvest of Medieval Theology: Gabriel Biel and Late Medieval Nominalism*. Cambridge: Harvard University Press, 1963.

O'Connor, Flannery. "Letter to A." September 6, 1955. In *Collected Works*, 951–54. New York: Library of America, 1988.

———. "Revelation." In *Collected Works*, 633–54. New York: Library of America, 1988.

———. "Some Aspects of the Grotesque in Southern Fiction." In *Collected Works*, 813–21. New York: Library of America, 1988.

O'Donovan, Oliver. *The Desire of the Nations: Rediscovering the Roots of Political Theology*. Cambridge: Cambridge University Press, 1996.

Origen. *Contra Celsum*. In vol. 4 of *The Ante-Nicene Fathers*. Edited by Alexander Roberts and James Donaldson. 1885. Repr., Peabody, MA: Hendrickson, 1994.

———. "Dialogue of Origen with Heraclides and His Fellow Bishops on the Father, the Son, and the Soul." Translated by Robert J. Daly, SJ. In *Origen: "Treatise on the Passover" and "Dialogue of Origen with Heraclides and His Fellow Bishops on the Father, the Son, and the Soul."* Ancient Christian Writers: The Works of the Fathers in Translation 54. Edited by Walter J. Burghardt, Thomas Comerford Lawler, and John J. Dillon. New York: Paulist Press, 1992.

O'Siadhail, Micheal. "Freedom." In *Poems, 1975–1995*. Newcastle upon Tyne: Bloodaxe Books, 1999.

Pelikan, Jaroslav. *The Riddle of Roman Catholicism*. Nashville: Abingdon, 1959.

Percy, Walker. *Lost in the Cosmos: The Last Self-Help Book*. New York: Farrar, Straus & Giroux, 1983.

———. *The Message in the Bottle: How Queer Man Is, How Queer Language Is, and What One Has to Do with the Other*. New York: Farrar, Straus & Giroux, 1975.

———. *Sign-Posts in a Strange Land*. Edited by Patrick Samway. New York: Farrar, Straus & Giroux, 1991.

Perkins, John M., ed. *Restoring At-Risk Communities: Doing It Together and Doing It Right*. Grand Rapids: Baker, 1995.

Peterson, Erik. *Theological Tractates*. Edited and translated by Michael J. Hollerich. Stanford, CA: Stanford University Press, 2011.

Pieper, Josef. *Living the Truth: "The Truth of All Things" and "Reality and the Good."* Translated by Lothar Krauth and Stella Lange. San Francisco: Ignatius, 1989.

Porter, Bruce D. *War and the Rise of the State: The Military Foundations of Modern Politics*. New York: Free Press, 1994.

Poteat, William H. *A Philosophical Daybook: Post-critical Investigations*. Columbia: University of Missouri Press, 1990.

———. *Polanyian Meditations: In Search of a Post-critical Logic*. Durham, NC: Duke University Press, 1985.

Power, David, and Herman Schmidt. "Editorial." In *Politics and Liturgy*, edited by David Power and Herman Schmidt. New York: Herder and Herder, 1974.

Putnam, Robert. "Bowling Alone: America's Declining Social Capital." *Journal of Democracy* 6 (January 1995): 65–78.

Raboteau, Albert J. *Slave Religion: The "Invisible Institution" in the Antebellum South*. New York: Oxford University Press, 1978.

Radner, Ephraim. *The End of the Church: A Pneumatology of Christian Division in the West*. Grand Rapids: Eerdmans, 1998.

Ratzinger, Joseph. *Church, Ecumenism, and Politics: New Essays in Ecclesiology.* New York: Crossroad, 1988.

———. *Salt of the Earth: Christianity and the Church at the End of the Millennium; An Interview with Peter Seewald.* Translated by Adrian Walker. San Francisco: Ignatius, 1997.

Rauschenbusch, Walter. *Christianizing the Social Order.* New York: Macmillan, 1912.

Rawls, John. *Political Liberalism.* New York: Columbia University Press, 1993.

Ritschl, Dietrich. *The Logic of Theology: A Brief Account of the Relationship between Basic Concepts in Theology.* Philadelphia: Fortress, 1987.

Robinson, Anthony B. "The Making of a Post-Liberal." In *Good News in Exile: Three Pastors Offer a Hopeful Vision for the Church,* by Martin B. Copenhaver, Anthony B. Robinson, and William H. Willimon, 5–26. Grand Rapids: Eerdmans, 1999.

Rorty, Richard. *Achieving Our Country: Leftist Thought in Twentieth-Century America.* Cambridge: Harvard University Press, 1998.

———. "The Priority of Democracy to Philosophy." In *The Virginia Statute for Religious Freedom,* edited by Merrill D. Peterson and Robert C. Vaughan, 257–82. New York: Cambridge University Press, 1988.

Rosin, Hanna. "Beyond 2000: Many Shape Unique Religions at Home." *Washington Post,* January 17, 2000.

Rouse, Joseph. *Knowledge and Power.* Ithaca, NY: Cornell University Press, 1987.

Rousseau, Jean-Jacques. *The Social Contract.* Translated by Willmoore Kendall. South Bend, IN: Gateway, 1954.

Ruether, Rosemary Radford. *Faith and Fratricide: The Theological Roots of Anti-Semitism.* New York: Seabury, 1974.

Sanders, E. P. *Judaism: Practice and Belief, 63 BCE–66 CE.* Philadelphia: Trinity Press International, 1992.

Sartre, Jean-Paul. *Being and Nothingness.* Translated by Hazel E. Barnes. New York: Gramercy, 1956.

Schindler, David L. "Christology and the *Imago Dei*: Interpreting *Gaudium et Spes.*" *Communio* 23 (Spring 1996): 156–84.

Schlabach, Gerald W. "The Correction of the Augustinians: A Case Study in the Critical Appropriation of a Suspect Tradition." In *The Free Church and the Early Church: Bridging the Historical Divide,* edited by Daniel H. Williams, 47–74. Grand Rapids: Eerdmans, 2002.

Schmemann, Alexander. *Church, World, Mission: Reflections on Orthodoxy in the West.* Crestwood, NY: St. Vladimir's Seminary Press, 1979.

———. *For the Life of the World: Sacraments and Orthodoxy.* Crestwood, NY: St. Vladimir's Seminary Press, 1973.

Sheehan, Jonathan. *The Enlightenment Bible: Translation, Scholarship, Culture.* Princeton: Princeton University Press, 2005.

Sheldrake, Philip. *Spirituality and History: Questions of Interpretation and Method*. Rev. ed. London: SPCK, 1995.

Sherman, Hazel. "Baptized—'in the Name of the Father and of the Son and of the Holy Spirit.'" In *Reflections on the Water: Understanding God and the World through the Baptism of Believers*, edited by Paul S. Fiddes, 101–16. Macon, GA: Smyth & Helwys, 1996.

Skinner, Quentin. *The Age of Reformation*. Vol. 2 of *The Foundations of Modern Political Thought*. London: Cambridge University Press, 1978.

Smith, Christian, with Melinda Lundquist Denton. *Soul Searching: The Religious and Spiritual Lives of American Teenagers*. New York: Oxford University Press, 2005.

Smith, Harmon L. *Where Two or Three Are Gathered: Liturgy and the Moral Life*. Cleveland: Pilgrim, 1995.

Smith, Ted A. *Weird John Brown: Divine Violence and the Limits of Ethics*. Stanford, CA: Stanford University Press, 2015.

Smith, Wilfred Cantwell. *The Meaning and End of Religion: A New Approach to the Religious Traditions of Mankind*. New York: Macmillan, 1962.

Soelle, Dorothee. *The Window of Vulnerability: A Political Spirituality*. Minneapolis: Fortress, 1990.

Southern, Richard William. *Western Society and the Church in the Middle Ages*. Harmondsworth, UK: Penguin, 1985.

Spruyt, Hendrik. *The Sovereign State and Its Competitors*. Princeton: Princeton University Press, 1994.

Stackhouse, Max L. "Public Theology and Political Theology in a Globalizing Era." In *Public Theology for the 21st Century*, edited by William F. Storrar and Andrew R. Morton, 179–94. New York: T&T Clark, 2004.

Stark, Rodney. *The Rise of Christianity: A Sociologist Reconsiders History*. Princeton: Princeton University Press, 1996.

Stendahl, Krister. "Biblical Theology, Contemporary." In *The Interpreter's Dictionary of the Bible*, edited by G. A. Buttrick, 418–32. Vol 1. Nashville: Abingdon, 1962.

Stevens, Wallace. *Letters*. Edited by Holly Stevens. New York: Knopf, 1966.

Stewart, James S. "On a Neglected Emphasis in New Testament Theology." *Scottish Journal of Theology* 4 (1951): 292–301.

Stout, Harry S. *Upon the Altar of the Nation: A Moral History of the American Civil War*. New York: Viking, 2006.

Strayer, Joseph R. "The Laicization of French and English Society in the Thirteenth Century." *Speculum* 15 (1940): 76.

———. *On the Medieval Origins of the Modern State*. Princeton: Princeton University Press, 1970.

Stringfellow, William. *The Politics of Spirituality*. Philadelphia: Westminster, 1984.

Stroumsa, Guy G. *Hidden Wisdom: Esoteric Traditions and the Roots of Christian Mysticism*. New York: Brill, 1996.

Swinburne, Richard. *The Existence of God*. Oxford: Oxford University Press, 1979.

Taylor, Charles. *A Secular Age*. Cambridge: Belknap, 2007.

————. *Sources of the Self: The Making of Modern Identity*. Cambridge: Harvard University Press, 1989.

Tertullian, *De corona*. In vol. 3 of *The Ante-Nicene Fathers*. Edited by Alexander Roberts and James Donaldson. 1885. Repr., Peabody, MA: Hendrickson, 1994.

Thiselton, Anthony C. *Interpreting God and the Postmodern Self: On Meaning, Manipulation and Promise*. Edinburgh: T&T Clark, 1995.

Thompson, Philip E. "Sacraments and Religious Liberty: From Critical Practice to Rejected Infringement." In *Baptist Sacramentalism*, edited by Anthony R. Cross and Philip E. Thompson, 36–54. Waynesboro, GA: Paternoster, 2003.

Tillich, Paul. *Dynamics of Faith*. New York: Harper & Row, 1957.

Torrell, Jean-Pierre, OP. *Saint Thomas Aquinas*. Vol. 1, *The Person and His Work*. Translated by Robert Royal. Washington, DC: Catholic University of America Press, 1996.

Toulmin, Stephen. *Cosmopolis: The Hidden Agenda of Modernity*. Chicago: University of Chicago Press, 1990.

Trocmé, André. *Jesus and the Nonviolent Revolution*. Edited by Charles E. Moore. Rifton, NY: Plough, 2011.

Troeltsch, Ernst. *The Social Teaching of the Christian Churches*. 2 vols. Translated by Olive Wyon. Louisville: Westminster John Knox, 1992.

Turner, Denys. *The Darkness of God: Negativity in Christian Mysticism*. New York: Cambridge University Press, 1995.

————. *Faith, Reason and the Existence of God*. Cambridge: Cambridge University Press, 2004.

Virgil. *The Aeneid*. Translated by Robert Fagles. New York: Viking, 2006.

Wainwright, Geoffrey. *Eucharist and Eschatology*. New York: Oxford University Press, 1981.

Ward, Graham. *Cultural Transformation and Religious Practice*. New York: Cambridge University Press, 2005.

Weber, Max. *The Protestant Ethic and the Spirit of Capitalism*. Translated by Talcott Parsons. London: Unwin, 1930.

West, Cornel. "Ethics and Action in Fredric Jameson's Marxist Hermeneutic." In *Postmodernism and Politics*, edited by Jonathan Arac, 123–44. Minneapolis: University of Minnesota Press, 1986.

Westerhoff, John H. "Fashioning Christians in Our Day." In *Schooling Christians: "Holy Experiments" in American Education*, edited by Stanley Hauerwas and John H. Westerhoff, 262–81. Grand Rapids: Eerdmans, 1992.

Wilken, Robert L. *The Christians as the Romans Saw Them*. New Haven: Yale University Press, 1984.

———. *John Chrysostom and the Jews: Rhetoric and Reality in the Late 4th Century*. Berkeley: University of California Press, 1983.

———. *The Spirit of Early Christian Thought: Seeking the Face of God*. New Haven: Yale University Press, 2003.

William of St. Thierry. *The Mirror of Faith*. Translated by Thomas X. Davis. Kalamazoo, MI: Cistercian, 1979.

Williams, Rowan. "Between Politics and Metaphysics: Reflections in the Wake of Gillian Rose." In *Rethinking Metaphysics*, edited by L. Gregory Jones and Stephen E. Fowl, 3–22. Oxford: Blackwell, 1995.

———. *Christ on Trial: How the Gospel Unsettles Our Judgment*. Grand Rapids: Eerdmans, 2000.

———. *The Edge of Words: God and the Habits of Language*. New York: Bloomsbury T&T Clark, 2014.

———. "Language, Reality and Desire in Augustine's *De Doctrina*." *Literature and Theology* 3 (July 1989): 138–50.

———. *Lost Icons: Reflection on Cultural Bereavement*. Edinburgh: T&T Clark, 2000.

———. *On Christian Theology*. Oxford: Blackwell, 2000.

———. "Politics and the Soul: A Reading of the *City of God*." *Milltown Studies* 19/20 (1987): 55–72.

———. *Resurrection: Interpreting the Easter Gospel*. New York: Pilgrim, 1984.

———. "Theological Integrity." *New Blackfriars* 72 (March 1991): 140–51.

———. "The Unity of Christian Truth." *New Blackfriars* 70 (February 1989): 85–95.

———. *The Wound of Knowledge*. 2nd ed. Boston: Cowley, 1990.

Wolff, Hans Walter. *Joel and Amos: A Commentary on the Books of the Prophets Joel and Amos*. Translated by Waldemar Janzen, S. Dean McBride Jr., and Charles A. Muenchow. Philadelphia: Fortress, 1977.

Wright, N. T. *The Climax of the Covenant*. Minneapolis: Fortress, 1992.

———. *Jesus and the Victory of God*. Vol. 2 of *Christian Origins and the Question of God*. Minneapolis: Fortress, 1996.

———. *The New Testament and the People of God*. Vol. 1 of *Christian Origins and the Question of God*. Minneapolis: Fortress, 1992.

———. *Who Was Jesus?* Grand Rapids: Eerdmans, 1993.

Wyschogrod, Michael. *The Body of Faith: God in the People Israel*. San Francisco: Harper & Row, 1983.

Yoder, John Howard. "Armaments and Eschatology." *Studies in Christian Ethics* 1 (1988): 55–58.

———. *For the Nations: Essays Public and Evangelical*. Grand Rapids: Eerdmans, 1997.

———. *The Politics of Jesus: Vicit Agnus Noster*. 2nd ed. Grand Rapids: Eerdmans, 1994.

———. *The Royal Priesthood: Essays Ecclesiological and Ecumenical*. Edited by M. G. Cartwright. Grand Rapids: Eerdmans, 1994.

Ziegler, Philip G. *Militant Grace: The Apocalyptic Turn and the Future of Christian Theology*. Grand Rapids: Baker Academic, 2018.

Zizioulas, John D. *Being as Communion*. Crestwood, NY: St. Vladimir's Seminary Press, 1985.

———. "The Early Christian Community." In *Christian Spirituality: Origins to the Twelfth Century*, edited by Bernard McGinn, John Meyendorff, and Jean Leclercq, 23–43. New York: Crossroad, 1997.

Zwingli, Ulrich. *Commentary on True and False Religion*. Edited by Samuel Macauley Jackson and Clarence Nevin Heller. Durham, NC: Labyrinth, 1981.

SCRIPTURE INDEX

Old Testament

Genesis

1:26–28 67
1:28 59
1:29 134
3 200
3:4–6 67
3:12–13 67
6:11 67
11:1–9 68
12:1–3 53
12:2–3 59
12:3 8, 58, 142
12:7 72
17:2 59
17:6 59
17:8 59
22:16–18 59
32:28 58

Exodus

19:6 53
34:18–22 66

Leviticus

25:1–55 66

Deuteronomy

4:28 24, 94
6:4–5 57

14:2 68n49
15:1–5 66
15:12–15 66
15:17 66
26:8 59
26:18 68n49

Judges

6:11–8:23 61

1 Samuel

8:4–8 62
8:5 94
8:7–9 97
8:19–20 97
8:20 94
12:14 74

2 Samuel

7:4–7 97

Nehemiah

9:36–37 73

Psalms

47:2 56
50:3–5 75
104:19–23 64
137:1 72
137:5–6 73

Isaiah

3:2–3 62
6:1 130
6:5 130
6:9–12 131
9:6 74
11:6–9 74
24:5 71
24:21–22 71
25:6–8 71
28:15 131
43:19 69
44:28–45:4 100
45:13 100
52:7–8 69
52:8 64
52:10 69
61 79
65:17 71

Jeremiah

4:23 70
4:26–27 70
29:7 57
29:11 64
29:12–14 63
31:32 70

Ezekiel

20:21 94
37:1–3 23
37:4–6 25

37:11 23
38–39 71
43:1–9 69

Daniel

2:35 74
7 76, 77
7:14 74
9:18–19 74
12:1–3 71

Hosea

8:3–4 96–97
10:13 131

Joel

2:17 69

Amos

5:11 97

Obadiah

15 70
17 70

Micah

4:1 74
4:4 62, 73

Zechariah

1:7–21 71
2:11 71
4:1–4 71
4:10–14 71
6:1–8 71

New Testament

Matthew

4:17 75
5:10–11 85
5:13–16 88
5:18 82
12:6 83
17:25 83
21:12–13 83
25:31–46 142

Mark

1:14–15 56
1:15 75
3:31–35 157
4:12 132
8:17–18 132
8:22–26 132
8:27–33 132
8:34 158
9:33 132n21
10:17 132n21
10:29–30 85
10:29–31 157
10:30 210
10:32 132n21
10:52 132n21
13 76–77
13:2 83
13:5–23 77
13:24–27 77
13:26 48
13:28–37 77

Luke

1:8–20 82
1:51–53 78–79
2:22 83
2:41–50 83
4:18–19 79
6:20–21 79
14:33 79
18:18–25 158
18:29–30 80
19:1–10 158
24:26 86
24:53 83

John

1:10 129
2:14–17 83
2:19 83
17:20–24 157

Acts

1:8 83
2:44–45 80
2:46 83
4 80
4:32 80

4:34–35 80
9:2 132n21
18:25–28 132n21
19:9 132n21
19:23 132n21
22:4 132n21

Romans

1:17 87
1:20 28
3:21 83
3:26 87
3:28 82
6:3–4 138, 158
6:5 186
9–11 84
11:17 29
11:17–24 54
12:1 84

1 Corinthians

1:24 194
3:16 83
4:20 38
10:6 95
10:11 95
10:17 78, 134, 207
11:20–34 126
11:26 48
13:12 46

2 Corinthians

2:14 86
3:17 192
4:11 84
5:17 85, 139
5:21 87
6:16 83

Galatians

1:3–4 86
3:11 82
3:24 100
3:27–28 133

Ephesians

1:9–10 137, 170
1:10 88, 144

1:20–23 137
2:11–14 53
2:11–20 137
2:12–13 29
2:21–22 83
3:10 38, 142
4:17–18 29
6:17 101

Philippians

2 188
2:5 86
2:8 86
2:12–13 141
3:20 12

Colossians

2:15 86
3:9–11 80
3:10 25
3:10–11 139

1 Thessalonians

1:6–7 85
2:14 85

Titus

2:14 68n49

Hebrews

2:10 86–87
2:14–15 86–87
9 199
9:8–9 83
9:24 83
11:1 194
11:1–40 116
11:9 49
11:10 12
12:1 116
13:12 21, 49
13:12–13 87
13:14 12, 77, 135

James

1:22 43

1 Peter

2:9 68n49
2:11 83

1 John

1:1 144

Revelation

2:17 189
5:9 84
5:10 169
21:16 83
21:22 83

SUBJECT INDEX

American dream, the, 30–31, 33–36
apocalyptic
  eschaton and, 8
  Eucharist and, 45–48, 78, 133–37
  history and, 69–75, 88–89
  interpretation and, 44–49
  Jesus and, 75–88
  pilgrimage and, 52–56, 202–3
  sacrament and, 45–48, 78, 126–37, 143–51
  sin and, 67–69
  sovereignty and, 7–8, 56–63
  the Spirit and, 82, 169–71
  See also sovereignty
authority, Christendom and, 100–105. *See also*
  state, the
autonomy. *See* freedom
away team, the. *See* pilgrimage

baptism, 133–34, 138–40, 148, 189–93. *See also*
  sacrament
Bible, 26–27, 56–75
body, Christ's
  Christendom and, 16–19, 106–7
  sacrament and, 140–43, 145–51
  truth and, 27–29, 37–42
bystanders, rescuers and, 91–93

canon law, 106–7
capitalism, 112–21, 144–51, 164–69, 195–97,
  207–8. *See also* economy
catechism, early, 162
catholicity, denominationalism and, 2–6
choice. *See* freedom
Christ. *See* Jesus; Messiah, the

Christendom, 6–7, 16–19, 95–108, 169–79
citizenship, Christian, 99–101, 195–211. *See*
  also sovereignty; state, the
civil religion, 119–20, 167–69, 199–202
Communion, Holy. *See* Eucharist, the
community, 16–19, 99–101, 151, 154–59,
  189–90
conformity, peculiarity and, 95–99
Constantinianism, 97–99, 101–5
consumption, 165–69. *See also* capitalism
contemplation. *See* mysticism
conversion, judgment and, 191
creation, 63–74, 133–37, 203–5. *See also* nature
cross, the, 85–87

democracy, church and, 33–36
denominationalism, 2–6
discipleship. *See* formation, spiritual
dissent, 148n64
distances, realism of, 202–3
divine right of kings, 105–8

earthly city. *See* economy; sovereignty; state,
  the; world, the
economy
  apocalyptic, 77–80, 205–10
  capitalist, 112–21, 195–97
  gift and, 205–10
  sacrament and, 144–51
  spiritual formation and, 164–69, 175–76
eschaton, apocalyptic and the, 8
Eucharist, the
  apocalyptic and, 45–48, 78, 133–37
  community and, 140–42, 145–47, 157–58

spiritual formation and, 193
truth and, 28–29, 124–26
See also sacrament
exile, the, 63–69
experience, religious, 123–26

fall, the, 65, 67–69
fear of God, 183–85
following, interpretation as, 42–49
foreshortening, apocalyptic, 76–77
formation, spiritual
  capitalism and, 164–69, 175–76
  gender and, 174, 188
  individualism and, 171–72, 174–79
  judgment and, 190–91
  politics of, 179–87
  process of, 162–64
  theology and, 171–75
  unselfing and, 9–10, 169–70, 187–94
  women and, 174, 178
freedom, 118–19, 150–54, 178–79, 192–93

Gnosticism, 152–54

hermeneutics, 13–16, 42–49, 172–75
historicism
  apocalyptic and, 63–69, 74–75, 88–89
  catholicity and, 4–5
  modernity and, 30–42, 112–21
hospitality, Eucharist and, 157–58

idolatry, 198–202
incarnation, 27–29, 204–5
individualism
  Christendom and, 16–19
  economic, 116–19, 164–69
  sacrament and, 130, 146–47, 150–51, 152–54
  spiritual formation and, 169–72, 174–79,
    182–83, 190
  the state and, 111–12
interpretation, 13–16, 42–49, 172–75
Investiture Controversy, 105–8
Israel, 52–75, 82–84

Jesus, 75–88, 137–43, 152, 203–5
Judaism. *See* Israel
jurisdiction, ecclesiastical, 106–7

kingdom, God's. *See* sovereignty
knowledge, 26–33, 204

law, canon, 106–7
libido dominandi, 10, 197–203
liturgy, sacrament and, 145, 157–58
local, church as, 154–59
love, God's, 184
Luther, Martin, 177. *See also* Reformation,
  Protestant

markets, value and, 112–21
mastery, lust for, 10, 197–203
matter, physical. *See* sacrament
Messiah, the, 74–78, 137–43. *See also* Jesus
metanarrative. *See* postmodernism
military, the, 100–105, 197–203
modernity, 16–19, 29–36, 152–59
monarchy, 61–63, 95–99, 105–8. *See also* state,
  the
multiculturalism, 19
mysticism, 174–76, 186–87

name, God's, 59
narrative, sacrament and, 154–59
nations, the. *See* state, the
nature, 29–30, 63–69, 203–5
necessity, worship of, 198–202
neoliberalism, 12n6
New Testament, 56–63, 72
nostalgia, Christendom and, 20

oikonomia. See economy
Old Testament, 56–63, 72
orders, religious, 164–65

peace, security and, 161–62
peculiarity, conformity and, 95–99
performance, sacramental, 154–59
persecution, messianic, 84–88
piety. *See* formation, spiritual
pilgrimage
  apocalypse and, 52–56
  modernity and, 20–22, 154–59, 195–211
  sovereignty and, 56–63, 99–101
  witness as, 9–10
pluralism, 19, 120
politics, 99–101, 179–87. *See also* state, the
postmodernism, 40–41, 154–59
power. *See* politics; sovereignty
prayer, 170–71
presence, Eucharistic, 46–48
progress, knowledge and, 30–31
property, use of, 112–21

Puritans, English, 178. *See also* Reformation, Protestant

race, sin and, 33
realism, apocalyptic, 202–3
reason. *See* knowledge
Reformation, Protestant, 2–3, 177–79
religion, 109–12, 164–65, 167–69, 199–202
res, signum and, 27, 127–37
rescuers, bystanders and, 91–93
restoration, Israelite, 69–75
resurrection, the, 87
ritual, cyclical, 65–66

Sabbath, the, 65
sacrament
    apocalyptic and, 45–48, 78, 126–37, 143–51
    Christ and, 137–43
    church and, 13–14, 28
    faith and, 7, 124–26, 189–93
    modernity and, 154–59
    theology and, 13–14, 152–54
sacrifice, war and, 199–202
salvation, 152–54, 178, 180
Scripture. *See* Bible
sesquiguous reality, 13n9, 48
seven, ritual cycle of, 65–66
sign, thing and, 27, 127–37
sin, apocalyptic and, 67–69
slavery, 33, 139
social gospel movement, 34
sovereignty
    apocalyptic and, 7–8, 56–63
    sacrament and, 130–33, 137–51

the state and, 105–8, 179–87, 195–210
    See also apocalyptic; state, the
Spirit, the, 82, 138, 169–71, 179–87
spiritual formation. *See* formation, spiritual
state, the
    church and, 6–7, 16–19, 33–36, 95–108
    individualism and, 111–12
    Judaism and, 56–63
    sovereignty and, 105–8, 143–44, 195–210
    the Spirit and, 179–87
    See also sovereignty
suffering, 84–88, 141, 183–86
supersessionism, 54–55
sword, power of the, 100–105, 197–203

tents, living in. *See* pilgrimage
theology, spiritual formation and, 171–75
thing, sign and, 27, 127–37
Torah, 60. *See also* Old Testament
truth, knowledge of, 26–29, 36–42

unnatural, the, 203–5
unselfing, 10, 169–70, 187–94

values, capitalism and, 112–21
violence, 100–105, 197–203
vulnerability, Christian, 163–64, 179–94

war, 100–105, 197–203
world, the, 169–74, 193, 195–211. *See also*
    economy; sovereignty; state, the